Preface Books

A series of scholarly and critical studies of major writers, intended for those needing modern and authoritative guidance through the characteristic difficulties of their work to reach an intelligent understanding and enjoyment of it.

General Editor: MAURICE HUSSEY

A Preface to Wordsworth	JOHN PURKIS
A Preface to Donne	JAMES WINNY
A Preface to Jane Austen	CHRISTOPHER GILLIE
A Preface to Yeats	EDWARD MALINS
A Preface to Pope	I.R.F. GORDON
A Preface to Hardy	MERRYN WILLIAMS
A Preface to James Joyce	SYDNEY BOLT
A Preface to Hopkins	GRAHAM STOREY
A Preface to Conrad	CEDRIC WATTS
A Preface to Lawrence	GĀMINI SALGĀDO
A Preface to Forster	CHRISTOPHER GILLIE
A Preface to Auden	ALLAN RODWAY
A Preface to Dickens	ALLAN GRANT
A Preface to Shelley	PATRICIA HODGART
A Preface to Keats	CEDRIC WATTS
A Preface to George Eliot	JOHN PURKIS

A Preface to Shelley

Patricia Hodgart

Longman, London and New York

LONGMAN GROUP LIMITED
Longman House
Burnt Mill, Harlow, Essex, CM20 2JE, England
and Associated Companies throughout the world

Library of Congress Cataloging in Publication Data

Hodgart, Patricia.
    A Preface to Shelley.

        Bibliography: p.
    Includes index.
    Summary: Discusses the life and work of Percy Bysshe
Shelley in the social and political context of the world
and time in which he lived.
        1. Shelley, Percy Bysshe, 1792–1822. 2. Poets,
English – 19th century – Biography.   [1. Shelley, Percy
Bysshe, 1792–1822.   2. Poets, English]   I. Title.
PR5431.H58 1985   821'.7[B] [92]   84–7190

ISBN 0 582 35369 6 Paper
            0 582 35370 x Cased

Set in 10/11 pt Baskerville, Linotron 202

Produced by Longman Group (FE) Ltd.
Printed in Hong Kong.

PATRICIA HODGART was a scholar of Girton College, Cambridge, and subsequently taught for several colleges in the university. For a considerable time she has been Chief Examiner in the Romantic period with the Cambridge Local Examination Syndicate. Together with Theodore Redpath she compiled *Romantic Perspectives* (Harrap, 1964).

Contents

List of Illustrations

Acknowledgements

I should like to thank Valerie Pitt, Nora Crook and Professor Cedric Watts for reading the manuscript, and of course Maurice Hussey for his help and encouragement. Among the pleasures experienced in writing the *Preface* was a visit to the Casa Magni Shelley Museum at Boscombe Manor; Miss Margaret Brown deserves special mention for her enthusiasm and energy in sharing her knowledge of Shelley and for having collected so many memorabilia. I must also thank Mr and Mrs Collins at Castle Goring for showing me that amazing house, surely one of the treasures of Sussex.

We are grateful to the following for permission to reproduce photographs:
BBC Hulton Picture Library, page 75; Bodleian Library, Oxford, pages 27, 40 and 140; Bristol Museum and Art Gallery, page 30; British Museum, page 144; Cambridge University Library, page 135; Fotomas Index, page 47; Keats-Shelley Memorial House, Rome, pages 93 and 191; Linnean Society of London, page 121 (plate DXLIV from Andrew's *Botanist's Repository*); Mansell Collection, page 128; Musée des Offices, Florence, page 98 (photo Giraudon); National Gallery, page 167; National Portrait Gallery, pages ii, 16, 56, 68 and 111; Newstead Abbey, Nottingham Museums, page 178; Oldham Art Gallery, page 79; University College, Oxford, page 8 (photo Thomas-Photos, Oxford); Victoria and Albert Museum, page 118; Walker Art Gallery, Liverpool, page 198.

The painting *The Bay of Baiae, with Apollo and the Sibyl* by Joseph Mallord William Turner is reproduced on the cover by permission of the Tate Gallery.

Foreword

It has been alleged that one of the culminations of literary scholarship is an ability to appreciate Milton and that the test of a gentleman is an ability to enjoy Walter Scott. Then perhaps an assessment of one's responses towards poetry may be tested rigorously by the work of that scholar and Romantic gentleman, Percy Shelley. His fortunes during and after the Victorian period reveal at least as much about his readers and critics (Karl Marx, Shaw and Hardy approved while Hopkins, T.S. Eliot and F.R. Leavis did not) as the poetry itself.

Patricia Hodgart, blessed with a long-lasting respect for the Romantic period, here begins to guide readers through many of the different areas that Shelley himself invaded and she does so with a most notable lucidity and sensitivity. As a good starting point for the whole book one might take a sentence (p. 114) which seeks to rescue the poet from baseless and untested statements of rejection: 'his perception of Nature was by no means vague and imprecise... his landscapes, however symbolic, were created from careful observation.'

As we read Shelley now we come to realize that he had a wide and up-to-date understanding of so many spheres of knowledge and opinion. His wife Mary, author of the celebrated *Frankenstein*, must have drawn to some extent upon his enthusiasm for chemistry, astronomy and technology while he in return listened to hers for women's rights. Also diffused in his mind were ideas upon politics, economics and religious agnosticism. The contexts that a modern student may ponder in this *Preface* are those most clearly outlined from the philosophies of Plato and Rousseau, the prevailing concepts about Nature and the Natural, and the different European literary works that helped Shelley formulate his deepest impressions. The reader may then pursue his reading as deeply and comprehensively as he wishes and in Part Two he will be usefully prompted by the discussions of the thought, techniques and emotional qualities present in the poems that Mrs Hodgart analyses. The examination candidate will find them especially helpful.

Finally Part Three offers the poet's several environments. Go to Oxford and see the infamous monument to the poet, naked and glistening as from the waters drowned, but spare time too for the collection that has returned from the continent to Bournemouth.

Finally as the Romantic fascination takes firmer hold ascend the famous Spanish Steps in Rome to the Keats-Shelley house: that is a true culmination.

MAURICE HUSSEY General Editor

Introduction

If you look in Hazlitt's collection of essays *The Spirit of the Age*, written to present the significant personalities and ideas of the early nineteenth century, you will not find any reference to Shelley. This is not surprising in view of the fact that Hazlitt did not like him, mistrusted his radical enthusiasm and in *The Plain Speaker* brushed him off as 'not a poet, but a sophist, a theorist, a controversial writer in verse'. But what an opportunity he missed:Shelley is in so many ways a man of his period, fully alive to contemporary thought and taste in the worlds of literature, politics, science and philosophy. His life-time saw some of the greatest changes of the century, covering as it did the years of the French Revolution and the rise and fall of Napoleon; the map of Europe was changed, there were movements for independence in Spain, Italy and Greece, while at home the anti-Jacobinism of the British Government during and after the war years had the effect of increasing the pressure for Reform, although this did not come until ten years after his death.

As an observer of political and social affairs, a campaigner for Reform and sometimes an active participant, as in his visit to Ireland, Shelley understood a good deal about that aspect of the Spirit of the Age in England and Europe. He shared the pessimism of those who saw the turn of events in France, but also the optimism of the Reformers who believed in a better future for England, not perhaps the millennium that he envisaged but a more egalitarian and free society. He was a voracious reader in all fields and knew some of the famous writers and philosophers of the period. He had wide scientific interests and even when he was away in Italy kept in close touch with literary affairs in England. In all these ways he was a man of his time, concerned with the world around him, possessing a remarkable intellectual grasp of what he saw and read and the ability to communicate it in his writing.

There was also the other Shelley, the private and isolated individual who was more at home in the Classical past of Plato and the Greek dramatists and who often felt the need to turn away from the complications and miseries of real life to a vision of the world as it might be, a Golden Age beyond possibility. This ideal connects with his political thought and Godwinian ideas of perfectibility, but more often than not goes beyond into the dreamland of a 'far Eden of the purple East' symbolized by his many images of islands and caves hung with flowers and trailing leaves, refuges from 'the sea of Life and Agony'. His romantic sensibility, fed on the literature of the past, on Shakespeare, Milton and Dante, as well as on the Gothic of his own time, was a rarefied one and his work at its best fulfils Pater's definition of great art in aspiring to the condition of music – the music of the lyric and of the fine symphonic passages of *Prometheus Unbound* and *Hellas*.

In this *Preface* I have tried to convey the many-sided Shelley, the man of his time and the sensitive oddity who shocked many by his behaviour and the extravagance of his ideas. He would certainly have fitted more happily into the Bloomsbury circles of the early twentieth century, where his opinions on free love and free speech, atheism, socialism and vegetarianism would not have raised an eyebrow. Sections of the book are designed to show the wide range of his intellectual interests, political, philosophical and literary, although much has had to be omitted, inevitably, since his tastes were so eclectic. Something, for example, could have been said of Zoroastrianism and his debt to Peacock's 'Ahrimanes'; much more on his literary debts to Milton and Spenser among others, and very much more on the details of his life and relationships, a story so absorbing and so well-documented that one is reluctant to sacrifice any part of it. But this is only a *Preface*, to encourage further exploration of one of the most fascinating and intelligent writers of the period; and for those who want to pursue the quest there is a mass of material at their disposal. The huge bibliography of Shelley scholarship indicates the force of the spell that he has cast on readers and critics.

The critical section takes a closer look at some of the poetry. The reference section at the end is intended to add a little more substance to people and places mentioned earlier in the text. The length of the gazetteer points to an essentially romantic aspect of Shelley, that of the wanderer continually in search of an ideal resting-place; and the list of his friends and acquaintances reminds one that, although he always emphasized his love of solitude, he knew many of his famous contemporaries, not least of them Lord Byron. He ends *A Defence of Poetry* with a tribute to the writers of his day: 'the electric life which burns within their words' is 'less their spirit than the spirit of the age'. And Hazlitt notwithstanding, this was manifestly true of Shelley himself.

Part One
The Writer and his Setting

Family trees

A Ancestral and fraternal

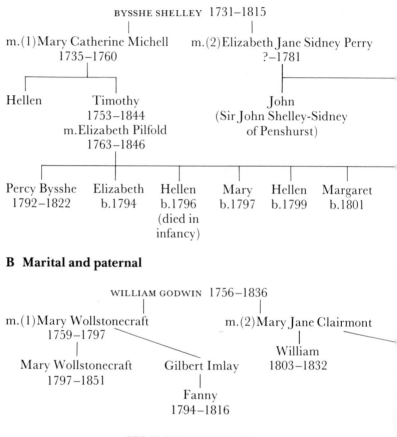

BYSSHE SHELLEY 1731–1815

m.(1) Mary Catherine Michell
1735–1760

m.(2) Elizabeth Jane Sidney Perry
?–1781

Hellen

Timothy
1753–1844
m. Elizabeth Pilfold
1763–1846

John
(Sir John Shelley-Sidney
of Penshurst)

Percy Bysshe
1792–1822

Elizabeth
b.1794

Hellen
b.1796
(died in
infancy)

Mary
b.1797

Hellen
b.1799

Margaret
b.1801

B Marital and paternal

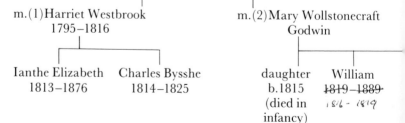

WILLIAM GODWIN 1756–1836

m.(1) Mary Wollstonecraft
1759–1797

m.(2) Mary Jane Clairmont

Mary Wollstonecraft
1797–1851

Gilbert Imlay

William
1803–1832

Fanny
1794–1816

PERCY BYSSHE SHELLEY

m.(1) Harriet Westbrook
1795–1816

m.(2) Mary Wollstonecraft
Godwin

Ianthe Elizabeth
1813–1876

Charles Bysshe
1814–1825

daughter
b.1815
(died in
infancy)

William
~~1819–1889~~
1816 – 1819

2

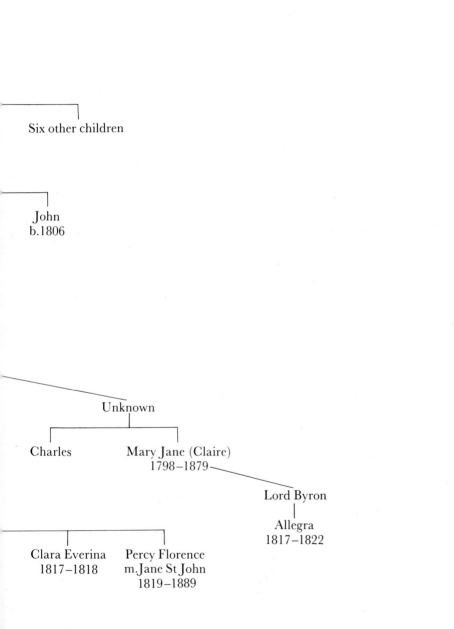

Six other children

John
b.1806

Unknown

Charles   Mary Jane (Claire)
                      1798–1879

Lord Byron

Allegra
1817–1822

Clara Everina   Percy Florence
1817–1818   m. Jane St John
                         1819–1889

Chronological table

1811	Meets Harriet Westbrook (January). *The Necessity of Atheism* (February); sent down from Oxford with Hogg (March). Begins to correspond with Eliza Hitchener (June); Elopes with Harriet, married in Edinburgh (29 August). To York, then Keswick where he meets Southey.
1812	Writes to Godwin (January). To Dublin; publishes there his two political pamphlets, and prints *Declaration of Rights*. Returns to Wales (April), then to Lynmouth. Travels to North Wales (September). Meets Godwin (October).
1813	Leaves Tremadoc, after episode at Tan-yr-allt (February). To Ireland, then to London. *Queen Mab* printed (May). Ianthe Shelley born (23 June). Settles in Bracknell (July) near Mrs Boinville.
1814	*A Refutation of Deism* printed. Elopes with Mary (27 July) and goes to France with Mary and Claire. They travel on Continent and return in September. Charles Shelley born to Harriet (30 November).
1815	Death of Sir Bysshe, his grandfather. Mary's child born and dies. They move to Bishopsgate, near Windsor Park.

1811	Prince of Wales becomes Regent. Luddite riots (March).
1812	Assassination of Spencer Perceval in the House of Commons. Napoleon invades Russia; the retreat from Moscow (May). Byron: first Canto of *Childe Harold* Beethoven: Seventh Symphony.
1814	Abdication of Napoleon and exile in Elba (April). Restoration of Bourbons. Louis XVIII enters Paris (May). Congress of Vienna (November).
1815	The Hundred Days (March–June). Waterloo (18 June). Return to Paris of Louis XVIII. Establishment of Lombardo, Venetian Kingdom under Austrian rule. Corn Laws passed.

1816	William Shelley born (24 January). *Alastor* published (February). Travels to Switzerland with Mary and Claire; they stay on Lake Geneva and meet Byron. Writes 'Mont Blanc' and 'Hymn to Intellectual Beauty'. Returns to England (September). Suicides of Fanny Imlay (October) and Harriet (November). Marries Mary (30 December).	1816	Spa Fields riot (2 December). Byron: *The Prisoner of Chillon.* Peacock: *Headlong Hall.* Coleridge: *Kubla Khan* and *Christabel.*
1817	Allegra, Claire's daughter, born (January). He is denied custody of Harriet's children. Settles at Marlow (March). Finishes *Laon and Cythna*, begins *Rosalind and Helen.* Birth of Clara Shelley (2 September). *History of a Six Weeks Tour* published. Writes *Address...on the Death of Princess Charlotte* (November).	1817	March of the 'Blanketeers' (10 March). Death of Princess Charlotte (November). Byron: *Manfred.* Death of Jane Austen.
1818	Leaves for Continent (11 March). To Italy. Meets Gisbornes. To Venice with Claire; death of Clara (24 September). Begins *Julian and Maddalo*, Act I of *Prometheus Unbound* and 'Euganean Hills'. Travels in Italy, settles at Naples (December). Birth of Elena Shelley, his 'Neapolitan charge'.	1818	Peacock: *Nightmare Abbey.* Jane Austen: *Northanger Abbey* (posthumous).
1819	Leaves Naples for Rome. Writes Acts II and III of *Prometheus Unbound.* Death of William Shelley (7 June). To Leghorn; writes *The Cenci* and *The Mask of*	1819	Peterloo (16 August.) Six Acts passed (December).

Anarchy; To Florence (October); Percy Florence Shelley born (12 November); writes *Peter Bell the Third*, 'Ode to the West Wind' and *A Philosophical View of Reform*; finishes *Julian and Maddalo* and *Prometheus Unbound*.

1820 To Pisa (January); writes 'The Sensitive Plant', 'Ode to Liberty', 'To a Skylark', and 'Letter to Maria Gisborne'. To Bagni di San Giuliano; writes 'Witch of Atlas', 'Ode to Naples', and *Swellfoot the Tyrant*. Returns to Pisa (October) and meets Emilia Viviani.

1821 Writes *Epipsychidion*. Meets Edward and Jane Williams; writes *A Defence of Poetry* (February–March) and *Adonais* (May–June). Visits Byron at Ravenna. Writes *Hellas* (October).

1822 Trelawny arrives in Pisa. Writes poems to Jane Williams. Death of Allegra (20 April). Moves to San Terenzo; writes *The Triumph of Life*. Sails to Leghorn with Williams to meet the Hunt family; on return is drowned in storm (8 July).

1824 *Posthumous Poems of Percy Bysshe Shelley* published by Mary.

1839 *The Poetical Works of P.B.S.* in four volumes published by Mary.

1820 Death of George III (January) and accession of George IV.
Beginning of Revolution in Spain (January).
Cato Street conspiracy (February).
Liberal revolt in Naples (July).
Keats: *Lamia and other Poems*.

1821 Greek War of Independence begins.
Restoration by Austrians of Ferdinand IV to throne of Naples.
Coronation of George IV (July) and death of Queen Caroline (August).
Death of Keats (February).

1822 Turkish invasion of Greece (July).
Suicide of Castlereagh (August).

The Shelley Memorial in University College, Oxford

1 Shelley's early biographers

The spider spreads her webs, whether she be
In poet's tower, cellar, or barn, or tree;
The silk-worm in the dark mulberry leaves
His winding-sheet and cradle ever weaves;
So I, a thing whom moralists call worm,
Sit spinning still round this decaying form,
From the fine threads of rare and subtle thought.
                    (Letter to Maria Gisborne)

The classic French distinction between 'Vie' and 'Oeuvre' as an approach to a writer and his work is not easy to apply to most Romantic poets since they, like the spider, must spin from their own entrails the 'fine threads of rare and subtle thought' and feeling which is the stuff of Romantic poetry. Keats made a similar analogy: 'Now it appears to me that almost any Man may like the spider spin from his own inwards his own airy Citadel', but Shelley moves on from the spider-image to the more unusual one of the poet as a silk-worm, wrapped in a self-created silken cocoon of thought, like the poet in 'To a Skylark' 'hidden in the light of thought' – an image of creation also suggesting isolation and concealment, particularly apt for a writer whose life-experience of thirty years is spun into the shining threads of his poetry to entangle many a biographer and critic.

'Ah, did you once see Shelley plain?', that familiar line from Browning's lyric, is often used as a starting-point for an investigation into his true character and work; but to see him plain was never an easy task, even for his family and friends. To most of them he was an elusive personality although able to arouse powerful reactions, and the lack of understanding he met with among his intimates as well as from the critics and general public was in some part responsible for his self-created myth of the persecuted solitary. After his death this image, fostered by Mary Shelley, 'the chosen mate of a celestial spirit' as she put it, helped to sentimentalize both the poetry and the man. The legend of the Divine Poet, the tragic youth doomed to an early death, was taken up by Lady Shelley, the wife of his son Percy; as a tribute to him she commissioned the dramatic monument of the drowned romantic figure, now in University College, Oxford, and she collected a mass of material about his life and work, editing and rejecting letters which might show him in an unfavourable light. Although her contribution to Shelley scholarship was of immense value, such an emotional approach was hardly conducive to an understanding of the poetry. Shelley, one of the most intellectual and philosophical of the Romantic poets, poses difficult problems for his readers, not to be solved by fulsome talk of his celestial and angelic qualities.

Victorian biographers, in particular Edward Dowden, who wrote the authorized *Life* in two volumes (1886), favoured this romantic version, but Shelley's contemporary critics took a more down-to-earth view. Their attitude to his radical ideas, his atheism and the confused conduct of his private life often conditioned their assessment of his stature as a poet. To an early reviewer of *Queen Mab*, overwhelmed by 'a mixture of sorrow, indignation, and loathing' he appeared as the Evil One himself, horns and all, 'as if a cloven foot, or horn, or flames from the mouth must have marked the external appearance of so bitter an enemy to mankind'. By 1888 he had become 'the beautiful *and ineffectual* angel' of Arnold's famous review of Dowden's *Life*, but even Arnold could not stomach his bohemianism and exclaims in distaste, 'What a set! What a world!' and dismisses him as a poet of undoubted charm but lacking the high seriousness of the great ones.

It is difficult to recognize the same man in two such extreme opinions, as difficult as it is to reconcile Francis Thompson's image of the golden child playing with the toys of Heaven, or the airy sprite of André Maurois' *Ariel*, with Peacock's Scythrop Glowry playing at Gothic horrors in the owl-haunted tower of *Nightmare Abbey*. And none of them does him justice as a poet or as a man. From the contemporary memoirs written by friends and admirers who knew him best, or thought that they did, we get a more authentic but fragmented picture, although certainly one of a flesh-and-blood man seen at first-hand. As an introduction to his work it might be useful to go back to look at their records; it will also serve to introduce characters who played a more or less important part in his life-story. They suggest some idea of the complexity of the man and of the experiences which formed his 'rare and subtle thought'. Shelley recognized the essence of his poetry when he wrote that 'Poets, the best of them – are a very camaeleonic race; they take the colour not only of what they feed on, but of the very leaves under which they pass'.

Chameleon, spider, silk-worm? Skylark, the blithe spirit hidden 'in the light of thought' or nightingale 'who sits in darkness and sings to cheer its own solitude with sweet sounds'? Or Aeolian lyre swept by the wild winds of inspiration? His images of the poet are as multiform as the facets of his personality. But he particularly liked the notion of the chameleon, magically changing its colour with the shifts of light and feeding on air, as it was once thought to do. He makes the comparison again in the short lyric, 'An Exhortation'; if poets corrupt their 'free and heavenly' mind with wealth and power they betray their nature as chameleons would if they ceased to 'feed on light and air'. Keats wrote, 'What shocks the virtuous philosopher, delights the camelion Poet'. Shelley would not have recognized the distinction: for him the chameleon poet *was* the virtuous philosopher or nothing.

Schooldays : Medwin and Shelley

> He had a gentle yet aspiring mind;
> Just, innocent with varied learning fed;
> (*Prince Athanase*)

Of the contemporary memoirs, the *Life* by Thomas Medwin was the first to appear, in 1847. Medwin, Shelley's cousin, was with him at his first school, Syon House at Brentford, but subsequently saw little of him until the last two years of the poet's life when he joined the Shelley circle in Pisa in 1820. In spite of his admiration, Medwin, a dull and rather boring man from all accounts, had little original to say about his hero. To fill out his inadequacies as a biographer he ransacked Mary Shelley's notes to her edition of the poems, as well as drawing freely on articles by Hogg and others, but the *Life* remains full of factual errors and painful misquotations.

There are a few memorable sketches, including one of Shelley as a little boy of ten, 'a strange and unsocial being', a daydreamer hopeless at games and dancing. As a child he is described as having 'a profusion of silky brown hair' and blue eyes very large and prominent, and Medwin speaks of his talent for drawing and his passion for reading 'blue' books, which were the cheap popular Gothic romances of the day, 'stories of haunted castles, bandits, murderers, and other grim personages'. Shelley read them all and was particularly devoted to Mrs Radcliffe's *The Italian* and Charlotte Dacre's *Zofloya*, later to become the inspiration for *Zastrozzi*, his own Gothic novel written in his Eton days.

Although according to Medwin Syon House was 'a perfect hell to him', Shelley acquired here his first taste for science when he attended the lectures of Adam Walker on astronomy and chemistry, a pleasure which was later renewed at Eton since Walker also went there to lecture and demonstrate.

After Syon House they lost touch with one another; Shelley, at the age of twelve, went to Eton and they met again only briefly. After the expulsion from Oxford, Medwin describes how, at four o'clock in the morning, Shelley knocked at his door in London, crying with 'a loud half-hysteric laugh' "Medwin, let me in, I am expelled"'; but after this, until the meeting in Pisa in the autumn of 1820, the *Life* is a hotchpotch of secondary sources.

Despite his shortcomings as a biographer, it must be said that

11

Medwin did have a feeling for literature and truly appreciated Shelley's poetry. When they met again in Italy he found that the boy he had known at school had not changed: 'a book was his companion the first thing in the morning, the last thing at night' and they were able to spend long hours together studying Spanish, Greek and Italian.

Oxford : Thomas Jefferson Hogg

> He is a complete infidel, and a scoffer at all things reputed holy.
> (Shelley's note to *Julian and Maddalo*)

Medwin is a dull writer, copiously inaccurate. The *Life* by Thomas Jefferson Hogg, although far from truthful in its detail is never for a moment dull. Hogg, who first met Shelley when they were undergraduates together, draws on the letters and documents provided by Sir Percy and Lady Shelley for the early material, since his memoir covers only the time at Oxford and the subsequent years of the marriage to Harriet, that is from 1810 to 1814, although he continued to see Shelley up to the time of his departure for Italy with Mary in 1818. His account of their days at Oxford together had already appeared in 1832 in the *New Monthly Magazine*, and contains the most vivid impressions of the Divine Poet, as Hogg calls him throughout the book. His description on their first meeting is worth quoting at length as it tells one more about the subject than any existing portrait.

> His figure was slight and fragile, and yet his bones and joints were large and strong. He was tall, but he stooped so much, that he seemed of a low stature. His clothes were expensive, and made according to the most approved mode of the day: but they were tumbled, rumpled, unbrushed. His gestures were abrupt, and sometimes violent, occasionally even awkward, yet more frequently gentle and graceful. His complexion was delicate, and almost feminine, of the purest red and white; yet he was tanned and freckled by exposure to the sun, having passed the autumn, as he said, in shooting. His features, his whole face, and particularly his head, were, in fact, unusually small; yet the last *appeared* of a remarkable bulk, for his hair was long and bushy, and in fits of absence, and in the agonies (if I may use the word) of anxious thought, he often rubbed it fiercely with his hands, or passed his fingers quickly through his locks unconsciously, so that it was singularly wild and rough. In times when it was the mode to imitate stage-coachmen as closely as possible in costume, and when the hair was invariably cropped, like that of our soldiers, this eccentricity was very striking. His features were not

symmetrical (the mouth, perhaps, excepted), yet was the effect of the whole extremely powerful. They breathed an animation, a fire, an enthusiasm, a vivid and preternatural intelligence, that I never met in any other countenance. Nor was the moral expression less beautiful than the intellectual; for there was a softness, a delicacy, a gentleness, and especially (though this will surprise many) that air of profound religious veneration, that characterises the best works... of the great masters of Florence and Rome.

In the Oxford section, too, his descriptions of Shelley's rooms at University College, full of scientific clutter and chemical smells, the carpets, books and furniture burnt with acids, and electrical equipment offering a constant hazard to unwary visitors, reveal yet another persona, a developed version of the little boy at Syon House and the forerunner of the writer who later so brilliantly transmuted science into poetry.

Hogg's book brings alive the early years of Shelley's marriage to Harriet Westbrook, although he shamelessly misleads the reader on the subject of his own attempted seduction of the new bride which led to a temporary break in the friendship. We hear from him of Eliza, Harriet's bossy elder sister, the 'loathsome worm' who was to become the bane of Shelley's life and whom he held responsible for the Chancery proceedings culminating in the removal of his children from his care after Harriet's death. But on the whole, the tone of the book is one of brisk comedy, in keeping with the picture of high-spirited youth which Hogg aims to portray; and they were all extremely young – Shelley not yet nineteen and Harriet sixteen at the time of their elopement. Their *vie de bohème* is nicely captured in the scene where the three of them sit in their dreary London lodgings with a shilling's-worth of penny buns for their tea 'spread out on an open paper upon a side table', a scene typical of the precarious existence of the hard-up young Shelleys.

Later he was introduced by Shelley to the household of William Godwin, author of *An Enquiry into Political Justice*, the book which was to have such influence on Shelley. Godwin had been previously married to the famous Mary Wollstonecraft, who had died in giving birth to Mary, later to become Shelley's second wife; he had married again by this time, acquiring with the new Mrs Godwin her two children, Charles and Mary Jane, who liked to be known as Claire. The ménage also included Fanny Imlay, the illegitimate daughter of Mary Wollstonecraft, born during her years in France.

Hogg gives us some idea of the unsettled years of Shelley's marriage to Harriet as they moved around England, Scotland and Wales in search of the ideal house to rent, Shelley constantly changing his ideas on the subject. Sometimes he thought of returning to Sussex: 'Let it be in some picturesque retired place – St Leonards Forest for instance' he wrote to Medwin (26 November 1811); at another time his heart was set on a farm in Wales, and later a cottage in Lynmouth in Devon, romantically entwined with roses and myrtles, seemed to satisfy his desire for tranquillity. There were visits to the Lakes and the politically inspired trips to Ireland, and the return south to live in houses in Bracknell and Marlow: a glance at the gazetteer and the maps of his travels in the British Isles shows the extent of his wanderings.

Although the *Life* covers only three or four years, it does establish the character of an eccentric, extremely intelligent and sensitive young man, a judgement confirmed by a reading of Shelley's own early letters. It is, of course, the portrait of an immature 'Divine Poet' whose divinity is somewhat diminished by Hogg's ironic pen and delight in the absurdities of his behaviour. So we have vignettes of Shelley flicking bread-pellets at unsuspecting customers in a coffee-house, Shelley addressing a goat 'What news from Hades?', Shelley convinced that he had caught elephantiasis from an old lady in a coach. And here too is the passionate health-food fanatic attacking Southey for his consumption of large quantities of currant-cakes, and subsequently demanding that Harriet bake them for him every day. Such realism, however lively, was not to the taste of Sir Percy and Lady Shelley, who were so displeased by Hogg's revelations that their idol was all too human that they took back the Shelley papers and the *Life* ended at the point where Shelley was about to leave Harriet for Mary.

Thomas Love Peacock : Memoirs of Shelley

He now became troubled with the *passion for reforming the world*. He built many castles in the air, and peopled them with secret tribunals, and bands of illuminati, who were always the imaginary instruments of his projected regeneration of the human species.

Peacock: *Nightmare Abbey*

Peacock's brief *Memoirs* were written much later, appearing in the pages of *Fraser's Magazine* as various reviews between 1856 and 1862, including those of Hogg's *Life* and Trelawny's *Recollections*. He carries the story a step further and covers the years from the spring of 1812, when he met Shelley and Harriet at Nantgwillt in Wales, through the Bracknell period until the time when Shelley and Mary left for Italy. Added to the *Memoirs* are the famous Italian letters describing the sublime scenery of Switzerland and Italy, intended for publication, as many letters of travel were in those days. Indeed, Mary adds a postscript to one of the letters, dated 9 November 1818,

'Take care of these letters because I have no copies, and I wish to transcribe them when I return to England'.

Peacock, novelist, poet, man of letters and enthusiastic Greek scholar, was a close friend of Shelley, shared many of his interests and was named as one of the executors of his will, together with Byron. Yet the *Memoirs*, recollected at a distance of some forty years, lack the exuberance of Hogg's. There are glimpses of Shelley the vegetarian among the cranks of Mrs Boinville's circle at Bracknell (who were later transformed into the crotcheteers of Peacock's novels), of Shelley sailing paper boats on the Serpentine and of the affectionate father walking up and down the room with his first child 'singing to it a monotonous melody of his own making, which ran on the repetition of a word of his own making. His song was "Yáhmani, Yáhmani, Yáhmani, Yáhmani"'. And at this time, too, Shelley became deeply involved in Greek studies under Peacock's guidance, and the winter of 1815–1816 was passed in this way.

Peacock much preferred Harriet to Mary, and gives a fresh and charming picture of her. With her light brown hair and simple manner, 'Her complexion... beautifully transparent; the tint of the blush rose shining through the lily', she seems the typical English rose, in contrast to Hogg's dramatic description of Mary on her first appearance when he was taken by Shelley to the Godwin household in Skinner Street:

> A door was partially and softly opened, a thrilling voice called 'Shelley!', a thrilling voice answered 'Mary!' – A very young female, fair and fair-haired, pale indeed, and with a piercing look, wearing a frock of tartan, an unusual dress in London at that time, had called him out of the room.

Peacock merely, and somewhat coldly, says of Mary that she 'was intellectually better suited to him than his first'. His sympathies were clearly with the deserted wife, left with her two children, Ianthe (born in 1813) and Charles, born in November 1814 after Shelley had gone off with Mary. Her death in the December of 1816, by drowning in the Serpentine, was deeply shocking to everyone concerned. The circumstances were mysterious: apparently she had been living in lodgings in Chelsea under the name of Harriet Smith, leaving the children with her sister, Eliza. Her last known act before her suicide was to write to Eliza expressing her despair and loneliness:

> Too wretched to exert myself, lowered in the opinion of everyone, why should I drag on a miserable existence? embittered by past recollections & not one ray of hope to rest on for the future.

For Shelley this was the second tragedy within the space of two months: in October Fanny Imlay, Mary Wollstonecraft's illegitimate

Mary Shelley: portrait painted in her widowhood by Richard Rothwell (1841)

daughter of whom he and Mary were very fond, had killed herself by taking an overdose of laudanum. She was in her early twenties and described by Harriet in a letter as 'very plain, but very sensible. The beauty of her mind fully overbalances the plainness of her countenance'. Writing to Byron about this 'series of the most unexpected and overwhelming sorrows', Shelley alleges that Fanny's death affected him far more deeply than that of Harriet; a strange comment in the circumstances, but explicable perhaps by his anger at Eliza, who had instituted a Chancery proceeding against him to gain possession of the children, in accordance with the wishes of Harriet set down in her suicide note.

Scythrop Glowry and others

The *Memoirs*, interesting as they are, do not stir the imagination as much as his *romans à clef*, novels based on easily identifiable characters of the period. The drama of Shelley's life, together with his eccentric personality, was an obvious gold-mine for any writer of fiction, and Peacock's novels abound in sketches and caricatures of the poet at various stages of his early career.

His five satirical novels (excluding *Maid Marian* and *The Misfortunes of Elphin*) all follow the same pattern of a country-house party with much good food, drink and conviviality. The guests hold strong opinions on every topic under the sun, or represent some freakish belief or 'crotchet', and Peacock sets one against another in animated and witty debate, a perfect vehicle for satire on all aspects of his age. Politicians, cranks, critics, poets, musicians and learned clerics all air their views, with the occasional malicious comment from the author. In the first of these novels, *Headlong Hall* (1815), Mr Foster, a perfectibilian, voices many of Shelley's theories, arguing his case with the rest of the guests at the Hall for the future of an enlightened society. Here we also have Shelley the amateur of the sciences: 'Look at the progress of all the arts and sciences – see chemistry, botany, astronomy –' while his exaggerated opinions of the evils of civilization are expressed by another character, Mr Escot, who resembles Shelley in other ways, in being susceptible to feminine charms and blushing like a poppy at the sight of the beautiful Cephalis. In a scene typical of Peacock's satiric method Mr Escot is seen denouncing the miseries of the Industrial Revolution and the consequent distress of children with 'pale and ghastly features' like denizens in Virgil's Hell. 'As Mr Escot said this, a little rosy-cheeked girl, with a basket of heath on her head, came tripping down the side of one of the rocks on the left.'

This novel was written at a time when Shelley and Peacock were close friends and in February 1817 Shelley and Mary moved to live near him at Marlow where they took a lease of Albion House. In that year the second novel, *Melincourt*, was published, and in it Sylvan Forester is modelled on the poet in the persona of the enlightened squire of Redrose Abbey; he is a lover of ancient books, a philosopher and campaigner for Reform, a sworn enemy of the Tories (as Peacock was), 'the friend of the poor, the enthusiast for truth, the disinterested cultivator of the rural virtues, the active promoter of the cause of human liberty' – a portrait only lightly touched with satire.

Peacock was obviously fascinated by the quirks of Shelley's personality and even as late as 1860 in *Gryll Grange*, written in his old age, he created Mr Falconer, in rural seclusion in his round tower full of books. This character, a learned dilettante well-read in the classics, English, French, Italian and Spanish, expresses unmistakeably Shelleyan sentiments: 'We are all born to disappointment. It is as well to be prospective. Our happiness is not in what is, but in what is to be. We may be disappointed in our every-day realities, and if not, we may make an ideality of the unattainable, and quarrel with nature for not giving what she has not to give' – an echo of 'To a Skylark':

> We look before and after,
>   And pine for what is not:

But of all the novels, *Nightmare Abbey* (1818) contains the most famous and most carefully drawn caricature of Shelley in Scythrop Glowry, a comic creation who shows up the absurdity of many of his ideas when carried to excess. It is also a novel dedicated to a satirical attack on the excesses of Romanticism, in particular its concentration on darkness and despair, the 'blue devils' which poison contemporary taste. Peacock's object is, as he wrote to Shelley (15 September 1818), to focus on 'a few of the morbidities of modern literature, and to let in a little daylight on its atrabilarious complexion' and he introduces into the dismal surroundings of the Abbey figures who are associated with the exaggerated Germanic Romanticism and the cult of the Gothic so popular at the time. Byron appears as Mr Cypress in full rhetorical flights of disillusionment ('We wither from our youth; we gasp with unslaked thirst for unattainable good'), as does Coleridge in the character of Mr Flosky the transcendental philosopher, a wickedly comic caricature of an obscurantist wrapped in metaphysical shadows. Godwin's novel *Mandeville* is dismissed as 'the morbid anatomy of black bile', and equally disparaging references are made throughout the book to Gothic novels, especially to one which set the pattern for the cult of despair – *The Sorrows of Young Werther*, completed by Goethe in 1787, which had extraordinary success in Germany and was responsible for a wave of suicides in sympathy with its hero. This young man, gifted with extreme sensibility, loses himself, as Goethe writes, 'in

18

fantastic dreams and undermines himself with speculative thought', and finally commits suicide because of his unrequited love. Goethe, when young, was a leading figure in the movement known as 'Sturm und Drang' (storm and stress) leading up to the full flower of Romanticism; it was not only a literary movement which had a strong influence on English literature, but it also had repercussions on the climate of late eighteenth-century political thought in that its ideas favoured the aspirations to freedom of the individual as opposed to the rationalistic ideals of earlier years.

In Scythrop, Peacock is hitting off a double satire of Shelley as a wildly romantic Werther figure, lost indeed in fantastic dreams in the ruinous tower of the Abbey amongst its secret passages and sliding panels. Here, he concocts plans to reform the world by setting up a perfect republic; he fancies himself as a conspirator and spends evenings in the garden 'on a fallen fragment of mossy stone, with his back resting against the ruined wall – a thick canopy of ivy, with an owl in it, over his head – and the Sorrows of Werther in his hand'. His political speculations are interrupted by the arrival on the scene of two ladies: Marionetta, gay and charming, and Celinda (or Stella, as she liked to be called in deference to Goethe, who had written a play of that name), a beautiful liberated woman who can recite passages from Schiller and Goethe and who shares his love of freedom. They are fictional versions of Harriet and Mary, and although Harriet was by this time dead Shelley was in no way distressed by the novel as it was written with such good humour and wit. He wrote to Peacock in June 1819, on receiving a copy: 'I am delighted with Nightmare Abbey. I think Scythrop a character admirably conceived & executed, & I know not how to praise sufficiently the lightness chastity and strength of the language of the whole.'

The susceptible Scythrop naturally falls in love with both ladies and in the end, losing both, decides to kill himself in the true spirit of Werther. At the last moment, he decides against it for philosophical reasons and calls for his valet. 'Scythrop, pointing significantly towards the dining-room, said "Bring some Madeira".' This absurd character, torn between two loves and obsessed with a passion for transforming the world through 'bands of illuminati, who were always the imaginary instruments of his projected regeneration of the human species' and yet incapable of conducting his own affairs, is a shrewd and delightfully witty comment on the young poet.

However, the novel does touch on something perceived by most of those who knew him – that is, his erratic and unstable behaviour which at times seemed to suggest a decidedly hysterical personality, especially in his early years. Peacock, of course, turns this into comedy. But the would-be suicidal attempt of Scythrop had some truth in it. Peacock, in the *Memoirs*, remembered him at the time of the separation from Harriet in a state of near-madness: 'His eyes were bloodshot, his hair and dress disordered. He caught up a bottle of laudanum and said "I never part from this"'; he did, in fact, at this time take an overdose which was almost fatal, and this was not the only attempt. In a letter to Godwin (3 June 1812) he confesses that 'Until my marriage my life had been a series of illness, as it was of a nervous, or spasmodic nature, it in a degree incapacitated me for study', and there is no reason to disbelieve him; he had at school been known as 'Mad Shelley' because of his violent reactions to bullying or oppression. Scythrop's eccentricity resulted from his over-indulgence in 'the darkness and misanthropy' of Romantic fiction, but in Shelley's case the cause lay deeper. At critical moments of his life, when financial or personal problems became too much for him, his melancholy became very marked and he was subject to strong feelings of persecution amounting almost to mania. A typical instance was the allegation that at Tan-yr-allt, when he and Harriet were living in Wales, a figure came into his room at night and fired a pistol at him, although no one could find evidence to prove that it had ever happened.

Mary Shelley

> I have ... the liveliest recollection of all that was done and said during the period of my knowing him. Every impression is as clear as if stamped yesterday.
>
> (Preface to the Second Collected Edition of Shelley's Poems)

One of the difficulties in trying to see Shelley plain is that of reconciling this distracted personality with the Divine Poet, the gentle, affectionate character who charmed so many men and women. The extreme sensibility of his imagination, the fount of his poetic greatness, meant that the tensions of everyday living often became almost unbearable to him. Mary, the one who knew him best over the eight years of their marriage, shows in her letters and Journal the concern she felt for his well-being. Frequently she speaks of his ill-health, of his weak eyesight and the pain he suffered from the 'nervous and nephritric' disease (so diagnosed by Vaccà, their Italian doctor). They left England in 1818 because he had been told by his doctor that he had to choose between living in Italy or by the seaside in England for his health. Mary's note on *Alastor* confirms that, when composing the poem in 1815, he thought that he was dying of consumption: hence the gloomy presentation of the Poet, whose bloodless hands, wan eyes and withered hair proclaim him destined for an untimely tomb. This doomed figure was, of course, part of the Romantic mythology in the Werther tradition, but Shelley, among the English poets, made it peculiarly his own, creating his own personal legend of the suffering outcast, the 'herd-abandoned deer struck by the hunter's dart'.

Shelley's meeting with Mary in May 1814 at Godwin's house was a turning-point in his life. She was then sixteen and a half years old, not merely a striking and intelligent girl but with the added attraction of being the daughter of two of Shelley's idols, Godwin and the famous Mary Wollstonecraft, author of *A Vindication of the Rights of Woman*, a book which he had ordered from his book-seller in July 1812 and which influenced much of his thought on feminism and the place of women in society. Cythna in *The Revolt of Islam*, the New Woman who

> doth equal laws and justice teach
> To woman, outraged and polluted long;

is modelled on her writings and in the Dedication to that poem he addresses her daughter:

> They say that thou wert lovely from thy birth,
> Of glorious parents, thou aspiring Child.
> I wonder not – for One then left this earth
> Whose life was like a setting planet mild,
> Which clothed thee in the radiance undefiled
> Of its departing glory; still her fame
> Shines on thee, through the tempests dark and wild
> Which shake these latter days; and thou canst claim
> The shelter, from thy Sire, of an immortal name.

She had died in giving birth to Mary, but Shelley felt that her spirit lived on in her daughter; it was appropriate that on 26 June, a month or so after their first meeting, the grave of Mary Wollstonecraft in St Pancras churchyard was the setting for the declaration of their mutual love. The next month they eloped to France, not to marry until December 1816, after the suicide of Harriet.

Their life together was satisfying and happy in that they shared intellectual interests and tastes. Mary was as voracious a reader as her husband, and coming from a literary family was also a writer. At nineteen she wrote *Frankenstein*, and after Shelley's death she kept herself and her son by writing, editing and continuing a literary career. Her other novels, in which Shelley can be easily recognized (in particular *Lodore*) are now mostly forgotten but she was a prolific and imaginative writer. Even so, in the last years in Italy there were shadows on their happiness. She suffered greatly from the loss of her children: one died in early infancy in 1815, Clara and William were both victims of Italian fevers or infections. After William's death she wrote to Leigh Hunt's wife: 'I feel that I am not fit for anything and therefore not fit to live.' Also her husband's undisguised interest in other women – Claire Clairmont (the daughter of Godwin's second wife), Emilia Viviani, Jane Williams and others – must have hurt her in spite of the brave ideals of free-love current in their circle.

Her letters and Journal are among the fullest records we have of the last eight years. Sir Timothy, anxious for the world to forget the scandal of his son's life, would not permit her to write any biography nor for some years would he allow publication of the poems which she meant to undertake as a memorial to him. However, her Journal is of great value in giving a day-to-day account of their life together, beginning with their elopement to France in 1814. The entries are usually short and factual, limited to a few lines in many cases, with notes on the weather, occasional sketches of their friends and a very full and formidable list of the books she and Shelley read, an indication of his extraordinary intellectual range, second only to that of Coleridge. The letters and Journal are discreet and say nothing of her husband's relationship with women; sometimes the letters reveal a little of the truth, as when she writes ironically to Maria Gisborne (7 March 1822) about Emilia Viviani's marriage which put an end to 'Shelley's Italian platonics', or when she expresses relief at the departure of Claire who took up so much of Shelley's time and attention.

Her notes to the 1839 edition of the poems are of special value in that they provide a commentary on the circumstances in which Shelley composed them. So, we learn that *Alastor* was written after his visit to Switzerland in 1814, followed by the trip down the Rhine, and that this was the scenery which inspired the sublime setting of the poet's journey. Similarly her notes to *Prometheus Unbound* reveal how much he was inspired by his Italian experience which 'helped to clothe his thoughts in greater beauty than they had ever worn before'. She gives many biographical details, but though she understood him well she was not always a good critic; her note to 'The Witch of Atlas' describes the poem as 'peculiarly characteristic of his tastes – wildly fanciful, full of brilliant imagery and discarding human interest and passion, to revel in the fantastic ideas that his imagination suggested'. True: it is a correct perception of Shelley's special imaginative flair. He knew it himself and in a letter to John Gisborne jokingly asserts 'you might as well go to a gin-shop for a leg of mutton, as expect anything human or earthly from me'. But when she tried to persuade him to write 'to suit popular taste', addressing his poetry to 'the common feelings of men' in order to be more sympathetically received by his readers, she showed some lack of understanding of the nature of his genius, although her well-meaning motive was to help him overcome the morbid feelings of persecution and isolation which led him to retreat to an unreal visionary world. Shelley's light-hearted dedication 'To Mary'

The Casa Magni, near San Terenzo

23

prefacing the poem, laughs at her desire to turn his poetry into something Wordsworthian, composed with 'slow, dull care' like *Peter Bell*, nineteen years in the making. As if to prove her wrong 'The Witch of Atlas' is a brilliant and witty tour-de-force, notable for its very lack of morbidity and self-pity, and close in spirit to the gaiety and speed of 'The Cloud'.

One could hardly expect her to be an objective critic of her husband's work and sometimes she made bad mistakes, as when she wrote of *The Cenci*: 'It is the finest thing he ever wrote' – not a view universally accepted, least of all by Dr F.R. Leavis who thought 'it takes no great discernment to see that *The Cenci* is very bad'.

But in the same note to that play she gives evocative pictures of their life together in the Villa Valsovano near Leghorn where they were living at this time (1819), just after the death of their son William:

> the peasants sang as they worked beneath our windows, during the heats of a very hot season, and in the evening the water-wheel creaked as the process of irrigation went on, and the fireflies flashed from among the myrtle hedges: Nature was bright, sunshiny, and cheerful, or diversified by storms of a majestic terror, such as we had never before witnessed.

It makes a sharp contrast to her description of their last days at Terenzo in Casa Magni, a house she greatly disliked:

> The natives were wilder than the place. Our near neighbours of San Terenzo were more like savages than any people I ever before lived among. Many a night they passed on the beach, singing, or rather howling; the women dancing about among the waves that broke at their feet, the men leaning against the rocks and joining in their loud wild chorus. We could get no provisions nearer than Sarzana, at a distance of three miles and a half off, with the torrent of the Magra between; and even there the supply was very deficient. Had we been wrecked on an island of the South Seas, we could scarcely have felt ourselves farther from civilization and comfort.

The last years : Trelawny and Shelley in Italy

and then all was hush'd,
Save the wild wind and the remorseless dash
Of billows;

(Byron: *Don Juan* Canto II)

What we know of Shelley in Italy comes from various sources – his own letters, the Journals of Mary and Claire, Leigh Hunt's

Autobiography and other reminiscences from people who met him in the years between 1818 and 1822. Medwin describes with his usual painstaking dullness the circle of his friends living in Pisa in 1821, but in the next year a visitor arrived there dynamic enough to enliven them all, a bold and romantic figure and a writer incapable of writing a dull word. True, Byron said of him that he couldn't tell the truth 'even to save his life', but with all his exaggerations and fabrications Trelawny's account of the last six months of Shelley's life once read remains vivid in the memory. Edward John Trelawny was born in the same year as Shelley, but there the resemblance ends: he was essentially a man of action, something of an adventurer but not such a desperate buccaneer as his *Adventures of a Younger Son* would have us believe. He had been in the navy briefly, and, a passionate reader of Romantic poetry, liked to think of himself as Byron's Corsair. In 1820 he met Medwin and Edward Williams, both then on half-pay from the Indian service and living near Geneva. Medwin enthused about Shelley, 'the inspired boy', and later Williams wrote and asked Trelawny to join them in Pisa where he could meet the poet whose *Queen Mab* he had already read.

Trelawny's literary style matched the flamboyance of his personality. Mary was immediately attracted by his slightly sinister charm: 'tired with the everyday sleepiness of human intercourse, I am glad to meet with one who, among other valuable qualities, has the rare merit of interesting my imagination', and both she and Claire found him an exciting companion. In *Recollections of the Last Days of Shelley and Byron* (first published in 1858) his reminiscences are brilliantly lit, from the moment of their first meeting when 'swiftly gliding in, blushing like a girl, a tall thin stripling held out both his hands', to the last gruesome rites on the beach near Viareggio. Their relationship was an odd one: he hero-worshipped the poet, and Shelley was easy and companionable with him, admiring him as a fine physical specimen, 'Our Pirate', and envying him his skill as a swimmer and sailor. From Trelawny we learn much of how Shelley passed his days in these last months. Unlike Byron, who was indolent, he would rise early 'at six or seven, reading Plato, Sophocles, or Spinoza, with the accompaniment of a hunch of dry bread; then he joined Williams in a sail on the Arno, in a flat-bottomed skiff, book in hand, and from thence he went to the pine-forest, or some out-of-the-way place. When the birds went to roost he returned home, and talked and read until midnight'.

Trelawny was a sympathetic and perceptive observer; not only did he note Shelley's love of water and woods and solitary places, but saw that he was more genuinely and unselfconsciously at ease in society than Byron, the poseur who always had to cut a fine figure. He also seemed to have a shrewd idea that the state of the Shelleys' marriage was less than perfect. In one particularly revealing episode he recalls a day spent with them on the sea-coast near Pisa in the pine-forest of the Cascine, the setting of 'We wandered to the Pine Forest That skirts the Ocean's foam'. Mary, tired by walking, sat under the trees while Trelawny went in search of Shelley, to find him deep in the gloomy forest, gazing into a pool of dark glimmering water in a profound day-dream. In this scene he seems to catch the essence of Shelley – the sadness, the imaginative brilliance as he fantasizes about the distorted shapes of the pines, and the sudden characteristic change of mood when, on rejoining Mary, he became almost hysterically euphoric – 'we talked, and laughed, and shrieked, and shouted as we emerged from under the shadows of the melancholy pines'. It is one of the memorable passages of the book, in which he conveys so powerfully the sense of landscape and the relationship of the characters, Shelley sighing 'Poor Mary! hers is a sad fate. Come along; she can't bear solitude, nor I society – the quick coupled with the dead', and Mary 'to hide her own emotions... chiding and coaxing him' in a half-joking manner.

Other more familiar set-pieces in Trelawny's *Recollections* are the descriptions of the storm which blew up when the *Don Juan* sailed out from Leghorn, and the cremation on the sands near Viareggio, given in all its grisly detail. At the beginning of July 1822 Shelley had sailed off to Leghorn to meet Leigh Hunt who, with his wife and six children had arrived for the purpose of arranging with Byron the production of a new journal, the *Liberal*. On 8 July, after a few trying days in Pisa ('Every body is in despair & every thing in confusion' he wrote to Mary) during which he had tried to settle the difficulties which were already beginning to arise over that journal, he sailed home from Leghorn with Edward Williams and another sailor. A fierce squall blew up, the *Don Juan* capsized in circumstances never fully resolved, and ten days later the bodies came ashore. By Italian law they were buried in quicklime on the beach without delay for fear of epidemic, to be exhumed later in August for cremation. Trelawny gives a long and detailed account, sparing nothing. Byron, writing to Tom Moore (27 August 1822) in a few lines gives some idea of the scene, bizarre enough for any Gothic novel and a truly fitting end for one who had so often prophesied his death by drowning:

> We have been burning the bodies of Shelley and Williams on the sea-shore, to render them fit for removal and regular interment. You can have no idea what an extraordinary effect such a funeral pile has, on a desolate shore, with mountains in the background and the sea before, and the singular appearance the salt and frankincense gave to the flame. All of Shelley was consumed, except his *heart*, which would not take the flame, and is now preserved in spirits of wine...

A sketch by Shelley drawn on the back of a letter addressed to Fanny Imlay and possibly representing steps leading to a grave

Nothing else remained of Shelley except the two books taken from his jacket pocket – Keats's poems and a copy of Sophocles – when his otherwise unrecognizable body was washed ashore.

It is significant that among all the shaken and appalled family and friends it was Trelawny, the man of action, who took charge of the practical details, who collected the ashes and arranged for the planting of cypresses beside the grave in the Protestant cemetery in Rome, where Keats was buried and Shelley's son, William; here he hired masons to build two tombs (one for himself, so that he could be buried beside his hero) and added to the Latin epitaph written by Leigh Hunt his own tribute, the lines from *The Tempest*, Shelley's favourite play:

> Nothing of him that doth fade,
> But doth suffer a sea-change
> Into something rich and strange.

These early biographers of Shelley had none of the resources of later researchers but they had the one supreme advantage of knowing the man at first-hand, and it is clear from their accounts that he was an extraordinary personality, not easy to understand. We have to rely on them for a physical description of him, since no proper portrait remains except one by an amateur, Amelia Curran, painted in 1819, an early picture of him as a child drawn by the Duc de Montpensier, and a sketch by Edward Ellerker Williams supposed to be of Shelley in the last years of his life.

However, all memoirs are necessarily subjective, each one reflecting the character and prejudices of the observer as much as of the observed. To come nearer to the truth one has to look at Shelley's letters, in themselves a fascinating revelation of the man in many moods and many situations, as well as of the poet and philosopher expounding his ideals and arguing out his theories with his friends. Within them, as in the letters of Keats, are contained the germs of the poetry, details of its composition and a valuable picture of a mind at work.

Equally revealing but less available to the general public are the 28 notebooks (most of them in the Bodleian in Oxford, the rest in the United States) in which he made drafts of poetry and prose, jotted down quotations from his reading and made notes of future projects. Many of the pages are decorated with pen and pencil sketches; Medwin speaks of his talent for drawing and here are scribbles of strange daemonic figures and the shapes recurring so obsessively in his poetry of rivers, islands, caves, trees and little boats.

2 The making of a gentleman

The Sussex Squire

I am independent, being the heir of a gentleman of large fortune in the County of Sussex, & prosecuting my studies as an *Oppidan* at Eton;

(Letter from Shelley to Longman and Company, London. Written from Eton College, 7 May 1809)

Elusive as his personality may be in the many guises of Godwinian radical atheist, Platonist, classical scholar, amateur scientist and poet, on one fact all opinions agree – that Shelley was a gentleman, by birth and breeding and in behaviour. Hogg says 'Shelley was uniformly a gentleman, eminently and strikingly such' and Shelley's friend, Horace Smith the banker, had no doubts on the subject:

His stature would have been rather tall had he carried himself upright; his earnest voice, though never loud, was somewhat unmusical. Manifest as it was that his pre-occupied mind had no thought to spare for the modish adjustment of his fashionably-made clothes, it was impossible to doubt, even for a moment, that you were gazing upon a *gentleman*; a first impression which subsequent observation never failed to confirm, even in the most exalted acceptation of the term, as indicating one that is gentle, generous, accomplished, brave...

Shelley's early years were formed in the pattern of the English landed gentry: an impeccable country-house background, followed by Eton and Oxford. As the oldest son he was brought up and educated to fill his position as heir to a large estate, and much of his father's anger against him was because of his failure to conform to the demands of his situation and class.

The Shelleys were an old Sussex family, and his Grandfather Bysshe had, by two advantageous marriages and the death of an older brother, become one of the wealthiest landowners in the County. In 1806 he had been given a baronetcy by the Duke of Norfolk for services to the Whig party, and Shelley was brought up in a resolutely Whig ambience. Medwin describes the old man as remarkably handsome and tall, an autocrat and in later years an eccentric, living simply in the centre of Horsham while spending a small fortune, said to be in the region of £80,000, on the construction of a country-house at Castle Goring, a few miles from Arundel, the seat of his patron the Duke. Designed by John Biagio Rebecca, it is

one of the more astonishing houses of the period, grandiose in conception with a heavily Gothic façade of turreted stone and flint at the entrance, and at the rear a beautiful Palladian south prospect with classical plaques of Pan, Ceres and Bacchus and a curving staircase. It still has a truly romantic air about it, but was unfinished at Sir Bysshe's death, and subsequently lay unoccupied and derelict, known locally as Rats' Castle.

Sir Bysshe's estates and baronetcy had established the family in a way that simple wealth alone could not have done. To be a big landowner was the important thing, as Professor H.J. Habbakuk's essay on 'England's Nobility' succinctly expresses in a way particularly pertinent to the affairs of the Shelley family:

> The basis of this class [the aristocracy and the gentry] was the family estate, which provided the family not only with its revenue and its residence, but with its sense of identity from generation to generation. What was it that gave a landowner more general consequence than a moneyed man of equal wealth? Not only the visible fact of the rolling acres, the psychic ease which ownership of an estate conferred, the greater security of land, the control of tenantry at election times, but the fact that land could be made the vehicle of family purpose; its ownership could be determined for long periods ahead by the exercise of the general will of the family, in a way which was not true of other forms of property. What a merchant did with his money was primarily a matter for him alone. What a landowner did with his land was determined by a complex of decisions, in origin reaching far back into the family history, in effect stretching forward to his grandchildren yet unborn.

To Sir Bysshe the land did indeed become the 'vehicle of family purpose'; he used it to consolidate the family fortunes, to establish the Shelleys as wealthy landowners and to prevail upon his grandson to carry on the tradition. Unfortunately his grandson had no affection for him and was not to be persuaded.

Timothy Shelley, the poet's father and son of Sir Bysshe's first marriage, had no doubts whatsoever that his duty was to preserve the family heritage. His life followed what was beginning to be the conventional routine for a young man of money at this period: in 1771 he went up to University College, Oxford, then set out on the Grand Tour (as Medwin observes, all that he brought back was 'a smattering of French, and a bad picture of an Eruption of Vesuvius'), became M.P. for Horsham in Sussex from 1790 to 1792 and then later for North Shoreham, and married in 1791 Elizabeth Pilfold, a beautiful and well-connected girl with whom he settled at

Boys sailing a little boat *by Francis Danby (c. 1821)*

Field Place, Warnham, part of the family estates. He was a typical Whig squire: like his father he was tall, handsome and marked with the eccentricity which is one of the accepted characteristics of the English gentleman. In the Shelley family it was certainly not lacking: old Sir Bysshe was known for his odd behaviour and Timothy, according to Hogg, talked to the two young men after their expulsion from Oxford 'in an odd, unconnected manner; scolding, crying, swearing, and then weeping again. No doubt, he went on strangely'. In this respect, at least, Shelley, never the most conventional of men, kept up the family tradition.

Bysshe, as his family always called him, as eldest son was destined to spend his life in much the same way, to follow his father as an M.P., to settle as a country squire, perhaps devoting his interests to politics, as the Duke of Norfolk encouraged him to do. In 1811 he wrote to Leigh Hunt: 'My father is in parliament, and on attaining 21 I shall, in all probability, fill his vacant seat', although his ideas would have certainly been more radical than his father's. His early life seemed conducive to such a career: he was the eldest of seven children of whom all survived but one, and from the letters and reollections of Hellen, his sister, it is clear that they lived a comfortable and happy country life in Field Place, a charming house with extensive gardens and grounds set in a particularly beautiful part of Wealden Sussex. It is necessary to remember that Shelley was a country boy, his childhood spent near the woods and hammer-ponds (a legacy of the iron trade which enriched the county in the sixteenth century), and that much of his time was spent in country pursuits. Hellen describes how he would go out at night to look at the stars and one of his own early letters to a local friend gives a picture of a satisfying social life:

> We are to have a cold dinner over at the pond, and come home to eat a bit of roast chicken and peas at about nine o'clock. Mama depends upon your bringing Tom over to-morrow, and if you don't, we shall be very much disappointed. Tell the bearer not to forget to bring me a fairing – which is some ginger-bread, sweetmeat, hunting-nuts, and a pocket-book. Now I end.
>
> I am not
> Your obedient servant,
> P.B. Shelley

Even at the tender age of eleven, there is no mistaking the social poise of the young squire.

In such a milieu he naturally acquired the attributes of the heir to the estate; he rode and was a good shot and a good walker. Peacock notes that when they lived at Marlow, he and Shelley very often walked to London, a distance of some thirty-two miles, but that he never saw Shelley tired in spite of his fragile appearance. Hogg, on first meeting him, observed that he was tanned from an autumn's shooting, and in Italy he proved to be as good a marksman as Byron. When he married Harriet in Scotland he appears on the marriage register as Percy Bysshe Shelley, Farmer, Sussex.

At the age of six he began to learn Latin from the local parson, at ten went to his first school at Syon House, and at twelve entered Eton College as an Oppidan, to mix with other young gentlemen of wealth. The Shelleys were not rich enough to provide him with a private tutor at home, as grander families often did, but his education was much better than that of his father and grandfather. Mr Shelley was very anxious for him to be well educated and well read, and after his son's expulsion from Oxford wrote sadly in a letter '...from six years of age he has never been kept *one day* from School when he ought to be there, and in his Holydays I read the Classics and other books with him in the full hopes of making him a good and Gentlemanly scholar'.

Eton, however, at this time, was hardly a centre of scholarship and learning, although it was a place where, as one noble lord advised his son, it was suitable 'to make a select acquaintance as much in your own rank as possible', and to lay the foundations of a future career. Shelley clearly failed to live up to such worldly precepts and by temperament was a misfit in the rough school life of bullying and fagging. Too odd to fit into the conventional pattern of social life, and labelled 'Mad Shelley' by his school-fellows, he found enjoyment in reading, boating, and such simple pleasures as he described in 'The Boat on the Serchio', written at the end of his life in Italy, a nostalgic memory of happy days on the river.

> Those bottles of warm tea –
> (Give me some straw) – must be stowed tenderly;
> Such as we used, in summer after six,
> To cram in greatcoat pockets, and to mix
> Hard eggs and radishes and rolls at Eton,
> And, couched on stolen hay in those green harbours
> Farmers called gaps, and we schoolboys called arbours,
> Would feast till eight.

After Eton he went up to University College, Oxford, his father's college, but at this point things began to go wrong. Mr Shelley was grieved to see the emergence, not of the perfect English gentleman, but of a radical atheist in rebellion against established society. *The Necessity of Atheism*, written in collaboration with his friend Hogg, was the fatal turning-point in Shelley's relationship with his family: Mr Shelley, on receiving a copy, wrote on the fly-leaf 'Impious' and rightly blamed it on the influence of Godwin. To his solicitor, Mr Whitton, he wrote: ...'he is such a Pupil of Godwin that I can scarcely hope he will be persuaded that he owes any sort of obedience or compliance to the wishes or directions of his Parents'.

To Mr Shelley the idea of atheism was unforgiveable. To be a country squire was to be an upholder of the established Church (although the Whigs were not so resolutely 'Church and King' as the Tories), and church on Sunday was as much part of the normal process of life as foxhunting and shooting. Also, many country gentlemen were in the position to grant Church livings, even if they were not the most devout believers themselves. For Shelley to attack the basis of Christian belief was extremely shocking to his father and laid him open to a charge of blasphemy, as the later fate of *Queen Mab* shows. Mr Shelley wrote to his son: 'The disgrace which hangs over you is most serious, and though I have felt as a father, and sympathized in the misfortune which your criminal opinions and improper acts have begot: yet you must know, that I have a duty to perform to my own character . . .'

In fact, *The Necessity of Atheism* is a relatively mild document, and hardly in the spirit of its doctrinaire title. It asserts that 'there is no proof of the existence of a Deity', either through the senses, reason or personal testimony, and that therefore it should not be considered wrong to proclaim disbelief. Shelley, defending his action to his father writes:

> You well know that a train of reasoning, & not any great profligacy has induced me to disbelieve the scriptures – this train myself & my friend pursued. We found to our surprise that (strange as it may appear) the proofs of an existing Deity were as far as we had observed, defective. We therefore embodied our doubts on the subject, & arranged them methodically in the form of 'The Necessity of Atheism', thinking thereby to obtain a satisfactory, or an unsatisfactory answer from men who had made Divinity the study of their lives.

Shelley's reading of Locke and Hume, as well as Godwin, had set his mind on a course of healthy scepticism with this result, and the whole business was an example, if anything, of the tactlessness which marked much of his early life. He must have known that in a University whose members had to subscribe to the Thirty-nine Articles, *The Necessity of Atheism*, by its very title, would give offence, yet he sent it to heads of colleges, professors and bishops, perhaps hoping, naively, that some interesting argument might ensue. It did not. And after his expulsion he wrote, in the same spirit of sweet reasonableness, a number of tactless and irritating letters to his father, who reacted in much the same way as the University authorities. The quarrel between them, not helped by the interventions of Mr Whitton, was exacerbated when Shelley wrote to say that he wished to break the entail and give up part of the property which was to come to him, in favour of his mother and sisters. In return, he would receive £100 as an annuity, which he badly needed; also, as a true pupil of Godwin, he would be free of the curse of property. As he was in no position to renounce his claim, being under age, his gesture was a fruitless one but it was symptomatic of his rejection of his destiny as a landlord. And yet, throughout his life he was conscious of the fact that one day he would become Sir Percy Shelley and that his son after him would inherit the Shelley estates.

Financial expectations

At this point it is necessary to consider the tangled and never-ending story of Shelley's finances and expectations, complicated enough to fill a whole volume. He had never been short of money, and at school and university had been able to indulge his fancy not only for scientific equipment but sometimes for elegant clothes. Hellen writes that 'Bysshe ordered clothes according to his own fancy at Eton' and speaks admiringly of his 'beautifully fitting silk pantaloons'. After Oxford and his elopement – an expensive undertaking in itself for a young man with a mere £200 a year settled on him – he met his expenses in the traditional aristocratic fashion, that is, by running up debts, and this he did to the end of his life, not by extravagant living but because he assumed that he would inherit a fortune on the death of his father. Ironically, and perhaps with wishful thinking, he expected this event at any moment, as his letters to Mary show. As early as 1818 he wrote to her: 'As yet I do not direct to you *Lady* Shelley', little guessing that Sir Timothy would outlive him by many years. So he left a trail of debts wherever he went, owing money to landladies, printers, booksellers, tailors and other tradesmen such as the coachmaker whose bill was not paid until years after his customer's death. When he was living in London with Mary in 1814 he was so much in debt that he had to hide from his creditors and could only stay with her at weekends when the bailiffs were not operating. He was twice arrested for debt, and perhaps because he had never been obliged to deal with financial affairs, seemed quite incapable of managing them, and at first, before reality was forced upon him, had an airy attitude to money. When Timothy had settled on him £200 a year he wrote to Hogg: '200£ per an [num] is really enough – more than I can want – besides what is money to me, what does it matter if even I cannot purchase sufficient *genteel* clothes'.

The elopement with Harriet in August 1811 caused the final break with his family. Harriet's father, although quite well-off and able to send his daughter to an expensive boarding-school, had made his money as proprietor of a coffee-house, and this was not the kind of connection thought desirable for the heir of the Shelleys. His allowance was cut off and by May 1815 he was in debt to the tune of

£2,900 or more. He raised money by post-obit agreements, in other words by borrowing from money-lenders on his expectations, to pay his own debts and those of Godwin, since he had by now left Harriet for Mary. In a desperate letter to Harriet at the end of 1814 he paints a dire picture of his predicament: 'If once in prison, confined in a damp cell, without a sixpence, without a friend... I must inevitably be starved to death. We have even now sold all that we have to buy bread.'

Sir Bysshe died in January 1815, leaving an estate of £200,000 to his son, now Sir Timothy, who would then settle it on Percy Bysshe, who in turn would resettle it on his son. The will had legal complications too technical to be dealt with here; but in effect, Shelley, by renouncing the entail and selling back to his father a part of the estate which would have become his outright, acquired a capital sum of £7,400, of which nearly £3,000 had to be spent on repayment of his debts. He would also receive £1,000 a year. From this he had to pay Harriet and the children £200 a year, and he was of course by now supporting not only Mary but her father, the importunate William Godwin, who naturally took a keen interest in his financial affairs. The large payments to Godwin made over the years illustrate another aspect of Shelley, the young aristocrat and patron of the arts, and one who felt it his duty to give charity to the poor and needy – so important a function in the conduct of a gentleman. Just as the traditional lady of the house and her daughters would visit the poorer homes to give assistance to their tenants, so Shelley felt the obligation in certain circumstances to do the same. The letters show how frequently he concerned himself with the sick and destitute and, according to Mary, he had contracted ophthalmia when visiting the homes of the poor near Marlow. To Godwin he gave much more than he could afford in gratitude to the one who had so strongly influenced his philosophical and political thought, and Godwin, a man hopeless about money matters, was always happy to be on the receiving end of charity, accepting it as his due as an important literary figure. This was a natural attitude in an age of patronage, and he had, in any case, in *Political Justice*, made it clear that the needy had a claim on society. Shelley's gratitude, however, finally turned to despair and misery as Godwin pressed for more and more. In a letter to Leigh Hunt, written from Livorno in 1819 (15 August) he speaks of 'this hard-hearted person' to whom he had already given over the years the incredible sum of £4,700; later, in 1820, he is described as 'my bitterest enemy'.

Shelley, who had the instincts but not the wealth of the English milord, could only honour his obligations by getting deeper into debt, and by continuing to write post-obit bonds in the expectation of his inheritance. He must have felt sadly inferior to Byron, that truly extravagant aristocrat who was able to indulge his eccentricities and his luxurious tastes in houses and women. The Shelleys, on the other hand, lived fairly simply in Italy, for example in a top floor apartment in the Tre Palazzi di Chiesa in Pisa, while Byron lived in splendour on the opposite side of the river in the Palazzo Lanfranchi; and at the end of his life, they were living in the small and crowded Casa Magni at Terenzo, which Mary found so unattractive. In these years his only real extravagance was in buying books, and in the purchase of the fateful *Don Juan* which cost him £80 and his life.

Two gentlemen in Venice : Julian and Maddalo

Shelley's friendship with Byron was not only the relationship of two literary men in exile but also of two gentlemen of aristocratic birth, of Julian and Count Maddalo: Count Maddalo a 'nobleman of ancient family and of great fortune' and Julian 'an Englishman of good family' (Shelley does not elaborate on Julian's financial situation). The character sketches in the Preface and in the poem itself are to the life, and the poem is, as Donald Davie notes, distinguished by the urbanity of its diction. The tone is, in fact, that of gentlemanly conversation as the two ride out one evening.

> Our talk grew somewhat serious, as may be
> Talk interrupted, with such raillery
> As mocks itself, because it cannot scorn
> The thoughts it would extinguish:

By temperament Julian and Maddalo are very different and they are of unequal wealth, but they obviously accept each other as equals, as they did in life. Shelley and Byron first met in Switzerland in 1816, when Shelley, Mary and Claire were staying at Sécheron on Lake Geneva and Byron at the Villa Diodati, further along the lake at Montalègre. Claire had already had a brief affair with Byron, and when, in 1817, she had his child, Allegra, Shelley took it upon himself to negotiate with Byron about her maintenance and upbringing. As a go-between he had a thankless task dealing with two determined characters both anxious to keep control of the little girl. Byron recognized Shelley's selflessness and wrote of him to Tom Moore as 'the *least* selfish and mildest of men – a man who has made more sacrifices of his fortune and feelings for others than any I ever heard of', adding 'with his speculative opinions I have nothing in common, nor desire to have' (Pisa, 4 March 1822).

But they had other things in common: both were exiles and both had made disastrous marriages, and, most important of all, they were both poets and connoisseurs of literature. They clearly enjoyed each other's company, rode together and went shooting and sailing, had similar radical views in politics and a deep appreciation of

Nature. Shelley was often shocked by the dissolute life led by Byron in Venice before La Guiccioli took him in hand, and Byron was often impatient with Shelley's unworldliness and the disordered bohemianism of his household. When told of the scandal put about by Elise, the Shelleys' nursemaid, that Shelley was the father by Claire of a child which he later adopted, he was not surprised, writing to his informant: 'It is just like them.' However, he recognized Shelley as a superior and unique being, a critic whose opinion he valued and in all ways a man of distinction. To his publisher, Murray, after Shelley's death, he wrote: 'You are all mistaken about Shelley. You do not know how mild, how tolerant, how good he was in Society; and as perfect a Gentleman as ever crossed a drawing-room, when he liked, and where he liked...', a fitting accolade from one English gentleman to another.

3   The historical background

The Sussex Whigs

What can be worse than the present aristocratical system? Here
we are in England ten millions only 500,000 of whom live in a
state of ease; the rest earn their livelihood with toil & care.
(Shelley to Eliza Hitchener, 26 July 1811)

Shelley's attitude to the affairs of his country was conditioned by his
upbringing and family background. As we have seen, he had been
brought up in an aristocratic Whig household; his father and
grandfather were supporters of the Duke of Norfolk and Shelley
himself was expected to take his place in the House as an M.P.

It should be remembered that the Whig party was at this time a
very broad party indeed, containing within itself men as disparate in
their political views as Burke and Charles James Fox. Burke, like
most of the Whigs, had supported the cause of American Independence but not that of the French Revolution. His *Reflections on the
Revolution in France* (1790) in reply to Dr Richard Price's famous
sermon, makes clear his commitment to traditionalism and the
established order. Charles James Fox, on the left of the party, was
for Reform and peace with France, having greeted the Revolution
with more warmth than many in his party but less ardour than the
radical Dissenters like Dr Price and Dr Priestley, although in 1791
he asserted in the House that it was 'one of the most glorious events
in the history of mankind'. It was to him that the Duke of Norfolk
owed allegiance and when Fox, at the end of his life, was Secretary of
State for War, the Duke was rewarded by becoming Lord Lieutenant
of Sussex in 1806, and in the same year Bysshe's baronetcy was
created. Both Timothy and Thomas Charles Medwin (the biographer's father and Shelley's uncle) were involved with the Duke's
political activities; ironically enough, though loud in his desire for
Reform, the Duke was a keen trafficker in boroughs and had a
number of local M.P.s in his pocket. Shelley as a young man was
therefore well aware of the double-think and corruption in party
politics, although much of the radical Whig programme was to his
liking. The Duke was kind to him, but Shelley, at the age of
nineteen, had no illusions about him: 'He desires, and votes for
reform, tho' he has not virtue enough to begin it in his own person.
He is in every respect a character of mediocrity... He merely
desires to gratify thro our family his own borough interests' (letter
to Eliza Hitchener, 29 January 1812).

Inscription inside the lid of Shelley's snuff-box

The ideals of the Whig party, at least of the radical wing of the party, were those of Shelley himself: religious toleration, abolition of the slave trade, reform of rotten boroughs. But he could not accept the demands and hypocrisy of political expediency, and when he read Godwin's *Political Justice* it was the purity of doctrine and lack of compromise which appealed so strongly to him. Godwin insisted throughout on the *morality* of politics – an austere approach far removed from the gross self-interest of the men Shelley had met in Horsham political circles. The philosophical utopianism and optimism which Godwin propounded found an echo in Shelley's own temperament, and to some extent formalized and carried to extremes the ideas he had always found so attractive, most of all the ideal of a society governed by reason and truth, in which men helped *hurrah* one another and cared for the weaker members of the community.

Rural England

> but the dell,
> Bathed by the mist, is fresh and delicate
> As vernal cornfields, or the unripe flax,
> When, through its half-transparent stalks, at eve,
> The level sunshine glimmers with green light.
> Oh! 'tis a quiet spirit-healing nook!
> (Coleridge: *Fears in Solitude*)

> The Price of Wheat being so very dear at present occasions very great grumbling amongst the Poor at this time, and makes them talk loudly. Three Pounds per Coomb for Wheat on Saturday last was said to be asked at Norwich Market.
> (James Woodforde: *The Diary of a Country Parson*, 25 February 1800)

The England of Shelley's day had been shaken both politically and economically by the ideas and events of the American and French Revolutions, and perhaps even more fundamentally by that other revolution, the Industrial, which brought with it increased national prosperity but also the new problems of developing town life and the mechanization of industry. England was still far from being a predominantly industrial country and by 1832, the year of Reform, agriculture still occupied a high proportion of the population. The enclosures of the eighteenth century and the improvement in agricultural methods had greatly advanced the agricultural economy, and during the war years this improvement continued as means had to be found to meet the growing demand for wheat, since it could no longer be imported. For the farmers and landed gentry they were boom years, but with the peace of 1815, the fall in prices and the possibility of a disastrous slump caused the Liverpool

Ministry to pass the Corn Laws as a protection to the growers. This controversial measure raised the price of bread and angered critics of the Government. Byron, in *The Age of Bronze*, has a few hard words for the country gentlemen who voted for their own interests in the House:

> For what were all these country patriots born?
> To hunt, and vote, and raise the price of corn?

William Cobbett, in his *Rural Rides*, is also satirical about the new post-war breed of farmers who are more concerned with aping gentility than looking after their labourers. He points with scorn at the house of one such farmer, 'all just in the true stock-jobber style' with its fancy furniture, glass and china. 'A "parlour"; Aye, and a *carpet* and *bell-push* too'.

Cobbett looks back to the enclosures which had so distressed Wordsworth and declares that they are the main cause of rural decay which he sees around him in some districts: 'In all the really agricultural villages and parts of the kingdom, there is *shocking decay*; great dilapidation and constant pulling down or falling down of houses. The farm-houses are not so many as they were forty years ago by three-fourths. The labourers' houses disappear also.' And like Wordsworth and Clare he laments the decline of the cottage industries, so essential to the fabric of country life and the well-being of the people.

Although the *Rural Rides* begin as late as 1822 they record conditions of life which had changed little over the last decade or so, and show how widely these conditions varied from region to region. For all his blustery attacks on the City (to him the source of all evil, the great Wen), on taxes and tithes and the iniquities of Government, his picture of rural England is one of a countryside largely untouched by industrial progress, rich in its great estates and farmlands. If his remedies for agricultural distress are not always necessarily the right ones, he can be relied on to give the truthful evidence of his eyes and his heart, and the *Rides* remain as a loving record of a landscape now partly vanished.

G.M. Trevelyan in his *English Social History*, writing on 'Cobbett's England', makes the same point that 'When Waterloo was fought, rural England was still in its unspoilt beauty, and most English towns were either handsome or picturesque', adding 'The factory regions were a small part of the whole'.

King Ludd and the road to Reform

> As the Liberty lads o'er the sea
> Bought their freedom, and cheaply, with blood,
>   So we, boys, we
>   Will die fighting, or *live* free,
> And down with all kings but King Ludd!
>   (Byron: Song for the Luddites)

Nevertheless by the beginning of the century Britain had become the most industrialized and the most technically advanced country in Europe. It had valuable raw materials in the form of iron ore and the highly productive coal mines; its cotton and wool industry in the north of England produced large quantities of export material for Europe and North America; its communications – roads, waterways and railways – were developing fast, and towns were expanding to accommodate the increasing population and the drift of agricultural labourers to the factories. All this meant wealth and a gradual rise in the standard of living, yet social historians have thoroughly documented the distress and miseries of the transition period, as country people were forced to come to terms with living conditions which were often appalling. The word 'slum' came into being in the 1820s and bad materials, bad workmanship and overcrowding all helped to bring about areas of squalid back-to-backs in many of the towns.

For many, the quality of life was radically altered; the factory system meant that workers lost their old independence and often had to work long hours in poor conditions, unregulated by any Factory Acts. Machinery was to them a mixed blessing. Robert Owen, the benevolent owner of the New Lanark Mills, said that in 1816 his work force of some two thousand 'completed as much work as sixty years before would have required the entire working population of Scotland' – which must have meant more prosperity. But as the men at less enlightened factories feared, the machines could also cause unemployment, and King Ludd was born. In Nottingham in 1811 a stocking-weaver called Ned Ludd smashed his machine and so started the wave of frame-breaking which spread across the North. It was declared a capital offence and Byron, in his famous maiden speech in the House of Lords, flayed the Government for introducing the Bill. The violence did not stop and in 1813 seventeen men were executed at York. Charlotte Brontë, in *Shirley*, vividly describes how mill-owners had to defend their property against this sort of vandalism; the Luddites in her novel are strongly independent Yorkshiremen who, rightly or wrongly, blame the bad state of the country on the Government: 'It is the Tories that carries on the war and ruins trade' – a view not entirely shared by the author since her hero, Robert Moore, is the unfortunate mill-owner under attack. But Shelley was on their side: in a letter to Eliza Hitchener (26 December 1811) he wrote: 'the military are gone to Nottingham – Curses light on them for their motives if they destroy *one* of its famine-wasted inhabitants', adding that 'Southey thinks that a revolution is *inevitablé*'.

The long French war, dragging on from 1793 to 1815 with little respite, was expensive and damaging to the economy, even that of a prosperous nation. The National Debt increased alarmingly, prices rose and taxes were imposed to pay for the army and the navy. In the first decades of the century, at the time of the Luddite troubles, bad harvests sent up the price of bread and since cheap grain could not be brought in from Europe there was great hardship among the poor. Wheat prices rose: in 1792 it was 43 shillings a quarter, by 1812 the price had trebled. Little wonder that in the towns and countryside the war was not always popular, especially as the Government adopted increasingly repressive anti-Jacobin measures to put down unrest and to stamp out dangerous liberal and radical ideas which had been encouraged by the French Revolution. In fact, after that great dawn of freedom and its subsequent progress, reaction had set in with a vengeance during the war and after its conclusion.

Shelley thus grew up in an age which seemed to him dominated by the forces of repression. The beginning of the Revolution had seen the spread of liberal ideas among those who felt deprived of democratic rights – the Dissenters, the new working-class and all who looked forward to Reform as essential to the liberty of the individual. The early nineteenth century is particularly rich in Reformers and men who hoped for a better future for Britain: Paine, Cobbett, Robert Owen, Francis Place, Major Cartwright, Sir Francis Burdett are a few of the names which are remembered in the cause of Reform. Although Pitt's Combination Acts of 1800 legislated against combinations of working-men to protect their interests, this period also saw the first stirrings of the Labour and Trades-Union movement in the proliferation of working-men's clubs and associations such as the Corresponding Societies and Constitutional Societies, founded for mainly educational purposes but becoming more and more politically active as the works of Tom Paine and Godwin were read and discussed and found to be relevant to people's needs. When Godwin's *Enquiry into Political Justice* was published, Constitutional societies would buy one copy for the benefit of their members, who could not afford the high price of such a book. And when Paine's *Rights of Man* came out, its hard-hitting prose and sentiments on such subjects as tax reform and pensions, as well as his enthusiasm for the French Revolution, were immensely stimulating to radical thought.

> The poem was written for the people.
> (Mary Shelley)

> You may call the people a mob; but do not forget, that
> a mob often speaks the sentiments of the people.
> (Byron: Maiden speech in the House of Lords,
> 27 February 1812, on the Luddite wreckers)

The years of the French war had seen many changes of government. Pitt, who had been saddled with a war he did not want, led the Tories in Government, with one brief break, until his death in 1806. Fox followed him but died within the year, leaving Grenville to run the coalition 'Ministry of all the Talents'. In 1812, after the assassination of the Prime Minister, Spencer Perceval, came the régime of Liverpool, Sidmouth and Eldon, with Castlereagh as Foreign Secretary – names certainly familiar to readers of Shelley. A glance at *The Mask of Anarchy* (1819) will make clear his views about these gentlemen:

> I met Murder on the way –
> He had a mask like Castlereagh –

Just as brutal is the appearance of Sidmouth and of Eldon, the Lord Chancellor who had decreed that, after Harriet's death, Shelley should not be given custody of the children. Castlereagh, the main enemy, was held responsible for Britain's reactionary foreign policy at the Congress of Vienna and for his policy in Ireland. Byron, in the Dedication to *Don Juan* was no less bitter about him:

> Cold-blooded, smooth-faced, placid miscreant:
> Dabbling its sleek young hands in Erin's gore.

The Mask, written on the occasion of Peterloo in 1819, is probably Shelley's most famous political poem, and the occasion of its composition is indicative of the state of the country at that time.

The Peterloo Massacre, as it came to be called in ironical reference to Waterloo, was the culmination of a number of incidents in which the military (this was before the days of an organized police force) clashed with the radical elements of the public. The Luddite troubles and the increasing demonstrations for Reform led to riotous scenes like the meeting at Spa Fields in London, when the mob marched on the Tower. This was in 1816, and in the same year was the march of the Manchester Blanketeers (so called because the men carried their blankets to sleep in), a demonstration about conditions in a bad period of recession for the cotton trade.

Three years later came the famous Peterloo affair, to which Shelley, now living in Italy, responded with a burst of hatred for Liverpool's reactionary Ministry. It was occasioned by the continuing post-war slump in the cotton trade. The Manchester and

Stockport area was overcrowded with Irish immigrants pouring in, together with disbanded soldiers; conditions and wages were poor, and resulting unemployment caused many strikes and labour troubles. The weavers, who earned less than the spinners, were in the front of the demand for a great protest meeting, claiming higher wages and political rights, that is Reform and universal suffrage. Manchester, Sheffield and Leeds, extraordinary as it seems to us now, had no representatives in Parliament, although many tiny country towns and villages had. There followed great activity among the radical movement: public meetings, meetings in clubs like the Union Societies (which ran an educational programme 'to instil in the minds of our children a deep and rooted hatred of our corrupt and tyrannical Rulers') and fiery articles in the Radical press. Pressure built up, and although middle-class liberals opposed violent action, the weavers spurred on by left-wing agitators, in particular Henry Hunt, a well known Reform orator, called a demonstration on 16 August at St Peter's Fields in Manchester. People came from miles around, from as far away as Leeds and Sheffield, and it was the most important meeting ever called in the cause of Reform. The magistrates, who had declared it illegal and seditious, over-reacted in the face of such a huge assembly, sent in troops and as a result eleven were killed, four hundred injured and military casualties were put at sixty-seven. Sidmouth, at the Home Office, had asked the magistrates not to use force unless the peace was disrupted, and it is likely that the resulting débâcle came from confusion and miscalculation rather than from the desire for the brutal repression that Shelley evokes in his poem. But *The Mask of Anarchy*, in its authentic note of outrage, is a stirring call to action (what action is not clear, as Shelley was, like Godwin, a determined believer in non-violence. Indeed, he advocates passive resistance, but the last lines belie that intention). It still has the power to inspire, and even today certain Labour leaders, at emotional moments, use it as a battle-cry to rouse their audience with

> Rise like lions after slumber
> In unvanquishable number

rising to the impassioned cry of 'Ye are many – they are few'.

The poem, a masque of the political deadly sins of Murder, Fraud, Hypocrisy and other destructive forces, is also a dance of death driven on by Anarchy, the skeleton riding a white horse 'Like Death in the Apocalypse', and laying waste to the country. Its crisp outlines have the impact and direct communication of a political cartoon, one of the popular art-forms of the period. Gillray, perhaps the greatest of political caricaturists, was dead by this time but Shelley must have known his work and may well have taken his vision of Anarchy from Gillray's famous cartoon of Pitt as Death on

Gillray's Presages of the Millenium *(1795), showing Pitt as Death on a White Horse attacking the left-wing politicians of his day*

the Pale Horse, drawn in 1795 and inspired by a painting by Benjamin West (p. 47). Gillray, a devout anti-Jacobin, would certainly have taken a different attitude to Peterloo; nevertheless Shelley's technique is the same and his figures appear as ugly grotesques, conceived in powerful images which leave no doubt as to their meaning. Hypocrisy, like Sidmouth, riding a crocodile, and Fraud in the ermine gown of Eldon, weeping mill-stone tears which knock out the brains of little children, are caricatures as vicious as any from Gillray's savage pen. Shelley shows himself a master of pictorial effect in his portrayal of the bloody army of Church and State – and the word 'blood' sounds through the poem like a drum-beat – in its triumphant progress with sword and cavalry. In contrast is the pitiful image of Hope, the maniac maid, and the beautiful Shape of the Spirit of Liberty which dispels the nightmare of the Mask, so that Hope will not be crushed by the horses' feet but can walk in safety, although 'ankle-deep in blood'. Also in the style of Gillray at his most flamboyant is the apocalyptic vision of the death of Anarchy with 'rushing light of clouds and splendour', but Shelley's message in the stanzas, 'Men of England, heirs of Glory', has a direct simplicity which eschews dramatic effects of a pictorial kind and relies on the force of popular oratory to make its appeal. Not surprisingly, 'Men of England' was taken up by the Chartists later on, as a hymn to Reform, and when Orwell parodied it in the song 'Beasts of England' in *Animal Farm* he was deliberately being offensive about one of the sacred left-wing anthems.

Peterloo was the most notorious incident in a period of agitation for Reform, which to those in Government looked more like agitation for revolution. As a direct result the Six Acts were passed, with even heavier penalties for Radical publications and meetings. The next year, in 1820, the Cato Street Conspiracy was organized by one Arthur Thistlewood, who had been imprisoned after the Spa Fields riot, with the intention of killing all the members of the Cabinet. The plot misfired, and Thistlewood and some of the conspirators were executed, but the episode shows the bitter feelings aroused by Government repression. Shelley, however, was deeply shocked by it; to Peacock he wrote 'Everything seems to conspire against Reform' (10 March 1820) and he saw that violent action of this kind would only delay its coming about.

It is hard to remember that these dark scenes took place against the background of what we think of as the elegant days of the Regency. The Prince of Wales, the future George IV, who became Regent in 1811 in place of his father, the 'old, mad, blind, despised and dying king' of Shelley's sonnet, was the centre of the brilliant world conjured up by the word Regency. His Pavilion at Brighton, the stateliest of pleasure domes, was a glittering symbol of extravagance and gaiety; the year before Peterloo Nash began constructing the great Indian domes and the fantastic Chinoiserie of the music-room and banqueting-room, ornately gilded with palms and dragons and Chinese painting. A year or two later he designed and built New Street, known now as Regent Street in London, and later, Regent's Park. The Prince and Mrs Fitzherbert, Beau Brummell and Sheridan, the Holland House set, Byron and his dashing ladies – these are the highly-coloured figures seen in contrast to the Blanketeers and the Luddites at the other end of the social spectrum. Like Disraeli's two worlds of *Sybil*, they seem like Dives and Lazarus with a great gulf between, and the gulf was to widen still further as the century went on. Shelley, who was not of this *beau monde*, was satirical about Carlton House and its magnificence on the occasion of a fête there, said to cost £120,000. 'Nor', he wrote to Eliza Hitchener (20 June 1811), 'will it be the last bauble which the nation must buy to amuse this overgrown bantling of regency.'

The Irish Question

> On our walk in Ireland we had too much opportunity to see the worse than nakedness, the rags, the dirt and misery of the poor common Irish.
>
> (Keats: letter to Thomas Keats, 9 July 1818)

The state of Shelley's England did not please him, but the state of Ireland was much worse. Its complicated history before the rising of 1798, centred on the never-ending conflicts of Catholic and Protestant and the poverty of the country, is too long to consider here. Wolfe Tone's rising of United Irishmen, inspired by the success of the Revolution in France, had struck at the Anglo-Irish landlord class and the British Government, whose rule would not give the Catholic population of over three million the right to sit in Parliament or to become judges. The rising was put down ferociously, adding yet another chapter to the story of Irish resentment of British rule. The Act of Union of 1800 gave Britain greater control there, and in England Catholic Emancipation became one of the Whig causes, although George III set his face against it. Pitt, who took a liberal view, resigned over it in 1801 and the Bill for Emancipation was not finally passed until 1829.

In 1818 Keats on his travels through Ireland was shocked by the conditions there. As a general comment on the age he writes: '... in Cities Man is shut out from his fellows if he is poor, the Cottager must be dirty and very wretched if she be not thrifty – The present state of society demands this and this convinces me that the world is very young and in a very ignorant state.' His feelings about 'the dirt and misery of the poor common Irish' are expressed most memorably in his famous sketch of the Duchess of Dunghill, an ancient crone carried on a sort of dog-kennel litter by ragged girls. Six years before Keats's visit, Shelley and Harriet had gone to Ireland, where he embarked on his first practical political activity, to bring enlightenment to the Irish, as his father satirically remarked. He had received much the same impression and found the poorer section of Dublin's population living in squalor, 'one mass of animated filth', in one of the most beautiful cities in Europe.

As he wrote to his faithful correspondent, Eliza Hitchener (27 February 1812), he considered 'the necessity of reform and the probability of a revolution undeniable'. Once settled in Dublin he published 1,500 copies of his *Address to the Irish People*, and he and Harriet occupied their days 'disseminating the doctrines of Philanthropy and Freedom' among the populace; in other words handing out pamphlets to passers-by in the street and in the public-houses, and even throwing them from their window: 'I watch till I see a man who looks likely. I throw a book to him.' In an attempt at popular appeal the style of his prose was 'adapted to the lowest comprehension that can read'.

Next came a much more ambitious paper, addressed this time to an educated middle-class audience; in *Proposals for an Association of those Philanthropists, who Convinced of the Inadequacy of the Moral and Political State of Ireland to Produce Benefits which are Nevertheless Attainable are Willing to Unite to Accomplish its Regeneration*, a high-sounding and somewhat cumbrous title, he advocates the virtues of sobriety and temperance: hardly the qualities, one might think, likely to appeal to the Irish. 'Do not', he wrote, 'spend your money in idleness and drinking.' Keats, a few years later, did not share his optimistic views and could not imagine how philanthropy offered hope for such people: 'with me it is absolute despair'. But not with Shelley. He stuck to his beliefs although his utopian projects of associations of philanthropists had little success with the public, and he was forced to defend his campaign to Godwin, who was fearful of anarchy and warned him, 'Shelley, you are preparing a scene of blood'. Shelley wrote to assure him that the pamphlets could not 'in the slightest degree lead to violence' and that he had insisted throughout on pacific measures, not rebellion.

In Dublin he addressed a public meeting of Catholics, reported in the press but not well received by his audience; his views on religion were hissed – 'more hate me as a free-thinker, than love me as a votary of Freedom' – and he found the Catholic aristocracy as intolerant as the Prince Regent himself and the gulf between rich and poor even wider than in England. The only person of note that he met was John Philpot Curran, a well-known orator and barrister (whose daughter Amelia painted a portrait of Shelley – see frontispiece – when they met in Rome). Godwin had given him an introduction but Curran's flow of Irish wit and conversational ebullience disconcerted Shelley, who had expected a more serious and committed character.

Little came of the expedition, but it brought Shelley to the notice of the Home Office. He had sent a packet of copies of both pamphlets together with a *Declaration of Rights* to Miss Hitchener ('a large Box', as Harriet wrote, 'so full of inflammable matter') and it had been opened and intercepted by the Customs at Holyhead. The *Declaration* seems a mild enough document, containing such unexceptionable sentiments as 'No man has a right to disturb the public peace, by personally resisting the execution of a law however bad' and 'No man has a right to do an evil thing that good may come', but one result of its publication was the arrest in Lynmouth in August 1812 of Daniel Healey, their Irish servant, for distributing the broadsheet. He was fined £200 but as Shelley had no money to pay this, Healey was sent to prison for six months and the Shelleys had to hastily depart, neglecting also to pay their landlady.

The Irish venture would have daunted a good many would-be Reformers, but for Shelley it was valuable experience and probably his first sight of real distress and hopeless ignorance which seemed invincible against his gospel of moderation and reason. It brought a sense of reality to his philosophical speculations; the illiterate poor of Dublin taught him a new lesson. 'These were the persons to whom in my fancy I had addressed myself; how quickly were my views on this subject changed! yet how deeply has this very change rooted the conviction on which I came hither.' And in a letter to Miss Hitchener he put the Irish Question in a nutshell: 'The spirit of Bigotry is high'.

The French Revolution and after

> A woeful time for them whose hopes survived
> The shock; most woeful for those few who still
> Were flattered, and had trust in human kind;
> They had the deepest feeling of the grief.
> (Wordsworth: *The Prelude* Book X)

In 1792, the year of Shelley's birth and the year in which France was declared a Republic, it was fashionable among radicals and well-wishers of the Revolution to visit France. Both Mary Wollstonecraft and Wordsworth were there to observe the brave new world and both were in touch with the Girondins who were the more moderate party, *les conventionnels*. A year or two before, Wordsworth had visited the liberated Bastille and

> gathered up a stone,
> And pocketed the relic, in the guise
> Of an enthusiast.

Yet he adds, perhaps with hindsight, he was not as moved as he pretended to be. Coleridge, who did not make the pilgrimage, celebrated the hopes of the period in 'France: an Ode' composed in disillusion in 1798:

> When France in wrath her giant-limbs upreared
> And with that oath, which smote air, earth, and sea,
> Stamped her proud foot, and said she would be free,
> Bear witness for me, how I hoped and feared.

His fears had proved all too real, and even in 1792 the first flush of euphoria was beginning to fade, except among those who were deeply committed. The setting up of the Revolutionary Tribunal, the subsequent execution of Louis XVI and his Queen in 1793 and the dreadful days of the Terror finally destroyed the allegiance of Wordsworth and many others to the régime in France. The guillotine in the Place de la Révolution became the symbol of the new tyranny:

> Head after head, and never heads enough,
> For those that bade them fall.
> (*The Prelude*, Bk. X)

The year 1793 brought the publication of Godwin's *Political Justice* and Paine's *The Age of Reason*, and suitably enough it was the year of the celebration of the Fête de la Raison in Paris, a great spectacle in Notre Dame in which an actress represented Liberty, to signify the substitution of the new humanist religion for the outworn ideas of Christianity. In the same year England went to war with France and Europe was in turmoil for the next twenty years.

Shelley was the child of this new era, spiritually of a different generation from those disillusioned enthusiasts, the early Romantic poets. Wordsworth, Coleridge and Southey all turned away from their early commitment to become, in the eyes of many of their younger contemporaries, political turncoats, lost leaders who had sold out to the Establishment. Shelley's delight in Southey's poetry, in particular *The Curse of Kehama*, was tempered by his recognition of the fact that (as he wrote to Leigh Hunt in 1811 after a visit to Southey in Keswick) 'he is now an advocate for existing establishments; he says he designs his three statues in Kehama to be contemplated with republican feelings – but not in this age – Southey hates the Irish, he speaks against Catholic Emancipation & Parliamentary reform'. And what was even worse, he had used his literary talents to glorify the Tory cause: 'to aggrandise the fame of Statesmen is his delight, the constitution of England with its Wellesley its Paget & its Prince are inflated with the prostituted exertions of his Pen' (letter to Miss Hitchener, 15 December 1811). It says much for Shelley's tolerance that he could still partly

forgive this falling away from grace and conclude that, nevertheless, 'he is a man of virtue'.

By the time Shelley was ten, in 1802, the figure of Napoleon had
arisen and the Peace of Amiens had momentarily halted the war,
only for it to break out again in the next year. Napoleon was
crowned Emperor and changed the face of Europe by his sweeping
victories and invasions. The first two decades of the century are a
catalogue of famous battles and campaigns – Marengo, Hohenlinden,
Trafalgar, Friedland, Borodino and the Peninsular War. Britain was
at war until 1814, when the Congress of Vienna met to settle the
conditions of a much-needed peace, but the tyranny of the French
Empire was not brought to an end until the next year with the
campaign culminating in Waterloo. Since Napoleon had made such
changes in frontiers and governments of Europe, the Congress of
Vienna had many problems to settle, not least those arising from the
new ideas of nationalism and democracy stimulated by the French
Revolution. The Treaty, drawn up by the Great Powers – Britain,
France, Austria, Prussia, Russia and the Papacy – redistributed
power in many parts of Europe. Austria, for example, acquired rule
over provinces of Northern Italy, and in Spain the Bourbon rule was
restored. The settlement, like that of many wars throughout history,
merely opened up new problems, and the causes of nationalism
rumbled on for many years afterwards, resulting in revolutions in
both Italy and Spain.

The Europe of Shelley's youth, that is until his early twenties, was
therefore one of war and unrest. Yet, curiously enough, his letters
mention very little of the great affairs outside the British Isles, nor
do his biographers indicate that he was much concerned with them.
His uncle, Captain Pilfold, who was extremely kind and sympathetic
to the young man (although he later had him arrested for debt), had
been very much involved in the wars and had served with Nelson at
the Battle of the Nile and at Trafalgar. In fact, his house near
Cuckfield, in Sussex, was called Nelson Place, but Shelley in his
letters refers to Nelson only once, and that in a scoffing manner
when, in one of the long rhetorical outbursts to Eliza Hitchener he
speaks of 'the narrowness that marked Nelson's dying hour' and
rephrases the famous last words to read 'The world expects every
being to do its duty'. Even in the momentous year 1815, the year of
the Hundred Days and Waterloo, he could write to Hogg: 'In
considering the political events of the day I endeavour to divest my
mind of temporary sensations, to consider them as already historical. This is difficult. Spite of ourselves the human beings which
surround us infect us with their opinions: so much as to forbid us to
be dispassionate observers of the questions arising out of the events
of the age.'

Wellington, that great bogeyman of the Radicals, is never mentioned and Napoleon very rarely. A sonnet, published in 1816, on 'Feelings of a Republican on the Fall of Bonaparte', blames him for the betrayal of liberty ('I hated thee, fallen tyrant!') but indicates that there are worse enemies such as

> old Custom, legal Crime
> And bloody Faith the foulest birth of Time.

Later, 'Lines written on Hearing the News of the Death of Napoleon' (published in 1821) make clear Shelley's feelings about the Emperor who had brought to Europe a torrent of 'terror and blood and gold', 'A torrent of ruin to death from his birth'.

As a student of Godwin he felt it necessary to be detached from the violence and irrationality of war. Nevertheless the spirit of liberty was the dominant spirit of the age, and Shelley was one of its most ardent enthusiasts. As Mary wrote in the Preface to the second collection of the poems: 'He had been from youth the victim of the state of feeling inspired by the reaction of the French Revolution' and his response to the anti-Jacobinism of the Government was always a fierce one. Wherever the cause of liberation arose he greeted it with fervour, not always realizing that revolutions rarely come about without bloodshed and tyranny. Byron, more practical, knew that 'revolutions are not made with rose-water' (Letters and Journals IV 358) but Shelley remained an optimist. Typical of his early, somewhat abstract attitude to liberty is the excited comment in the letter to Eliza: 'Have you heard, a new republic is set up in Mexico', with an impassioned (and very bad) poem written 'in tribute to its success'. Like many a young left-wing intellectual, then as now, his response to the cause of freedom in faraway places was automatic, although not always based on a proper understanding of the issues involved.

The master theme – a Vision of the Nineteenth Century : The Revolt of Islam

It was not until July 1814 that he began to understand what had happened to Europe. In that year he eloped with Mary to Switzerland and, taking Claire with them, they journeyed through France. They crossed France to find the country ravaged by war and starvation:

> I cannot describe to you the frightful desolation of this scene. Village after village entirely ruined & burned; the white ruins towering in innumerable forms of destruction among the beautiful trees. The inhabitants were famished; families once perfectly independent now beg for bread in this wretched country. No provisions, no accommodation; filth, misery & famine everywhere.

54

So he wrote to Harriet, and the Journals of Mary and Claire bear out the unhappy details of their *via dolorosa* across the country. The inns were dreadful, the food worse. At one point Claire could not sleep for the rats running across her bed, and of one village she records 'Perhaps never dirt was equal to the dirt we saw'.

The next visit in 1816 was more agreeable and he wrote to Byron describing a visit to Versailles and Fontainebleau, 'those famous Palaces, which, as I will hereafter tell you, are worth visiting as monuments of human power; grand, yet somewhat faded; the latter is the scene of some of the most interesting events of what may be called the master theme of the epoch in which we live – the French Revolution'.

The 'master theme' is given more extensive consideration in the Preface to *The Revolt of Islam* (originally issued as *Laon and Cythna*) composed in 1817 when the Shelleys were living at Marlow. Here he gives a perceptive and balanced account of the years of the Revolution, 'the tempests which have shaken the age in which we live', acknowledging that it had given rise to excesses of feeling on both sides, but that now the intense reaction to the Terror and to the Napoleonic Wars 'is gradually giving place to sanity'. Shelley, although by temperament a natural rebel, was always conscious of the terrible consequences when revolutionary ideals fall into anarchy because of over-precipitate action: 'Can he, who the day before was a trampled slave suddenly become liberal-minded, forbearing, and independent?' and he speaks of the 'gloom and misanthropy' which have resulted among those who hailed the Revolution as a liberating force. But while recognizing that disillusionment he optimistically sees change for the better: 'Methinks, those who now live have survived an age of despair' and the poem is intended to foster the sentiments of liberty and justice necessary to bring about that change.

The poem itself is one of his longest and most ambitious, but by no means his most successful. Some discussion of it is relevant here since it expresses so much of his thought on revolution and its purpose. The vaguely Middle Eastern setting hardly disguises the fact that the scene is Revolutionary and post-Revolutionary Europe in the full ugliness of bloody battles, famine and ruined countryside. Indeed, the original title was to be *The Revolution of the Golden City: a Vision of the Nineteenth Century*. The long and confused story of Laon and Cythna teems with ideas and images somewhat naively presented but later to be transformed into the splendours of *Prometheus Unbound*, and it develops at length his conception of liberty and its uses, first sketched out in *Queen Mab*.

The Revolt of Islam is conceived on the grand epic scale, inspired partly by Tasso's *Gerusalemme Liberata* and written in the Spenserian stanzas of *The Faerie Queene*. Like both these poems it is concerned

Mary Wollstonecraft

with the conflict of good and evil; the struggle for the Golden City embodies Shelley's vision of the world as it is and the world as it could be if men would learn the Godwinian lessons of love and reason. Laon, the hero and champion of good, and Cythna, the ideal woman who emerges as the stronger character of the two as the New Woman in the mould of Mary Wollstonecraft, are the Shelleyan Illuminati, the enlightened propagandists for the brave new universe:

> a nation
> Made free by love; a mighty brotherhood
> Linked by a jealous interchange of good.

In the original version of *Laon and Cythna* they were brother and sister, but this was changed in case of further attacks on a poem already radical enough to cause offence. Shelley stresses the sufferings they must undergo in the name of liberty: he, like Prometheus, chained on a high precipice to feed on carrion, and she, carried away by the agents of the evil tyrant who has raped her, to the solitude of a sea-cavern. In many details the poem prefigures *Prometheus Unbound*, not only in its theme of liberty but in the scenery of mountains, caves and wild oceans as fantastical as that of the Arabian Nights, and in the dream-landscapes of the voyage to the Temple of the Spirit. The message of the regeneration of mankind also looks forward to the prophecies of the Spirit of the Hour in the later poem and to the birth of 'a diviner day' when love and hope bring their own reward and man becomes 'Equal, unclassed, tribeless and nationless'. For Shelley this would be the achievement of the ideal revolution, and for a brief moment in the poem good does triumph over evil, as was the case in France in the first glorious days of 1789. Laon and Cythna, miraculously freed from captivity, return to the Golden City to see the overthrow of the tyrant Othman, brought down like Napoleon or Louis XVI from an emperor's throne. The liberation of the City is celebrated with a great festival, an occasion similar to the festivals of the French Revolution such as the Fête de la Raison, with banquets, garlands and speeches. For one moment it is indeed bliss to be alive, but the armies of evil return and Laon and Cythna escape, riding on a huge black horse to a far-off hill where they consummate their passionate love-affair and subsequently witness the return of tyranny in a vision of Europe at war. Kings and their armies ravage the land, plague and famine ensue and priests declare that sacrifices are essential to appease the god of war. The horrifying descriptions of 'the death-polluted land' recall Shelley's first shock at seeing the ruined countryside of France in 1814, and form a powerful argument for his attack on the wickedness of war. His old enemies, the kings and priests and tyrants, first seen in *Queen Mab*, give proof of their malevolent strength and subject the two lovers to a martyr's death by burning at the stake, a fiery consummation of their love. Evil has triumphed, but their spirits, freed by death, embark in an enchanted boat for the paradise of the Temple of the Spirit where they reign in bliss. In the complicated and circular framework of the poem this ending harks back to Canto I where the two sit enthroned in the Temple and tell their story to the anonymous poet who has just witnessed the battle of the Serpent and the Eagle and seeks an explanation. They 'pour fresh light from Hope's immortal urn' and say that they will relate to him 'A tale of human power – despair not – list and learn'. And the message 'despair not' takes us back to Shelley's Preface and to the dedication 'To Mary' which is, in a sense, a statement of self-dedication as he recalls a significant moment of his schooldays when, weeping, he made the vow

> I will be wise
> And just, and free, and mild, if in me lies
> Such power, for I grew weary to behold
> The selfish and the strong still tyrannise
> Without reproach or check.

The dedication expresses his debt to Mary, 'thou Child of love and light', and his reverence for her parents, Godwin and Mary Wollstonecraft, whose ghosts haunt the poem and whose ideas direct much of its thought.

The Revolt of Islam, for all its masochistic posturing in the face of tyranny, is an optimistic poem. Although death is the only answer for Laon and Cythna and the world goes on its wicked way, the final message is 'despair not', and we have been shown what could be when good prevails. Unfortunately at this stage of his poetic development Shelley was not fully capable of handling the complications of a poem extending over twelve cantos. The narrative is unnecessarily involved and the symbolism becomes confused from the start, with the conflict of the Snake and the Eagle. The serpent is meant as an image of Wisdom; it is Lucifer, the Morning Star, fallen to become 'a dire Snake, with man and beast unreconciled' after combat with a blood-red Comet. In making the fallen angel a representative of Wisdom and Good, he is deliberately reversing the traditional values, but in the course of the poem serpents recur as images of real evil, as the 'two dark serpents tangled in the dust' (Canto II, st. 4) and the 'rabid snakes, that sting some gentle child' of Canto V, st. 7. The Comet confusingly becomes an eagle which soars aloft 'with overshadowing wings of evil' and is an image of Cain who 'turned and shed his brother's blood'. One might suppose that he is also a symbol of Napoleon, since the imperial eagle was his personal emblem, but the connection is never made explicit. Shelley's exposition of the beginning of the world and the clash of the two warring forces of good and evil, half-Miltonic, half-invented and owing much to the Zoroastrianism he had absorbed from Peacock, is as vague and unresolved as the process of events in the poem, and suggests that his theories had not been fully thought out but are poured out in a torrent of excited idealism.

Nevertheless, *The Revolt of Islam* is a deeply-felt expression of his political thinking at that time, and makes clear his attitude to the French Revolution and its outcome, the 'master theme' of his generation. His hope for the future, although belied by the events in the poem, seems more than mere rhetoric and can hardly be written off as the easy optimism of youth; Shelley was twenty-six when he wrote it, the same age as Coleridge was when he wrote in *France*:

> The Sensual and the Dark rebel in vain
> Slaves by their own compulsion

and turned aside from the disillusionment of the political scene to the benefactions of Nature.

Shelley's optimism, that is, the optimism that takes a long view into a distant future, changed very little over the years, although it comes more and more to be clouded with despair at the irrationality of mankind. The pattern of thought in *The Revolt of Islam* is repeated in 1818, a year later, in 'Lines Written Among the Euganean Hills'. In this poem, composed in great sadness after the death of his little daughter Clara, he contemplates the 'waveless plain of Lombardy' spread beneath him as he stands on the hill. Venice and Padua, the cities of the plain, are seen as subject to the tyrannical rule of the Austrians, and he mourns the inability of men to awake from the nightmare of history:

> Men must reap the things they sow
> Force from force must ever flow,
> Or worse; but 'tis a bitter woe
> That love or reason cannot change
> The despot's rage, the slave's revenge.

It is the same cry that sounded through *The Revolt of Islam*, and again the same personal solution is offered. Not this time by death but by embarking for 'other flowering isles' in the sea of Life and Agony, carried there by boat to a ravishing landscape, a healing Paradise reminiscent of the Temple of the Spirit. Even the language is the same: the 'lawny hills' like 'the lawny islands fair' near the Temple, 'the flowering isles' like the 'flowering meadows', 'the old forests and scent of flowers' like the 'blosmy forests' of the earlier poem. Here, Shelley and a few chosen soulmates who share his desire to escape, will, like Laon and Cythna, live in brotherhood and peace and watch 'the earth grow young again'.

His Odes 'To Liberty' and 'To Naples', both written in 1820, celebrate positive victories for the freedom of nations. As paeans of praise for what he calls 'the glorious events' in Spain (the revolution which brought about a liberal government after the despotic rule of the Bourbon Ferdinand VII) and the new but short-lived constitution in Naples, which followed the Spanish success, these Odes strike a triumphant note far removed from the personal meditations on the Euganean Hills. Technically they are splendid in their use of the ode form, the Pindarics of the 'Ode to Liberty' being handled with exceptional dexterity; but the diction, rising to the demands of the public theme, inclines to shrill and over-heated personification:

> Indignation
> Answered Pity from her cave;
> Death grew pale within the grave;
> And Desolation howled to the destroyer, Save!

Odes to Liberty were, of course, a kind of compulsory exercise for Romantic poets, a response to the surge of feeling which swept Europe. Mary's letter to Maria Gisborne about the Spanish revolt ('The Inquisition is abolished, the dungeons opened and the patriots pouring out') recalls the spirit of Beethoven's *Fidelio* and its great chorus of *Freiheit*, just as the Odes and *Hellas* look forward to the joyous celebration of victory over the forces of evil in Schiller's Hymn to Joy which concludes the Ninth Symphony.

'Morals and politics'

Shelley as a cultivated man in touch with European affairs, could not help but respond to the spirit of the age in its desire for new ideals of freedom and democracy. For him as for the rest of the Continent the patterns of life were changing. But the question remains: how much of a radical was he? Despite claims to set him up as Red Shelley, an unremitting left-wing fanatic, it is hard to believe that his early political activity in Ireland and his attachment to the Leigh Hunt circle were more than the natural enthusiasm of a young man at a time when liberal ideas were under attack. If alive today he would no doubt have been involved in his early years in left-wing student activities, CND rallies, demonstrations by Friends of the Earth or similar concerned bodies hoping to change the Government, the environment, society in general, the world. But as early as 1816 he wrote to Hunt: 'I am undeceived in the belief that I have powers deeply to interest or substantially to improve mankind'. However, since his political opinions were based on morality rather than on narrow party interests ('Morals and politics can only be considered as portions of the same science', he wrote in *A Philosophical View of Reform*), his humanitarian and egalitarian beliefs remained unchanged throughout his life.

His Whig background, the political atmosphere he had absorbed from his earliest days in Field Place, conditioned his ideas on Reform, and his reading of Godwin took him a step further to consider economic equality and its social effects. His political prose writings reveal the extent of his commitment to a more or less radical programme on the affairs of his time, but they also show his ability to take a wider theoretical view, to set the contemporary movements for liberty in a historical perspective. Of these prose works the most emotional was the *Address to the People on the Death of Princess Charlotte*, signed 'The Hermit of Marlow' and written in November 1817 when he was living there. England was mourning the young Princess who had died in childbirth, but on the day after her death three agricultural labourers in Derbyshire were hanged and beheaded for plotting armed insurrection. Shelley saw this as a greater cause for mourning; not only was capital punishment wrong (and he paints a dreadful picture of the event) but the background to their actions was one of inequality and oppression leading inevitably to 'that anarchy which is at once the enemy of freedom'. In other words, if men are pushed too far, bloodshed and revolution will follow – the point he had made in the Preface to *The Revolt of Islam* in reference to the excesses of the French Revolution. Like Cobbett and the other radical Reformers he blames the 'unequal distribution of the means of living [that] saps the foundation of social union and civilized life' and points to the post-war breed of financiers and stock-jobbers which had been created, a new aristocracy more despicable than the old traditional one. Their profits had increased the poverty of the labouring classes who were thus forced to achieve justice at any cost. It is a fine rhetorical piece, ending with a dramatic flourish of which Dickens would have been proud: 'Mourn then People of England. Clothe yourselves in solemn black. Let the bells be tolled.' The Spirit of Liberty is dead but may reappear on a throne 'of broken swords and sceptres and royal crowns trampled in the dust' like some glorious phantom, the 'Shape arrayed in mail' to spring up two years later in *The Mask of Anarchy*.

A more thoughtful excursion into political philosophy was begun in 1819 with *A Philosophical View of Reform*, an unfinished essay scribbled as a first draft in one of his note-books and left unrevised. This must be the basis for any consideration of Shelley as a serious political thinker, since it contains a long theoretical discussion of Reform developing some of the ideas in the *Address* and viewing the whole movement as part of the evolutionary process of history. Through an examination of past governments and republics (Italy, Spain, France, the Americas, among others) and of the philosophical ideas which accompanied or gave rise to them, he shows the historical struggle of humanity against tyranny towards an inevitable system of liberty. England is 'at a crisis in its destiny' in its desire for political and social change, and reform *must* result. The cause of the crisis is economic inequality, the inefficiency of the Government, and most of all the fact that 'the rights of all men are intrinsically and originally equal' and must be given recognition.

Shelley, writing at the end of a long and expensive war period, was conscious that taxation laid a crushing burden on the poor. Like Cobbett he blamed the National Debt, although he was even more radical than Cobbett in his suggestion that it be absolutely cancelled. In plans for Reform they both call for the abolition of sinecures and reform of the legal system. Shelley adds to these measures the abolition of the standing army and the necessity of making all religions 'equal in the eye of the law'. He again attacks the post-war profiteers but is less severe to his own class, the hereditary landowners: 'Connected with the members of it is a certain generosity and refinement of manners and opinion' – the hallmarks of the English gentleman, infinitely preferable to the crude commercialism of the *nouveaux-riches*. Like many liberal thinkers of his time he had divided views on the working-classes: suffering victims of an inequitable system, they were at the same time the menacing mob with insurrection as their final weapon resulting in the awful retribution seen in the French Terror. To him this was one of the strongest arguments for Reform: 'Men having been injured, desire to injure in return', and the only solution lies in equality and justice for all. He hoped for a non-violent outcome, brought about by petitions and reasoned argument from philosophers and other writers, but his fears are expressed in the image of the volcano at the end of *The Mask of Anarchy*, suggesting an uncontrollable catastrophe. Violence breeds violence, and for Shelley gradual change to Godwinian perfectibility was a more desirable answer. 'I am one of those', he wrote to Leigh Hunt in 1819, 'whom nothing will fully satisfy, but who am ready to be partially satisfied by all that is practicable.' For this reason he was against universal suffrage and votes for women, premature measures too sweeping for the contemporary conditions of what he called 'the difficult and unbending realities of actual life'. But this pragmatism did not cloud his ultimate view of the perfect society as seen in *Prometheus Unbound*, which looks forward to the classless world as visualized by Marx, although achieved by a change of heart rather than by the full force of economic revolution.

His emphasis on the morality of politics led him to despise the 'vulgar agitators' who fomented ideas of retribution and anarchy. He had nothing in common with the *sans-culotte* brand of revolutionary ideology; unlike Byron his temperament was not suited to the rough reality of political in-fighting, although *The Mask of Anarchy* has the authentic note of popular appeal. His final political position seems to have been that respectable and very English one of the aristocratic radical like his contemporary Lord John Russell. Mary's note to *The Mask* summarizes his views: 'He was a republican and loved a democracy'; and as a hopeful fellow-traveller rather than a committed activist he came to see himself perhaps more in the role of the liberal and compassionate Prince Athanase. A few days before his death he wrote to his friend Horace Smith and, on the subject of the 'desperate condition' of England and Ireland, added, 'I once thought to study these affairs & write or act in them – I am glad that my good genius said *refrain*'.

4 Shelley's philosophical beliefs

Shelley and the Enlightenment : Queen Mab *and the* philosophes

> The doctrine of Necessity tends to introduce a great change into the established notions of morality, and utterly to destroy religion.
> (Shelley's note on *Queen Mab*)

> Yet have I found no power to vie
> With thine, severe Necessity!
> (T.L. Peacock: 'Necessity')

The light and delicate structure of Shelley's verse is deceptive: he is, with the possible exception of Coleridge, the most intellectual of all the Romantic poets. Hogg tells us that at Oxford he would read for sixteen hours a day, and the book-lists given in Mary's and Claire's Journals, together with the testimony of his own letters and note-books establish him as one of the most widely-read of English poets. Much that seems strange and extravagant in his writing can be traced to his study of philosophy or of treatises on many obscure and scientific subjects. From an early age he read everything he could lay hands on: Gothic romances or Sir Humphrey Davy's *Elements of Agricultural Chemistry* were equally fascinating to him, but although a keen student of science and history, his main love was for philosophy. Mary even suggested that he might have become an important philosopher had he not been a poet, and he himself had written to Peacock in 1819 saying 'I consider Poetry very subordinate to moral and political science, & if I were well, certainly I should aspire to the latter'. Fortunately he did not, but his poetry has a solid ground-work of these disciplines. Sir Leslie Stephen, in his study of 'Godwin and Shelley' (*Hours in a Library*, vol. 3) dismisses the idea of Shelley as 'an originator of philosophic thought or even as a moderately profound student of philosophy' but recognizes that to understand his poetry it is necessary to be aware of the philosophic element in it.

His philosophical ideas from the outset were inevitably linked to those relevant to the French Revolution, the great event which had most profoundly affected the affairs of his lifetime. From his reading of the English empirical writers he had early on acquired the habit of scepticism. To Godwin he wrote in 1812 that after his early reading of romances and tales of natural magic and ghosts 'I read Locke, Hume, Reid & whatever metaphysics came my way'. Then, as Mary tells us in the note to *Queen Mab*, he temporarily became a convert to the more extreme ideas of the French philosophers of the Enlightenment, and the poem itself, written when he was eighteen, shows his interest in their propositions; many of these he rejected as his tastes developed, some he retained as essential elements in his maturer work.

As his flirtation with the eighteenth-century *philosophes* was a brief one, only a brief account need be given here of their influence on his thought. In any case, many of their ideas came to him by way of Godwin's *Political Justice*, whose Preface acknowledged the author's indebtedness; and it is certain that Godwin's speculations had a more lasting effect on him.

For Shelley the importance of the *Encyclopédistes* lay in their anti-clerical, rationalistic and scientific views, which appealed to his already radical turn of mind. They take this name as contributors to the great Encyclopaedia, the *Dictionnaire raisonnée des arts et des métiers*, the inspiration of Diderot resulting in a vast work of some thirty-five volumes based on the English *Cyclopaedia* by Chambers. Its first volume was published in 1751, the concluding one in 1780; intended as a work for furthering universal education, it was not merely a manual of practical information and instruction on manufactures, technical processes and so on, but it also contained long articles on religious, philosophical, scientific and political matters with many illustrations. These, commissioned by the editors Diderot and d'Alembert, were for the most part written by free-thinkers, whose chief ideological purpose was to promote the importance of reason as the highest of the human faculties. Consequently their arguments concentrated on an attack on the Church and the iniquities of revealed religion, since in their opinion priestcraft merely fostered superstition and dogma, inhibiting the processes of free thought and scientific investigation. The Encyclopaedia was thus an extremely powerful manifesto of the ideas of the Enlightenment, a monument to the Age of Reason, and by the very nature of its propaganda for religious and political freedom, a forerunner of the ideology of the Revolution. Indeed, the material in it was thought to be so subversive of the *Ancien Régime*, that efforts were made by the Government of France to stop its publication.

In 1812 Shelley had ordered the works of Diderot from a bookseller, and intended to acquire the whole Encyclopaedia itself. In that same year *Queen Mab* was written, his first long and important poem, the outpouring of all his youthful intellectual excitement. Full of ardent speculation, contradictory theories and material gathered from his eclectic reading, it is his salute to the philosophers of the Enlightenment, both French and English. As the copious notes show, he had responded with enthusiasm (an enthusiasm which also embraced Lucretius, Bacon, Hume, Spinoza and many others named there) to the more provocative views of the French *philosophes*, citing among his sources d'Holbach and Cabanis, the most materialistic and atheistic of them all.

Queen Mab has for its epigraph Voltaire's famous words '*Écrasez l'Infame*', a starting point for Shelley's assault on the enemies of society – the monarchy, religion and warfare. But by '*l'Infame*' Voltaire merely meant intolerance; he was not an enemy of the monarchy in the sense that he wanted to destroy it. Rather, his writing proposed a progressive and enlightened government under which religious toleration and freedom of thought and expression could flourish. He was certainly not an advocate of revolution nor was he an atheist, but as a deist believing in reason he tirelessly battled against the power of the Church and the superstitions disseminated by it. Shelley makes his own violent protest against religion:

> prolific fiend
> Who peoplest earth with demons, Hell with men
> And Heaven with slaves

and his polemic against the horrors of war is as powerful if not as biting as that of Voltaire in *Candide*. But his indignation carries him on to take an extreme stand, anti-monarchical and atheistic, as shown by the long quotations in the Notes to the poem from the Baron d'Holbach. This philosopher, in his *Système de la Nature* (1770), from which the extracts are taken, rejects all forms of religion and proposes a deterministic view of Nature (the Necessity so often referred to in the poem) in which there is no place for a God or for anything so tenuous as soul or spirit, or for free-will. For him religion is born of ignorance; Nature is the only worthwhile study:

> *Si l'ignorance de la Nature donna la naissance aux dieux, la connaissance de la Nature est faite pour les détruire.* [If ignorance of Nature gave birth to the gods, the understanding of Nature is given to destroy them.]

By Nature d'Holbach means here the laws of the physical world, not the spiritual force which animates Wordsworth's poetry. It is the knowledge of and control of the physical universe which will bring happiness to mankind, not idle speculations on concepts like spirit, predestination or grace. Shelley as a passionate amateur of science was in total sympathy with this premiss, although to him knowledge, or science, was the key to the perfectibility of man and a resulting golden age – an idealistic conclusion which would not have been that of d'Holbach, who held that human nature was ruled by pure self-interest.

Shelley's version of Necessity, 'the great chain of Nature', in *Queen Mab*, is given in a panorama of Past and Present, leading on to a Future in which 'the habitable earth is full of bliss', and man lives in harmony with all its creatures. The Spirit of Nature, which accompanies the fairy Queen Mab in the magic car, demonstrates the

predestined undying force of 'Eternal Nature's law' in a vision of the
universe in which the planetary systems circle in 'Nature's unchanging harmony' and the earth below is a mass of interlinked
particles and impulses. Queen Mab's rôle is to show what monarchs
and conquerors in their pride have made of the earth, in building and
destroying cities, making war and enslaving their subjects; and
Ahasuerus, the Wandering Jew, is testimony to the malicious cruelty
of God and His son. Nature, on the other hand, is a mindless,
impartial force:

> all that the wide world contains
> Are but thy passive instruments, and thou
> Regardst them all with an impartial eye . . .

and Shelley seems to believe that in the course of Nature's necessary
progress the Golden Age will return, as he prophesies later on in
Prometheus Unbound and *Hellas*. By this time, as we shall see, his views
had been modified and transformed by his study of Plato. So, in
Prometheus Unbound the millennium is brought about through the
force of love rather than through the mindless and soulless operations
of Necessity, although Necessity in the person of Demogorgon has its
part to play. In that poem, too, Christ is seen by Panthea in a vision
as 'a youth With patient looks nailed to a crucifix', a pitiful sight
with little resemblance to the suffering Christ of *Queen Mab* who
looks on Ahasuerus with 'a smile of godlike malice' as He condemns
him to his eternal wanderings.

Queen Mab is often dismissed as a piece of intellectual showing-off
about the subjects dear to Shelley as a young man – philosophy,
astronomy, vegetarianism and so on. But it also shows Shelley as a
Romantic poet: even while committed to the materialist programme
of the *philosophes* his poem has a magic and dream-like framework,
and its imaginative brilliance and airy essence seem to deny the
earthbound opinions of his masters.

Godwin : the true foundation of virtue

The Enquiry concerning Political Justice may, unknown to me, be
a mass of false principles and erroneous conclusions; to me it
appears otherwise: there is one principle that lies at the basis of
that book: 'I am bound to employ my talents, my understanding,
my strength, and my time, for the production of the greatest
quantity of general good. I have no right to dispose of a shilling of
my property at the suggestion of my caprice'. There is no
principle, as it appears to me, more fundamental to a just morality
than this last . . .

(Godwin: letter to Shelley, July 1812)

William Godwin

After the initial excitement, Shelley quickly tired of the mechanistic approach of philosophers like d'Holbach and La Mettrie. However, he never seemed to tire of the book which he first read in his schooldays and afterwards almost annually. *An Enquiry concerning Political Justice* had a deep and lasting effect on his thought, and H.N. Brailsford did not exaggerate when he said that 'to attempt to understand Shelley without the aid of Godwin is a task hardly more promising than it would be to read Milton without the Bible'. For Shelley in his early years *Political Justice was* his Bible, and his relationship with Godwin (in spite of much coolness about money and the elopement with Mary) was that of a student at the master's feet.

In November 1810 he ordered *Political Justice* from a bookseller, and on 3 January 1811 he wrote from Keswick the fateful letter expressing his admiration and desire for friendship with the philosopher, little guessing the consequences of his action. Godwin could not have been flattered to hear from his disciple that 'I had enrolled your name on the list of the honourable dead. I had felt regret that the glory of your being had passed from this earth of ours'. Godwin was, after all, only fifty-five and hardly yet ready to pass from the earth: he was to survive for another quarter of a century. But after the early fame of *Political Justice* (a fame backed with a publisher's advance of 700 guineas) his reputation had diminished with the changing political climate and he was now living quietly in London in Skinner Street as a bookseller and publisher.

Political Justice on its first appearance in 1793 struck the optimistic note of the day and achieved a *succès fou* among intellectuals and working-class circles alike. Wordsworth, Coleridge, Southey, Hazlitt, Robert Owen, Crabb Robinson and many more famous men all bear witness to the inspiring effect of his gospel of reason and benevolence. But, as Hazlitt observes in his astute essay on Godwin in *The Spirit of the Age*, 'he raised the standard of morality above the reach of humanity', and his inflexible doctrines of perfectibility, universal benevolence and justice were too far removed from the experience of the common man. Nevertheless these were the virtues which attracted Shelley and he found in *Political Justice* a source of political and philanthropical action: 'I did not truly *think & feel* — until I read *Political Justice*' he wrote to Godwin, and tried to carry out its precepts in his daily life and writing:

> I will publish nothing that shall not conduce to virtue, and therefore my publications so far as they do influence shall influence to good.

Godwin, who came from a classic English Jacobin background of Dissenters, had been much influenced, as he says in his Preface, by current radical ideas, by the French philosophers and by Rousseau; hence his elevation of Reason, 'that impartial estimate of things which is the true foundation of virtue', his proposals for a tolerant society and his arguments against authority, established religion and state education. To him all men are equally rational, although not necessarily equal in intellectual power, therefore in the ideal society neither laws nor governments imposed from above are needed: morality is 'that system of conduct which is determined by a consideration of the greatest general good' rather than any system based on Christian teaching. 'Man is an intellectual being. There is no way to make him virtuous but in calling forth his intellectual powers' and (here he is following the assumptions of Helvétius) man is a product of his environment, having no innate principles or innate feelings. All feelings and passions and powers of the mind, too, arise from sensation; hence his chapter headed 'The characters of men originate in their external circumstances'.

All this would have been familiar to Shelley from his reading of the English empiricists, but Godwin clarified these ideas for him, driving the arguments on to logical conclusions at once revolutionary, egalitarian and philanthropic, which strongly appealed to Shelley's temperament. As we have seen, it was the austerity of Godwin's political views based on morality which attracted him; and the asceticism of *Political Justice* must have touched the puritanical streak in Shelley, the part of his nature which made him a vegetarian (Godwin recommends 'a frugal and wholesome diet'), careless of the luxuries of life and shocked by the excesses and gross talk and behaviour of men like Byron. Also attractive was Godwin's insistence on truth and sincerity in social relationships instead of the falsehood of social convention.

As a practical guide to living, *Political Justice* had its uses: Godwin on Property must have struck home to Shelley: 'It is a gross imposition that men are accustomed to put upon themselves, when they talk of the property bequeathed to them by their ancestors.' Godwin on Marriage, though, had its problems. In spite of his attack on the evil institution of marriage, 'the worst of monopolies' unless the partners are free to go their own ways, Godwin had married twice and had refused to see Shelley after the elopement with Mary until she was made an honest woman. Nor was he placated until the moment of their marriage; on that occasion he wrote to his brother exulting at his daughter's alliance with 'the eldest son of Sir Timothy Shelley, of Field Place, in the county of Sussex, Baronet', and expressing pleasure at 'so good a match': somewhat surprising in the stern philosopher who had set his face against both property and aristocracy.

Shelley himself had to overcome his principles about marriage when he first eloped with Harriet Westbrook, and discovered the gulf between theory and practice when Hogg attempted to seduce her; free love, exalted in the rapturous union of Laon and Cythna, was something less divine in these circumstances, although later Shelley was prepared to share Mary with his friend as a token of his belief in the concept of marriage as the union of free spirits.

It is easy to recognize throughout Shelley's poetry the values and ideals of Godwin's philosophical anarchism, particularly in the constant vision of a future age after the withering away of the state and the establishment of a free and loving society in which all men are equal. Shelley elevates the idea of perfectibility above Godwin's rather pedestrian definition of it:

> By perfectible, it is not meant that he [Man] is capable of being brought to perfection. But the word seems sufficiently adopted to express the faculty of being constantly made better and receiving perpetual improvement; and in this sense it is here to be understood.

To see what Shelley took from Godwin and how magnificently he transformed it, we need only turn to the Spirit of the Hour's proclamation of the new world at the end of Act III of *Prometheus Unbound*:

> The loathsome mask has fallen, the man remains
> Sceptreless, free, uncircumscribed, but man
> Equal, unclassed, tribeless, and nationless,
> Exempt from awe, worship, degree, the king
> Over himself; just, gentle, wise ...

Rousseau : the language of the heart

> There are very few of our automatic reactions whose cause we cannot discover in our hearts, if we are really capable of looking for it.
>
> (Jean-Jacques Rousseau: *Reveries of the Solitary Walker*, Sixth Walk)

So far we have looked at Shelley as an intellectual, reacting to the ferment of the philosophical and political ideology of his time. But the Encyclopédistes and the virtuous Houyhnhnms of Godwin's ideal community, living out their lives in the pursuit of impartial and rational justice, seem chilly inspiration for the Romantic poet of *Alastor* and 'The Sensitive Plant'; rather they form the foundations of his work, shifting in emphasis as his thought matured. What made 'the mere touch of cold philosophy' come alive in his poetry was feeling, the introspection and subjective response to Nature which characterize the Romantic sensibility. Sensibility, as distinguished from the sober sense of Godwin, is the cult of emotionalism, a well-established trend in the eighteenth century: the plight of

Richardson's Clarissa Harlowe (1747), betrayed, seduced and dying a lingering death beside her coffin, installed in her room as an emblem of mortality, had brought tears to the eyes of her readers as copious as those shed over Little Nell in later years. Henry Mackenzie's *Man of Feeling* (1771) is a novel in which tears are shed on every page; and Jane Austen's Marianne Dashwood in *Sense and Sensibility*, herself a creature of pure instinct and impulse, brought near to death by the agonies of unrequited love, is only one among the many fictional characters of the period who listen to the language of the heart rather than that of reason.

Of this cult of feeling Jean-Jacques Rousseau may well be described as the high-priest, although he had begun his philosophical career as a subscriber to the Encyclopaedia and had frequented the *salon* of d'Holbach. He soon broke with that circle, leaving Paris to write in quick succession in the 1760s *Émile* and *La Nouvelle Héloïse*, the works which so strongly affected Romantic literature in their appeal to a return to *le sentiment intérieur* and a morality dictated by natural, even primitive, instinct.

The effect of *Émile* on Wordsworth is well-known: that impulse from a vernal wood and his rejection of 'the dull and endless strife' of book-learning represent ideas lifted straight out of Rousseau. In Émile's education Nature really is the teacher and her lessons are learned through the application of sensibility, a heart that watches and receives. No meddling intellect intervenes: 'the life contained in the sight of Nature lies in man's heart; to see it he must feel it'. So Rousseau expressed it, years before Wordsworth adopted that message for one of his basic concepts. For Rousseau the first lesson of the child of Nature is that of self-love and self-preservation; in extending this to others he develops the social virtues of pity, generosity and so on. Morality therefore begins with the cultivation of self, and Rousseau turns his gaze inwards to self-analysis and introspection in order to define the true nature of feeling; almost totally given over to this end are the *Confessions*, an analysis of his own inner life, and his novel in letter-form, *La Nouvelle Héloïse*, in which the nature of love is examined at length.

The integrity of self, the preservation of one's primitive instincts and passions, is more easily maintained in contact with Nature, away from the corruption of so-called civilization and the specious opinions to be found in books: again a sentiment familiar to readers of the earlier Romantics. Such a belief is also central to the idea of the Noble Savage, a figure frequently encountered in Romantic literature in many forms. The monster of Mary Shelley's *Frankenstein*, for example, is one of the more striking variants on the theme, a creature educated by his instincts but perverted by the cruelty and misunderstanding of civilized man. His early days are passed in Rousseauistic simplicity and his education, like that of

Émile, evolves through sensation and physical experience. This novel, written when she was only nineteen, for all its suspense and macabre Gothic quality, is very much a *roman à thèse*, a story with a powerful message to communicate, and it is particularly interesting in a consideration of Rousseau's influence on Shelley himself. Although the original inspiration for the plot was her own, many of the ideas incorporated in it owe much to Shelley and, of course, to her father whose doctrines of reason and justice form the positive basis for the turns of the plot. But equally strong is the influence of Rousseau, whose *La Nouvelle Héloïse* has its setting on Lake Geneva, where the Shelleys were staying in the summer of 1816 and where she began to write *Frankenstein* after a suggestion of Byron's that they should each write a ghost story to while away the wet summer.

Shelley had read Rousseau's novel years before (he mentions it in a letter in 1811) but now they were both reading it again in the authentic surroundings: 'It is inconceivable what an enchantment the scene itself lends to those delineations, from which its own touching charm arises', he wrote to Peacock, and the spirit of Rousseau is alive in the many descriptions in *Frankenstein* of sublime mountain and lake scenery, ranging from the Vale of Chamouni to the mountains of the English Lake District where the scientist Frankenstein travels to find solace from his mental anguish. As the Modern Prometheus of the sub-title he has to suffer for overstepping the bounds of what is permitted, in creating a monstrous human being from the parts of dead bodies, but this is not the only sin he has to expiate: his real tragedy, the novel implies, comes not so much from the pursuit of knowledge but that it has led him to turn away from the dictates of the heart. In his scientific work he had neglected human relationships and failed in his duty to his creation, whose natural goodness and desire for affection is rejected. For this he pays dearly and sees the destruction of his family, wife and friend. In his aspiration to create, bringing its dreadful result, he becomes a version of the doomed romantic hero, the pursued and pursuing, to die at last in the sterility of the Arctic wastes, as symbolic a landscape as the ice-bound ocean in which the Ancient Mariner is stranded. The monster, losing its primitive innocence to become a vengeful killer, finally repents after the death of its creator, and goes away to end its miserable existence. The tension of the novel lies in the conflict between these two characters, and the moral implication is that the single-minded scientist (or artist) in his pursuit of an ideal must not reject the simple feelings of humanity natural to mankind.

The myth of primitivism was a powerful and attractive one, but, for writers committed to political ends, a dangerous one since its logical conclusion was a denial of progress, a turning away from the problems of 'real' life to a concentration on the self. Shelley, in

Alastor, although obviously seduced by the lures of the primitive ideal, shows an awareness of its inherent dangers.

The Poet in *Alastor* is a true child of Jean-Jacques. His infancy was nurtured by

> Every sight
> And sound from the vast earth and ambient air

and he makes his home among savage men, in wild country where the animals and birds feed from his hand. Untouched by civilization, except that of the dead past and the primitive Arab maiden, a female Noble Savage who tends him, he keeps 'mute conference With his still soul', driven on by a dream of spiritual beauty until his death in solitude. But Shelley points the warning moral: solitude and introspection are not enough. The Poet's self-centred seclusion brings its own doom: 'those who attempt to exist without human sympathy, the pure and tender-hearted, perish through the intensity and passion of their search after its communities, when the vacancy of their spirit suddenly makes itself felt'.

Keats in *The Fall of Hyperion* is concerned in the same way with the predicament of the Romantic poet. The Shade warns him as he approaches the altar steps that none can attain the sacred shrine of poetry

> But those to whom the miseries of the world
> Are misery, and will not let them rest.

The dilemma was a real one; over-indulgence in sensibility led to the ivory tower and both Keats and Shelley could see its dangers. Nevertheless, Rousseau was heady stuff, and Shelley like many of his contemporaries fell under his spell. On his travels in 1816, he went by boat to Clarens on Lake Geneva, the setting of *La Nouvelle Héloïse*. On the way (as he wrote to Peacock) 'I read Julie all day', and on arrival he walked the sacred soil where Julie and St Preux, the two lovers, had walked, saw the mountains that they had seen and was shown 'le bosquet de Julie'. Like the villagers he seemed to believe that 'the persons of the romance had actual existence', so strongly had the novel impressed him. Significantly at Lausanne when he visited Gibbon's house, although Byron picked some acacia leaves in memory of the great man, Shelley did not, 'fearing to outrage the greater and more sacred name of Rousseau, the contemplation of whose imperishable creations had left no vacancy in my heart for mortal things'. In other words, in the full flood of sensibility he had momentarily turned his back on 'the cold and unimpassioned spirit' of rationalism.

Lac Léman (the Lake of Geneva)

From Rousseau Shelley learned something of '*le sentiment intérieur*', the sensibility leading not only to self-knowledge and love of others but to a heightened feeling for wild natural scenery, the mountains and lakes of Switzerland which had excited him on his visits to that country. He also responded sympathetically to Rousseau's ideas of small communes of intelligent and sensitive people who would live, like the little community at Clarens in *La Nouvelle Héloïse*, in high-minded simplicity – an ideal which has haunted generations of intellectuals, usually ending, alas, in disillusionment. Such was the Bracknell household of Mrs Boinville which he had admired so much, and he himself had similar plans in mind when he pressed Eliza Hitchener to join him and Harriet, her sister and Hogg, as the nucleus of such a coterie of kindred spirits.

His visit to Clarens was an idyllic time. In Rousseau's novel he found a romantic expression of a love-affair as passionate as his own with Mary, and in St Preux he recognized his own devotion to the ideal woman. As Mary was to write later: 'There was something in the character of Saint-Preux, in his abnegation of self, and in the worship he paid to Love, that coincided with Shelley's own disposition.'

It might be added that he would also have responded sympathetically to the feelings of persecution, amounting almost to mania in Rousseau; the Romantic outcast, spurned by society for his principles, was a rôle in which Shelley was perfectly at home.

The Triumph of Life

In Shelley's last poem, *The Triumph of Life*, unfinished but potentially one of his finest, the great Rousseau has dwindled to the terrifying apparition on the hillside where the pageant of Life passes by in unholy frenzy. Distorted like an old root, with white hair and eyes like the hollows of a skull, he makes himself known to the poet.

I feared, loved, hated, suffered, did and died,
And if the spark with which Heaven lit my spirit
Had been with purer nutriment supplied,

Corruption would not now thus much inherit
Of what was once Rousseau, –

and explains to him the meaning of the triumphal procession. Why Shelley chose him for this rôle is not immediately clear. As one of the world-famous, like Napoleon or Voltaire, he is proof of the vanity of human wishes and cannot escape the cruel chariot which drives on the captive multitudes, humble and powerful alike. He is certainly ranked among the great, although not among the great thinkers who, like Plato and Bacon, are chained to the chariot; even these were unable to reach the highest human virtue of self-knowledge, of 'solving the mystery within' because intellectual power alone does not solve the mystery of life. Rousseau is not included among the thinkers because

> I was overcome
> By my own heart alone . . .

Like Shelley he has suffered: 'I have suffered what I wrote' – the fate according to Count Maddalo of many poets and writers who 'learn in suffering what they teach in song'.

At least for Rousseau there is some immortality:

> If I have been extinguished, yet there rise
> A thousand beacons from the spark I bore

and this is perhaps the clue to his function in the poem. Shelley recognizes his importance as a writer, 'one of those who have created, even If it be but a world of agony', and a writer whose works will light the future. In *A Defence of Poetry* he is included among the philosophers who liberated humanity, but Shelley adds: 'Although Rousseau has been thus classed, he was essentially a poet', and a poet with whom he could identify.

In the narrative (lines 300 and following) in which Rousseau attempts to explain how he had come 'to this dread pass' he speaks to Shelley as an equal and as one who will understand. His story opens with a dream-setting, parallel to the one at the beginning of the poem, except that Rousseau has passed beyond Lethe, the river of forgetfulness, beyond 'All pleasure and all pain, all hate and love', into a magical countryside at sunrise, in a light 'diviner than the common sun'. A Shape appears to him, a spirit with a crystal glass of Nepenthe, a draught to bring even more forgetfulness; she is an unmistakeably Shelleyan vision of ideal Beauty but what she represents here is not certain. She may be Intellectual Beauty (the images of light, mist and water suggest this), or she may be the Muse, more seductive than Keats's Moneta in *The Fall of Hyperion* but just as lethal in her effect. In *The Fall* the poet drinks a potion which induces a 'cloudy swoon'; in *The Triumph of Life* Rousseau's 'brain became as sand' as he quenches his thirst from the glass. The Shape fades, and a new vision, that of the 'cold bright car' which had appeared in the early part of the poem, sweeps on with its shadowy train of captives, the grotesques of death. The narrative has the hallucinatory confusion of a nightmare and by the time the final words are uttered: 'Then, what is life? I cried', the two poets, as in a dream, seem to have merged into the single agonized figure of the creative artist, confronted with the inevitable process of death and decay, the apparent senselessness of life.

From *The Triumph of Life*, his last poem, it is clear that Shelley had not lost his early love for Rousseau. In the beautiful and sad lyrics of his last years he seemed more attuned to the language of the heart, even its more exotic accents of the 'Italian Platonics' of *Epipsychidion*, than to the cool calm voices of the Enlightenment philosophers.

Plato : 'We are all Greeks'

EAGLE! why soarest thou above that tomb?
To what sublime and star-ypaven home
    Floatest thou?
I am the image of swift Plato's spirit,
Ascending heaven; Athens doth inherit
    His corpse below.

               (Shelley's translation from the Greek of an
                          Epigram by Plato)

Much as Godwin and Rousseau contributed to Shelley's thought, they did not fully meet the demands of his temperament. The ultimate satisfaction came from his study of Plato whose influence is seen throughout his major poetry and who alone was capable of satisfying both his intellectual and spiritual needs. Why this was so is explained in the Preface to his translation of the Symposium, *The Banquet of Plato*: 'Plato exhibits the rare union of close and subtle logic with the Pythian enthusiasm of poetry' – for Shelley the perfect combination to which he aspired in his own work.

His education at Eton and Oxford had not prepared him to read much Greek in the original, although he read a great deal in translation; and when in 1812 he ordered the works of Plato from a bookseller, it was an edition with a translation. Not until the years of 1815 and 1816, when he and Mary lived at Bishopgate, did he begin to read Greek seriously in the original, encouraged by Peacock, a learned and enthusiastic Greek scholar known to his friends as Greeky Peaky for his devotion to the subject; that winter, Peacock said, was 'a mere Atticism' as he and the poet read their way through the classics.

Shelley had an instinctive love for things Greek, art as well as literature. His long descriptive letters to Peacock, written after he and Mary had visited the Graeco-Roman cities of Herculaneum and Pompeii in 1818, tell how moved he was by the architecture and statues and by the setting of these cities so perfectly in harmony with Nature: 'If such is Pompeii, what was Athens?' He was thinking of such cities when he wrote in *Prometheus Unbound* (Act II, sc. 4)

The ruins at Paestum *by J.R. Cozens (1782)*

> Cities then
> Were built, and through their snow-like columns flowed
> The warm winds, and the azure aether shone,
> And the blue sea and shadowy hills were seen.

A Defence of Poetry returns to the theme: '...yet never at any other period has so much energy, beauty and virtue, been developed...Of no other epoch in the history of our species have we records and fragments stamped so visibly with the image of the divinity in man'.

The discovery of these cities in the 1730s and 1740s had excited a renewed interest in the civilization of Ancient Greece. In the latter half of the century were published the magnificent volumes of engravings, such as the *Antiquities of Athens* prepared by 'Athenian' Stuart and Revett for connoisseurs of the archaeological splendours of the Classical world. Travellers brought back their own antiquities, not least of which were the Elgin marbles, the 'Grecian grandeur' so overwhelming to Keats in 1816 when they arrived in London and Haydon took him to see them.

This aesthetic revival had its political counterpart in the sympathy felt by many for Greece in her long struggle with Turkey for independence, the subject of much of Byron's poetry and echoed by Shelley in his 'Ode to Liberty' and *Hellas*. Byron died in the fight for that independence; Shelley never saw Greece but always in his mind's eye had an idealized picture of it and, as the Preface to *Hellas* makes plain, he recognized it as the foundation stone of Western culture: 'We are all Greeks. Our laws, our literature, our religion, our arts have their root in Greece.'

Immortality

> When I have drunk the poison I shall no longer remain with you, but shall depart to some happy state of the blessed.
>
> *(Phaedo)*

In such a short study one can do no more than look at the mere outlines of the 'close and subtle logic' of the Platonic system. It is a logic deployed on a set of assumptions about the nature of the world which are mystical and not always easy to comprehend, although expressed in language of great beauty and freshness. Putting aside Plato's political arguments to be found in *The Republic* – the definitions of justice, the organization of the state, the purpose of education and other social matters – it is of interest to consider briefly the philosophical ideas that most influenced Shelley.

First of all is Plato's belief that beyond our world, which we know only through the senses, is another world, eternal and unchanging, and it is to this, the real world, that the philosopher aspires, seeking it through the love of wisdom and knowledge. 'Those who see the absolute and eternal and immutable may be said to *know*.' In our physical (or phenomenal) existence there is nothing permanent; all is in a state of flux and all change is illusory. The only unchanging things are those in the timeless reality beyond. This is the assumption on which all Plato's thinking is based; with it goes his belief that the body and soul are separate, expressed most beautifully in *Phaedo*, the great dialogue on Immortality of the Soul between Socrates and his pupils in the last hours before his death in prison. Here Socrates argues that for those in pursuit of wisdom, the body is a hindrance: therefore 'those who pursue philosophy rightly study to die; and to them of all men death is least formidable', because in death they will obtain 'what we desire; and this, we say, is truth'. In *Adonais* Shelley almost paraphrases this: 'Die If thou wouldst be with that which thou dost seek.'

Socrates, having proclaimed his belief in immortality, 'a great mystery which I do not quite understand', then speaks of pre-existence: we are born, he says, with knowledge of certain things, like the good, the beautiful, the just and the holy, and he demonstrates that this knowledge must have come from an earlier existence of the soul. In Romantic poetry Wordsworth's 'Ode on Intimations of Immortality' is the finest presentation of this concept:

> Our birth is but a sleep and a forgetting:
> The Soul that rises with us, our life's Star,
>   Hath had elsewhere its setting,
>   And cometh from afar:
>   Not in entire forgetfulness,
>   And not in utter nakedness,
> But trailing clouds of glory do we come
>   From God, who is our home . . .

Shelley, too, in *Adonais* thinks in Platonic terms of the soul and the body:

> Dust to dust! but the pure spirit shall flow
> Back to the burning fountain whence it came,
> A portion of the Eternal, which must glow
> Through time and change, unquenchably the same . . .

Although logical in argument Plato's philosophy is mystical and religious in its nature. His theory of knowledge and of ideas springs directly from this approach. Knowledge is the road to virtue and truth: but if in the phenomenal world objects are only shadows of the eternal reality, how can knowledge be acquired from shadows? Plato's answer, given at length in the last book of *The Republic*, is that objects have their ideal counterpart in eternity: God's creations were the originals, man merely makes and sees copies of them. So, there are many tables and beds, all different but recognized to be tables and beds, and the words 'table' and 'bed' are used as a general definition. But God has in the beginning created one unique table, one unique bed which is the real and ideal one; the ones we see are only apparent, approximations of the ideal. Thus, in 'The Sensitive Plant' the garden and the lady 'In truth have never passed away' because they are only images of the real which exist for ever in eternity.

The prisoners in the cave: illusion and reality

Most readers will know something of Plato's famous metaphor from *The Republic* of the shadows on the cave, and since this explains his concept of reality more fully, a closer look at it may be useful.

In Book VII Socrates, in a discussion of human nature, pictures men as prisoners chained in an underground cave from childhood, and able to look in one direction only; they see on a wall facing them, reflected from the firelight behind them, the shadows of life passing like a shadow puppet-show, and these they believe to be real things. If a prisoner were to be released and led towards the outside world, he would still believe that the shadows were more truly 'real' than what he can now see of the world beyond. If he were forced to look directly at the light outside, his eyes would ache and he would try to turn back to captivity; and if he were forced out of the cave into the sunlight, his eyes would be so dazzled that he would be unable to see 'a single one of the objects we now call true', but would need time before he could adjust his vision to see them properly. Then he might pity those who were his fellow-prisoners, but if he went back to tell them of the 'real' world outside they would mock him and persecute him even to death.

The purpose of this fable of 'the upward journey of the soul' to the true reality of life is to show the difficulty of perceiving the Good (or the True), although its perception is essential to both public and private virtue. The shadows are the reflections of the ultimate and immortal reality, known only to the Gods; thus in our world we live among images, copies of the original, shapes which correspond to a higher reality. Man's life should be (but rarely is) passed in the strenuous pursuit of virtue in order that he may perceive the 'real' as opposed to the phenomenal existence.

Once this has been understood, much of Shelley's thought and imagery becomes explicable. His poetry is in itself a pursuit of the ideal, a search for the reality beyond the shadows. Over and over again he uses the same images of life as an insubstantial pageant, Plato's puppet-show, as, for example, in the lyric 'Invocation to Misery':

Let us laugh, and make our mirth,
At the shadows of the earth,
As dogs bay the moonlight clouds,
Which, like spectres wrapped in shrouds,
Pass o'er night in multitudes.

All the wide world, beside us,
Show like multitudinous
Puppets passing from a scene . . .

Better known is the sonnet 'Lift not the painted veil' and its reference to the unreal shapes of what 'those who live call life', a mimic existence so gloomy that the poet although enlightened, 'a splendour among shadows', cannot break through to the ultimate truth. Again, in 'The Sensitive Plant', as we have seen, the fable of the garden and its decay has a Platonic moral; the garden is like the world

Where nothing is, but all things seem,
And we the shadows of the dream . . .

and the ideal beauty of the garden and the lady cannot die, since

For love, and beauty, and delight,
There is no death, nor change . . .

The Beautiful and the Good are immortal, but we, as unperceiving mortals, like the prisoners in the cave, can 'endure no light' on our dark existence. As in *Adonais*, 'Heaven's light forever shines, Earth's shadows fly'.

From a reading of this same fable in *The Republic* we can see not only the force of Shelley's constant references to shadow and light, but also the reason for the insistence in his poetry on the enlightened man, the one who has had a vision of the real, the ultimate beauty.

One of the aims of *A Defence of Poetry* is to show that poets, because of their sensitivity and imaginative powers, are more likely to have this vision than ordinary men. 'To be a poet is to apprehend the true and the beautiful, in a word, the good which exists in the relation subsisting, first between existence and perception, and secondly between perception and expression.' In other words, they can perceive the highest good and have the understanding and ability to convey it to others. They are thus able to lead men to virtue and are 'the unacknowledged legislators of the world'.

For this reason in his poetry the enlightened (and the enlighteners) are as often as not poets, usually thinly-disguised representations of himself. Much of what readers take to be egotistical self-pity in his poetry is his expression of the difficulty of the quest, the difficulty the prisoner experiences in making his way to

the light. Certainly Shelley had from early days felt a sense of
persecution, as the first few stanzas of *The Revolt of Islam* reveal ('The
harsh and grating strife of tyrants and of foes'), and self-pity had its
place in his character; but the emphasis on weakness and pain in the
poems reflects much more his sense of the inadequacy of mortal man
to aspire to the Platonic beauty which seems always to elude him. So
we have the frail form in *Adonais* wandering 'with feeble steps o'er
the world's wilderness' after his tantalizing vision of 'Nature's naked
loveliness', and the sad poet of *Alastor* who dies in his quest for the
image of beauty he had seen in the veiled maid. Again in
Epipsychidion Shelley speaks of how, in his own pursuit of the 'veiled
Divinity' he had become 'wounded and weak and panting like a
hunted deer'.

The Banquet of Plato : *'The great secret of morals is love'*

> Then Plato's words of light in thee and me
> Lingered like moonlight in the moonless east,
> For we had just then read – thy memory
>
> Is faithful now – the story of the feast;
> And Agathon and Diotima seemed
> From death and dark forgetfulness released...
>   (*Prince Athanase*)

To understand more of Shelley's debt to Plato we should turn to his
translation of the *The Symposium*, which he entitled *The Banquet of
Plato*, a work known from his schooldays and singled out by him as
the writer's finest achievement.

The Banquet at the house of Agathon in Athens is described by
Apollodorus, a pupil of Socrates, and consists of a number of debates
and dialogues on the subject of Love. Love, incidentally, in this
context is not heterosexual love. Pausanius, one of the guests, speaks
in praise of Love, but distinguishes between its two deities, the
Pandemian Venus and the Uranian Venus: the Pandemian represents earthly sensual love, that worshipped 'by the least excellent of
mankind', but the Uranian is the love of the soul rather than of the
body, a devotion to the wisdom and virtue embodied in the beloved.
Another guest, Eryximachus, adds that Uranian love through the
inspiration of its spirit can change 'the nature of the vicious' and
thus promote the highest social happiness. Aristophanes, the dramatist, continues the discussion with an extraordinary fable of the
original state of mankind: it began, he says, not with two sexes but
with male, female and a third androgynous sex having the attributes
of both. Human beings were first created in the round, strange
creatures with four arms, four legs, two faces and so on, standing

upright but when in haste tumbling over and over, cart-wheeling like acrobats. They warred against the gods, and Jupiter as a punishment cut them in half 'as people cut eggs before they salt them', and turned them into the human shapes we now know. From then on, each had to seek his or her other half, 'to heal the divided nature of man'. This is the desire and pursuit of the whole, 'that which we call love'.

Agathon follows this comic fable with a paean in praise of Love, the author of all the arts and sciences – music, poetry, medicine, politics. Questioned by Socrates he admits that Love is the desire for 'that which is absent and beyond his reach', and the desire for the Good and Beautiful. Socrates then relates to him a discourse he held with the prophetess Diotima on the nature of Love, one of the most important sections of *The Banquet* and one of which Shelley was particularly fond. She argues with him to prove that

> Love is the desire of men for the Good, 'the desire that good be for ever present to us'; of necessity, Love must also be the desire for immortality. To love rightly is a discipline: the lover must contemplate 'beautiful forms, and . . . make a single form the object of his love, and therein to generate intellectual excellences'.

This contemplation ultimately leads to the supreme beauty, 'from beautiful forms to beautiful doctrines': in other words, to knowledge and wisdom, Virtue itself, no longer the shadow but the reality.

The central topic of *The Banquet*, Love, is the constant theme of Shelley's poetry, Love both earthly and divine, the Pandemian and the Uranian. This distinction, so Mary Shelley's notes say, was to be the substance of *Prince Athanase* (1817) and in this poem is a direct acknowledgement of Plato's influence. Athanase's old friend, the philosopher Zonoras (a portrait of Dr Lind who had introduced Shelley to Plato's works when he was a schoolboy at Eton) reminds him of their reading of 'Plato's words of light', and talks of 'the story of the feast' and the noble words of Agathon and Diotima.

The story was to be the quest of Athanase for the one ideal woman. He was to meet 'the earthly and unworthy Venus' who deserts him, and on his deathbed (although the word 'Athanase' means 'deathless') the true Venus, the Uranian, comes and kisses him as in *Adonais* Urania kisses the dead poet. Athanase, like the Poet of *Alastor*, is a romanticized self-portrait of a youth, grey before his time, suffering a secret grief; but unlike the solitary in *Alastor* 'he loved and laboured for his kind', a benevolent Godwinian philanthropist, although now he is no longer the strident radical of *Queen Mab*, but one whose 'soul had wedded wisdom', Philosophy's accepted guest. And the philosophy is that of Plato: truly Platonic, Athanase 'loved good more for itself alone', but his friends, in attempts to discover the cause of his sorrow, offer garbled versions of

Platonic ideas which he scorns as 'vain words and fond philosophy' when they make half-understood references to the veil, the 'shadow of a dream', the cave and 'memories of an ante-natal life'.

Here, then, Shelley makes use of some of the ideas from *The Symposium* – the two Venuses, the notion that the pursuit of wisdom and virtue leads to social benefit, and the quest for the ideal beauty which, if found, will result in the acquisition of the highest virtue. But *Prince Athanase* is a mere outline of what was to be given much finer expression in *Prometheus Unbound*, *Adonais* and *Epipsychidion*.

Adonais : *death and resurrection*

> Those who instituted the mysteries for us appear to have been by no means contemptible, but in reality to have intimated long since that whoever shall arrive in Hades unexpiated and uninitiated shall lie in mud, but he that arrives there purified and initiated shall dwell with the gods. 'For there are', say those who preside at the mysteries, 'many wand-bearers, but few inspired'.
>
> (Plato: *Phaedo*)

Adonais, the elegy on Keats, most poignantly gathers together all Shelley's feelings about death and immortality and shows how deeply he had been influenced by Plato's teaching. As with Milton's 'Lycidas' it is a poem essentially Greek in conception, inspired by the pastoral poetry of Theocritus and more particularly by Bion's *Lament for Adonis*: 'I weep for Adonis; "Beautiful Adonis is dead." "Beautiful Adonis is dead," the gods of Love weep in answer.' In Bion's elegy Venus weeps for her lover, but in *Adonais*, the chief mourner is the Uranian Venus, a mother figure representing Love, Beauty and the Spirit of Poetry. She is 'Most musical of mourners', possibly a reference to Milton's 'Il Penseroso' in which the nightingale is 'most musical, most melancholy'. If so, it would be highly appropriate to the author of the 'Ode to a Nightingale', and the funereal mood of Milton's verse may well have been in Shelley's thoughts.

Shelley took immense trouble over what he called 'my least imperfect poem'. It is in effect not so much an elegy on Keats as an assertion of faith in the high art of poetry: poets – and he is very conscious of his own destiny – are in contact with the divine and as 'mirrors of the gigantic shadows which futurity casts upon the present' their function is of great importance. In it too are expressed his own personal grief and guilt over Harriet's death ('his branded and ensanguined brow'), and the bitterness over the blind ignorance of the reviewers who persecuted Keats and were scornful of his own work.

The death of the beautiful young hunter of Greek legend is, as Sir James Frazer fully demonstrates in *The Golden Bough*, part of the mythology of seasonal fertility cults: the hero dies, is mourned and rises from the dead in springtime. On it Shelley builds a complex structure of legend, personal feeling, and Platonic thought, rich also in literary reference. The seasonal pattern is followed, and in ritual elegiac mood the darkness and despair of mourning give way to the final 'white radiance of Eternity'.

After the opening lament and its reference to winter, 'the frost which binds so dear a head', the spirits of poetry gather, the traditional attendants of Aphrodite:

> Desires and Adorations,
> Winged Persuasions and veiled Destinies,
> Splendours, and Glooms, and glimmering Incarnations
> Of hopes and fears, and twilight Phantasies;

the dreams and symbols of 'All he had loved, and moulded into thought'. They make ritual gestures of mourning, and homage is paid by Shelley to some of Keats's poems: to 'Isabella' in the image of the 'pale flower by some sad maiden cherished', to the 'Ode to Autumn' in 'Like pageantry of mist on an autumnal stream' and to the 'Ode to a Nightingale' in the lorn nightingale of Stanza XVII.

Stanza XVIII announces the return of spring, and earth and all its creatures awaken from winter sleep; the swallows, seen departing in the 'Ode to Autumn', are back. The joyousness of the season adds particular irony to the poet's death and provokes the painful question:

> Whence are we, and why are we? of what scene
> The actors or spectators?

and Shelley surely had in mind not only the death of Keats but of his own son, William, buried in the spring of 1819 in the same cemetery in Rome:

> Where, like an infant's smile, over the dead,
> A light of laughing flowers along the grass is spread ...

The coming of spring heralds the rebirth motif of the fertility myth: the 'leprous corpse', ugly in death, is transformed with 'flowers of gentle breath', the wind-flowers or anemones sacred to Adonis in the rituals described in *The Golden Bough*. 'Nought we know, dies.' With spring, too, comes Urania to the death-chamber, where for a moment the corpse seems to revive; she kisses him but cannot restore him to life by any sacrifice she could make as she is 'chained to Time', an immortal being. The mourners come dressed as mountain shepherds, and are the poets who survived Keats – Byron, Moore, Leigh Hunt and Shelley himself. Urania curses the reviewers thought to have caused his death; their short forgotten lives, like those of ephemeral insects, are contrasted with the glory of a poet who, like a Platonic philosopher, enlightens the dark world, 'the spirit's awful night'.

Then comes the turning point of the poem:

> Peace, peace! he is not dead, he doth not sleep –
> He hath awakened from the dream of life –

The ritual mourning is over and the sad rites in the death-chamber end in a glorious new birth, following the pattern of the fertility cults of the Eleusinian mysteries or the ancient Orphic mysteries, and in keeping with the rebirth myth of Adonis. The mysticism of much of Plato's thought derives from these cults; from Orphism he took the ideas of the transmigration of souls and the duality of the soul and the body. He shared, too, their belief that life is dark and painful and that union with God is the much desired reward for the ascetic life of the philosopher. When Shelley describes himself as one of the mourners his appearance suggests the symbolism of the mysteries: his spear is topped with a cone from the cypress, a tree dedicated to Pluto, god of the underworld, and used in funeral ceremonies; it is twined with ivy, sacred to Bacchus, an everlasting evergreen plant. The violets and pansies of his wreath have a different symbolism, pansies traditionally representing thought, and violets love of truth, particularly suitable to a devotee of Plato.

Shelley is therefore in *Adonais* evoking a truly Greek attitude to death in combining the old primitive religion with the more sophisticated philosophy of the great age of Athens. The ancient rituals of the death-chamber are now superseded by the joy which sweeps the earth now that he 'is made one with Nature' and has become part of the eternal like the young poets of the past. Chatterton, Sidney and Lucan among many others are now immortals on thrones 'Far in the Unapparent', a purely Platonic conception. Their majesty is reminiscent of 'the Great who had departed from mankind', seated on sapphire thrones in the Temple of the Spirit, in the first Canto of *The Revolt of Islam*.

The darkness of the twilight chamber gives way to the brilliant image of the soul returning to 'the burning fountain whence it came', and for the remainder of the poem Shelley celebrates the ecstatic ascent of the poet's soul to 'the abode where the Eternal are', in words of light and radiance. The note of consolation for the mourners is a strong one. Contemplating the tombs in the cemetery he cannot deny the pain of loss which he has personally endured; the bitter wind of grief is hard to avoid, all is transient, Earth's shadows fly but the One remains, immutable and eternal as a beacon for mankind. The soul of Adonais, now among the immortals, burns like a star as an inspiration to others, a recollection of the ending of 'Lycidas'. Lycidas, too, is not dead although drowned:

So sinks the day-star in the ocean bed,
And yet anon repairs his drooping head,
And tricks his beams, and with new-spangled ore
Flames in the forehead of the morning sky . . .

Lycidas has ascended to the Christian Heaven with sweet societies and songs of saints, a less grandiose company perhaps than the Platonic Senate of Immortals that Shelley has in mind.

In the spirit of the *Phaedo* Shelley looks forward to his own end as something not to be feared but as 'The fire for which all thirst', that is, the element from which, according to the Greek philosopher Heraclitus, all things sprang and to which all will return. And since Socrates had taught that 'those who pursue philosophy rightly study to die' he thinks of embarking on his own voyage to eternity, in his favourite image of a boat sailing out into the dark – not the 'fatal and perfidious bark' of Lycidas but like Asia's enchanted boat in *Prometheus Unbound*, bound for 'a diviner day'. As a poet he is one apart from 'the trembling throng' of the mass of mankind, and he must fulfil his destiny. But as a man he is conscious of its loneliness and terrors as he is borne 'darkly, fearfully, afar'.

Italian Platonics : Epipsychidion

Oh Plato! Plato! you have paved the way
    With your confounded fantasies, to more
Immoral conduct by the fancied sway
    Your system feigns o'er the controlless core
Of human hearts, than all the long array
    Of poets and romances:
                    (Byron: *Don Juan* Canto I)

Epipsychidion, like *The Banquet of Plato*, is dedicated to Love, in Emilia's words 'L'anima amante', the soul that loves. Shelley's Italian Platonics, in Mary's rather bitter phrase, elevate the unfortunate lady imprisoned in her convent to the embodiment (if such a physical word can be used for a Seraph of Heaven) of Ideal Beauty conceived in terms of Dante and Plato. She is identified with the highest forms of beauty – a moon, a star, 'Thou Harmony of Nature's Art', a 'Metaphor of Spring and Youth and Morning' among other supremely flattering images. Some of these are images of light: she is a lamp, a splendour, 'soft as an incarnation of the Sun', an 'Image of some bright Eternity', and her radiance is so dazzling that she is a 'Veiled Glory' too brilliant to look upon. Shelley is thinking of the prisoner freed from Plato's dark cave, unable to look at the bright new sunlight; he makes this quite explicit when he speaks of

> this glorious One
> Floated into the cavern where I lay

and

> I knew it was the Vision veiled from me
> So many years.

He too has been a prisoner in the cave, or in an 'obscure forest', Dante's *selva oscura*, until he sees the light of reality.

Emilia is the incarnation of the Platonic ideal, at 'the height of Love's rare universe'. She is also the missing half of his being, and he is the lover absorbed in the desire and pursuit of the whole. Early in the poem he says to her: 'I am part of thee', and when they retreat to their island paradise he hopes

> We shall become the same, we shall be one
> Spirit within two frames, oh! wherefore two?

She is also the true Uranian Venus, 'The Vision I had sought through grief and shame', glimpsed before 'In the clear golden prime of my youth's dawn', a vision of ideal Beauty such as Rousseau describes in *The Triumph of Life*. Shelley's search to find her again led him along many trails to false Venuses: 'One, whose voice was venomed melody' and others in 'many mortal forms' who seemed to be 'The shadow of that idol of my thought' but proved not to be so. At this point the poem becomes more overtly autobiographical, a note signalled earlier by the famous passage:

> I never was attached to that great sect,
> Whose doctrine is, that each one should select
> Out of the crowd a mistress or a friend,
> And all the rest, though fair and wise, commend
> To cold oblivion . . .

It seems a jarring interpolation in the erotic rhapsody which precedes it, but in the fragments connected with the poem Shelley attributes such a creed to 'Socrates, the Jesus Christ of Greece' who urged 'all living things to love each other'.

Figures are introduced to prove his point, identifiable as his first love Harriet Grove, Harriet Westbrook and Mary, none of whom for one reason or another completely fulfilled the role of the One ideal woman. However, the Platonic path had its difficulties and Emilia, the reigning goddess, fell from her pedestal. A year or so after the composition of the poem Shelley wrote to John Gisborne (18 June 1822):

> The Epipsychidion I cannot look at; the person whom it celeb-
> rates was a cloud instead of a Juno; and poor Ixion starts from the
> centaur that was the offspring of his own embrace . . . It is an

idealized history of my life and feelings. I think one is always in love with something or other; the error, and I confess it is not easy for spirits cased in flesh and blood to avoid it, consists in seeking in a mortal image the likeness of what is perhaps eternal.

For Shelley it had always been so; in his essay 'On Love', written in 1815, he had said, 'I have found my language misunderstood, like one in a distant and savage land...I have everywhere sought sympathy, and have found only repulse and disappointment.'

Trelawny, in a letter to Claire after Shelley's death, puts it more bluntly: 'he was inconstant in Love as men of vehement temperament are apt to be – his spirit hunting after new fancies: nothing real can equal the ideal. Poets and men of ardent imagination should not marry – marriage is only suitable to stupid people.'

The episodes of Emilia and Jane Williams are symptomatic of the breakdown of his marriage, since Mary, after the loss of her children, had become increasingly withdrawn and cold. In his strong need for affection he looked elsewhere, much as he had turned to Mrs Boinville and Cornelia at the outset of his break from Harriet. The late poem 'The serpent is shut out from paradise' expresses his envy of the happiness of Edward and Jane Williams:

> When I return to my cold home, you ask
> Why I am not as I have ever been.
>   *You* spoil me for the task
> Of acting a forced part in life's dull scene –

and is fairly explicit about the difficulties of his own marital relationship.

Nevertheless *Epipsychidion* is his most clearly expressed commitment to the Platonic belief in the power of Love, as described in *The Banquet*. Asia had been the Uranian Venus herself, a divine and unearthly figure presented in a mythological context. Emilia, all too human as it turned out, shares some of Asia's divinity but is brought a little nearer to earth as the lady of a tale of courtly love. The poem owes much to Dante in its worship of feminine beauty, and an entry in one of Shelley's note-books which contains drafts of letters to Emilia makes it plain that he has courtly love in mind. He writes '*Tu Emilia ch'era più bella a vedere Che il giglio bianco sul verde stelo E più fresca che la Maia quando...*', a direct translation into Italian of lines from Chaucer's *Knight's Tale*:

> That Emelye, that fairer was to sene
> Than is the lylie upon his stalke grene,
> And fressher than the May with floures newe –

and Emelye in this tale, taken from Boccaccio's *Teseide*, is the archetypal lady of high degree and object of a lover's adoration.

The last part of the poem, the love-idyll among the flowers and beautiful scenery of the Elysian isle, moves away from high-minded Platonism to a purely romantic world of the imagination, yet still more earthly than the paradise of Asia's cave in which she and Prometheus 'will sit and talk of time and change'. For all its exquisite imagery of light and colour the isle in the 'far Eden of the purple East' where Shelley and Emilia are to find a haven, suggests rather more than the union in Heaven of twin-souls: overcome by erotic fantasy as fevered as that in *Alastor* when he encounters the veiled maid, Shelley confesses failure:

> The winged words on which my soul would pierce
> Into the height of Love's rare Universe,
> Are chains of lead around its flight of fire –
> I pant, I sink, I tremble, I expire!

The spirit is indeed 'cased in flesh and blood' and like Emilia he is all too human for the Platonic rôle.

Prometheus Unbound : *'The image of one warring with the Evil Principle'*

In this section on Shelley's philosophical thought, *Prometheus Unbound* has been left till last. Although earlier in composition (1818–1819) than *Adonais* and *Epipsychidion*, it represents the culmination of his moral and political ideas, expressed with a maturity and strength of conviction and a magnitude unequalled in the rest of his poetry. It was his own favourite, 'the most perfect of my productions', written 'in the merest spirit of ideal poetry', but although he knew its worth he also knew that it was a work 'very few will understand or like'; in 1820 he told Leigh Hunt that 'it is written only for the elect' and later in a letter to John Gisborne (26 January 1822) the elect were narrowed down to five or six persons. Mary's note to the poem echoes the warning: 'It requires a mind as subtle and penetrating as his own to understand the mystic meanings scattered throughout.'

Cautioned in such strong terms the unconfident reader approaches it with some apprehension. Esoteric it certainly is: Greek myth, Platonic and Neo-Platonic thought, Godwinian perfectibility and scientific theories of much complexity operate in dream-landscapes of extraordinary and unearthly beauty. The temptation is only to half-listen to what Shelley is saying and to luxuriate in the poetry; it is astonishing to remember that a year after its composition, in 1820, Keats was to write to him, 'you might curb your magnanimity, and

Joseph Severn's imaginary painting of Shelley writing 'Prometheus Unbound' in the Baths of Caracalla *(1845)*

93

be more of an artist, and load every rift of your subject with ore'. In *Prometheus Unbound* the ore seems to be loaded into every line. The lyrics and choruses are among the most splendid things he ever wrote, the blank verse a noble instrument. His inspiration takes wing from the majesty of Greek tragedy, and from the flowers and blue skies of the Roman spring which stirred his spirits 'even to intoxication' as he wrote in the Preface. The intoxication is infectious, rising to the cosmic symphony of Act IV, the height of Romantic prophetic rapture.

However, *Prometheus Unbound* stands as the finest of Shelley's works not merely as an outpouring of sublime verse and impassioned rhetoric. It has the high seriousness which Arnold seemed to deny him, in its concern with the philosophical problems of good and evil, the redemption of fallen man and the promise of a new golden age once men have learned the lessons of love and compassion. Shelley, in the full Romantic panoply of poet, prophet and philosopher, is aiming at Miltonic heights (the Preface compares Prometheus with Milton's Satan) in his most ambitious and important undertaking.

We have already seen in what ways his thought was influenced by Godwin and by Plato. In *Prometheus Unbound* Godwin's optimistic message of the perfectibility of man is essential to the theme, and firmly stated at the end of Act III in the Spirit of the Hour's vision of man:

> Equal, unclassed, tribeless, and nationless,
> Exempt from awe, worship, degree, the king
> Over himself; just, gentle, wise.

A year or so before, Godwin had been one of the guiding stars of *The Revolt of Islam*, and the subject had been a similar struggle between the forces of good and evil, although imperfectly resolved. In 1818, while composing *Prometheus Unbound*, Shelley was also translating *The Symposium* and his mind was full of Plato; the effect on him was powerful and the prosaic Utopia of *Political Justice* was transformed into the prophecy of a radiant new world, 'great and joyous, beautiful and free'. The dialogues of *The Banquet*, especially that of Diotima, are central to an understanding of the drama of Prometheus and Asia, and Love, not Godwin's reason, is the mainspring of the action. The Preface puts reason in its place: it is necessary for the advancement of mankind – Shelley the amateur of science and lover of knowledge for its own sake would not deny this – but there are other lessons to be learned.

> ... until the mind can love, and admire, and trust, and hope, and endure, reasoned principles of moral conduct are seeds cast upon the highway of life which the unconscious passenger tramples into dust, although they would bear the harvest of his happiness.

This is the essence of the drama, to be played out at the level of the gods. Prometheus is the supreme example of knowledge, science and virtue, 'the type of the highest perfection of moral and intellectual nature', the masculine principle of rationality and power of the will. After his fall he suffers alone on the cold mountain, apart from Asia, the female instinctive principle, the true Uranian Aphrodite of Love and Pity, and the embodiment of that supreme Beauty spoken of by Diotima in *The Banquet*. Until these two are united, like Plato's halves in the fable told by Aristophanes, cosmic chaos cannot be resolved. The world, like Prometheus, has to remain in chains under the tyrannous reign of Jupiter, the usurper and symbol of all the malevolent authority of the kings and priests attacked in *Queen Mab* and *The Revolt of Islam*. Mary notes that 'the subject he loved best to dwell on was the image of One warring with the Evil Principle, oppressed not only by it, but by all – even the good, who were deluded into considering evil a necessary portion of humanity'.

Indeed, in *Prometheus Unbound* Shelley repeats and reworks the dominant theme of these earlier poems, but with much greater confidence and unity of purpose. *Queen Mab*, clumsy as it is with its formal eighteenth-century device of the guided tour through past, present and future, contains the seeds of many ideas and images to be found in the drama. Here is the first of Shelley's magic chariots, and his first attempt, so brilliantly achieved in Act IV, to convey the majesty of the Universe, the earth and skies swarming with 'count-less spheres', and when the future is revealed by the Fairy Queen, and 'the habitable earth is full of bliss' we see Shelley's blueprint for a new heaven and a new earth, later to be idealized even more gloriously after the Spirit of the Hour has blown the conch-shell. It is interesting to read these two poems side by side and to see not only verbal echoes but the development of Shelley's poetic and intellec-tual abilities and the direction in which he was moving.

The drama, then, is a philosophical one transforming on a metaphysical level the political arguments for the overthrow of tyranny and the establishment of a fair and free society into a great discourse on the power of Love. 'The great secret of morals is love; or a going out of our own nature, and an identification of ourselves with the beautiful.' The well-known sentence from *A Defence of Poetry* expresses the dominant mood of *Prometheus Unbound*. Prometheus, sustained by the love of Panthea, Asia's sister, is saved from endless torment by a 'going out' of his nature in his repentance for the curse on Jupiter and compassion for his torturer. At his word 'pity' the last Fury vanishes, and blessed spirits appear to comfort him. The magic of Love begins to work at once, and he is transfigured, as Panthea tells in the next Act; the troop of spirits are 'Like flocks of clouds in spring's delightful weather' and their last chorus develops the image:

> As buds grow red when snow-storms flee,
>   From Spring gathering up beneath,
> Whose mild winds shake the elder brake,
> And the wandering herdsmen know
> That the white-thorn soon will blow . . .

The foretelling of the soft warmth of Spring comes as a fresh note of hope to Prometheus chained to the icy precipice where the 'crawling glaciers' pierce him with 'the spears of their moon-freezing crystals'. Spring is the visible symbol of his change of heart and it is a moment as poignant as that in *The Rime of the Ancient Mariner* when the mariner, also visited by a troop of angelic spirits, is freed from his punishment and the horrors of the deep give way to the images of the skylark and the hidden brook singing a song 'in the leafy month of June'.

The change of heart in Prometheus is the act of reversal on which the rest of the action hinges; Shelley chooses to place it at the beginning instead of at the end of the drama, more usual in Greek tragedy, so that *Prometheus Unbound* has very little dramatic tension. After the first act containing the story of Prometheus's fall and his repentance, the drama merely consists of the journey of Asia, released from her exile by this momentous event, to her union with him and the overthrow of Jupiter. Her journey can be seen as the Platonic progress of the soul to the completion of its identity, and suitably the language changes from the lucid masculine verse of Act I to ecstatic poetry filled with images of light and colour. When Act II opens it is morning in the 'far Indian vale' where Asia is exiled, and the Spring, already heralded, has come. Asia, lured on by unseen echoing voices calling her, follows them with Panthea who has now joined her. Then, in a pastoral scene of great beauty, choruses of spirits sing that the echo-voices are those of 'Demogorgon's mighty law' urging the travellers towards 'the fatal mountain' where he is.

Prometheus Unbound is a lyric drama, and as in a musical composition certain motifs recur. In this scene the two listening fauns speak of the songs they love to hear:

> Of Fate, and Chance, and God, and Chaos old,
> And Love, and the chained Titan's woful doom . . .

and of how, on his release, the world will become 'one brotherhood' – the second intimation of the new world to come, for which the last chorus of Act I has prepared us with its prophecy of 'Wisdom, Justice, Love, and Peace'.

The last three scenes of Act II are the most significant in the drama, and are possibly Shelley's greatest poetic achievement. The first is in the realm of the dreaded Demogorgon, a terrible deity who, according to Spenser's *Faerie Queene* lived in a deep abyss with the three fatal sisters; but Shelley, following Ariosto, sets his cave in the Himalayas, presumably near Asia's far Indian vale. His cave is like that of a sibyl where 'the oracular vapour is hurled up' and the spectacle from the high rock where Asia and Panthea stand is a breath-taking one of mountain peaks shining in the dawn above a great plain of mist which rolls across the valley and breaks 'in crimson foam' as the sun rises. It is Shelley's homage to the majesty of the Alps, already powerfully described in 'Mont Blanc', but his description here of the sublime landscape has a purpose, to prepare us for the awesome descent to the underworld and its veiled shape of darkness on the ebon throne.

The Song of the Spirits intensifies the mystical atmosphere necessary for the portentous scene about to come. They sing of the might of Demogorgon in his timeless kingdom beyond life and death and beyond

> The veil and the bar
> Of things which seem and are . . .

and they reassure Asia that in the depths below 'A spell is treasured but for thee alone', like a diamond shining in a mine (an echo of *Queen Mab*, Act VIII, lines 235–7 in which the 'gem of truth' is dragged from its dark mine). But 'the deep truth is imageless' and her questions about the nature of the Creation are answered by the 'mighty darkness' with Delphic brevity. 'God', he answers, is the Creator of all things good – the living world, the seasons and the noble mind of man. When she asks who created 'terror, madness, crime and remorse' and 'who rains down Evil', the response is vague: 'He reigns.' But Jupiter, she says, is only the slave of some greater master. To this Demogorgon has no real solution other than to assert that all is mutable except 'eternal Love', and to proclaim that by the law of Necessity (and perhaps because of her faithful love, the 'patient power In the wise heart' he speaks of at the end of Act IV) the destined Hour has come for the downfall of Jupiter.

Shelley's dramatic sense is at its most inspired in this Act, more original in conception than Act I. After the sombre questioning in the dark cavern the scene suddenly and symbolically breaks into brilliant light with the appearance of the immortal Hours, the wild-eyed charioteers driving their 'rainbow-winged steeds', and the arrival of Asia's own chariot 'An ivory shell inlaid with crimson fire'. Just as Prometheus was changed

> The overpowering light
> Of that immortal shape was shadowed o'er
> By love

so Asia becomes the incarnation of the Uranian Aphrodite, regain-

The Birth of Venus by *Botticelli*

ing the glory she had at birth. Panthea describes her, as in the famous Botticelli painting opposite, standing 'within a vèinèd shell' which floats on the Aegean sea, and her transfiguration is accompanied by a spirit voice singing in praise of her beauty. She is, in purely Platonic terms, the Child of Light, the Lamp of Earth, veiled and half-hidden from mortal eyes as she is too dazzling to look at; she is now what Diotima called 'the divine, the original, the supreme Beauty'.

This lyric and Asia's 'My soul is an enchanted boat', expressing Shelley's deepest thoughts in language of incomparable lightness and grace, are among his most sublime achievements and make a fitting climax to the second act. The lyric spell is momentarily broken at the opening of Act III with the deposition of Jupiter but almost at once the effect of his downfall is seen in Ocean's speech describing how the music of Love has quietened the seas, no longer bloodstained by slavery and commerce. The lovely image of the Nereids 'with garlands pied and starry sea-flower crowns' suggests a triumphant festival in honour of the new world heralded by Earth in the next scene, after the release of Prometheus by Hercules. She speaks ecstatically of the revival of her 'withered, old and icy frame' by the power of joy which will give nourishment to all the living world, and the great change becomes fully evident when the Spirit of the Hour blows the conch-shell

> And behold, thrones were kingless, and men walked
> One with another even as spirits do

as the painted veil of life is torn aside to reveal the real world beyond.

The golden age has returned and Prometheus and Asia reign in bliss in the cave near a temple

> Where we will sit and talk of time and change
> As the world ebbs and flows, ourselves unchanged.
> What can hide man from mutability?

Man, although restored to his lost nobility, is still subject, as the Spirit of the Hour says, 'to chance, and death and mutability' from which only the gods are immune.

In Act IV, a later addition to the drama, Prometheus and Asia are reunited in their bower of bliss and do not appear. Nearby, Ione and Panthea wake from sleep and are the audience for a great cosmic epithalamium, a symphonic celebration of the wedding of the gods, sung and danced by choruses of Spirits and Hours. The Moon and the Earth act out their own nuptials in a kind of masque analogous to the marriage of Prometheus and Asia; and Demorgorgon, Necessity, the master of them all returns to greet them and to round off the Act with the reminder that Love, Gentleness, Virtue, Wisdom and

Endurance – the protagonists of the drama – are the qualities to overcome 'the snake-like Doom' of tyranny.

This act is a display of Shelley's lyric virtuosity and brilliant imaginative invention; the spirit songs and the whirling dance-measures communicate in images of speed and energy the joy which is felt throughout every part of the living world. Particularly original is the wooing of the Moon and the Earth, in which much of his scientific knowledge is shown off to astonishing effect. The great *tour-de-force* of the Act is the entry of the Moon's chariot and the Earth's crystal sphere, 'two visions of strange radiance' described in detail like the ingenious machinery of a Jacobean masque. Within the Moon's chariot, thin and curved like the new moon, sits a winged infant, a supernatural white apparition with dark eyes, surrounded with 'cold and radiant air' and 'fire that is not brightness'. The Spirit of the Earth, also in the form of a child, is enclosed in the sphere and from its forehead shoot rays of light, penetrating the ground to show its rocks and minerals, and the ruins of past civilizations back to prehistoric times. Infants they may seem, but the erotic excitement of their encounter, rising to a wild Bacchanal, is hardly child-like; the snow on the Moon's cold sterile mountains is melted by Earth's passionate embrace, and she becomes its 'crystal paramour', 'an enamoured maiden', a Bacchante

> Gazing, an insatiate bride,
> On thy form from every side
> Like a Maenad, round the cup
> Which Agave lifted up
> In the weird Cadmaean forest.

The Spirit of Earth (not the Mother Earth of Act III), a masculine dominant force, feels the shock of the power of love and in a hymn of praise glorifies Man:

> Man, oh not men! a chain of linkèd thought,
> Of love and might to be divided not

the love and might, that is, of Prometheus and Asia whose union signifies universal harmony.

Part Two

Critical Survey

5　The writer and his craft

The world of letters

> You are now
> In London, that great sea, whose ebb and flow
> At once is deaf and loud, and on the shore
> Vomits its wrecks, and still howls on for more.
> Yet in its depths what treasures!
> ('Letter to Maria Gisborne')

Shelley's image of himself as an outcast, a solitary like the wandering poet of *Alastor*, is not entirely a convincing one. Always we seem to see him at the centre of a group – the Godwin household, Mrs Boinville's Bracknell *salon*, the Marlow circle, and in Italy the little Pisan group of friends and admirers – and as we have seen, he had early dreams of forming a commune of enlightened souls like the one in *La Nouvelle Héloïse*. And yet he was never part of a literary circle as the earlier Romantic poets had been. Wordsworth, Coleridge and Southey, for all their differences, had enough in common to be members of what came to be called the Lake School of poetry. 'They were', as Hazlitt said, 'for bringing poetry back to its primitive simplicity and state of nature' and were a literary movement with certain shared aims and critical axioms, although each poet was later to go his own way.

From this point of view Shelley was indeed a solitary; his aims and ideas were his own and it is hard to imagine him as part of a group of writers or even as a regular participant in such social events as Lamb's literary evenings, as described by Hazlitt in 'On the Conversation of Authors'. He was too original and eccentric a talent: Byron wrote to him in 1821, 'You...know my high opinion of your own poetry, – because it is of *no* school'.

He did, of course, meet many of the writers of his time, and particularly during the Marlow period there were pleasant social occasions when he dined with Hunt, Lamb, Keats and Hazlitt. Although deeply concerned with the literary affairs of his day – and the correspondence he kept up with Hunt, Peacock and his publisher Charles Ollier during his years in Italy shows how closely he continued to follow them – he was always something of an outsider in London circles. His aristocratic background and the intransigence of many of his opinions distanced him to some degree from the passionate controversies of the Grub Street scene fought out in the prestigious reviews and magazines. Nor had he much in common with the fashionable and successful world of letters with which Byron was connected and which gathered around Holland House and the cultivated Whig aristocracy. This would have been the natural ambience for one of his particular background, but the lightweight verse of Samuel Rogers and Tom Moore, dear to these circles, was not for him. Shelley was perfectly capable of turning out Regency album verse quite as charming as the Odes to Anacreon which opened the doors of so many salons to Moore; but his serious poetry was addressed to an audience of a rarer kind, a few select souls like the Illuminati of his dreams, who would understand and respond to his message.

In the first half of the century the market for the thrilling, the exotic and the sentimental was booming. The Gothic, at its height in the 1780s and 90s in the novels of Mrs Radcliffe and Monk Lewis, still flourished and Shelley when young had been an ardent devotee of the supernatural romances, the 'frantic novels' castigated by Wordsworth in his 1800 Preface to *Lyrical Ballads*. In 'Hymn to Intellectual Beauty' he looks back on the days when

> While yet a boy I sought for ghosts, and sped
> > Through many a listening chamber, cave and ruin,
> > And starlight wood, with fearful steps pursuing
> Hopes of high talk with the departed dead.

Indeed, he had himself composed two of these thrillers: *Zastrozzi*, full of bloody incident and inflamed passions, and *St Irvyne, or The Rosicrucian*, much the same but notable for the character of Ginotti whose confession of atheism and interest in 'the latent mysteries of nature' which led him to search for the elixir of life, is a key to Shelley's own intellectual development at this time. Ginotti's obsession with natural magic also points the way to Mary's Frankenstein who was to suffer similar Promethean torments in the name of science in his quest 'to explore unknown powers and unfold to the world the deepest mysteries of creation'. This prevailing passion for the horrid is mocked by Jane Austen in *Northanger Abbey* as Catherine Morland delights in 'the luxury of a raised, restless, and frightened imagination over the pages of Udolpho'; and in the same year (1818) Peacock's *Nightmare Abbey* makes Shelley the centre-piece of his Gothic parody, although by this time he had moved on to less frivolous interests.

Even more in vogue were what Wordsworth called the 'idle and extravagant stories in verse', culminating in the Eastern tales of Byron: in 1814 10,000 copies of *The Corsair* were sold on the day of publication, outdoing the sucess of the first cantos of *Childe Harold* which in 1812 had sold out in three days. The oriental fantasy of Moore's *Lalla Rookh* in 1817, another best-seller, was seized on by a public avid for exotic entertainment. Moore records with pride that the Prince Royal of Prussia 'always sleeps with a copy of the poem under his pillow'. Scott's early verse romances, *The Lay of the Last Minstrel* (1805), *Marmion* (1808) and *The Lady of the Lake* (1810) offered the excitement of a historical past rich in superstition and legend, as did many of the enormously successful Waverley novels. By contrast the sober realism of Crabbe's verse-tales met the demands of another large market described by Jeffrey in 1812 as 'the middling classes of society' who are 'below the sphere of what is called fashionable or public life'.

To be a fashionable writer was to have a ready-made market and sales which brought in a large income. Scott in 1807 received 1,000 guineas as an advance on *Marmion*; his novels earned him many thousands more and were, as he said, 'a mine of wealth' for him. Moore took £3,000 for *Lalla Rookh* and Byron, probably the most highly-paid poet of his time, had 500 guineas apiece for *The Bride of Abydos* and *The Corsair* – all unthinkable figures to a poet today. The highest advance Shelley ever had was thought to be £40 for *Zastrozzi*, the Gothic novel published during his Eton days. If not a successful writer the next best thing was to be a critic and reviewer, and many of the writers of the period, including Coleridge, Hazlitt and Southey, earned considerable sums of money by contributing to the great reviews and magazines like the *Edinburgh Review*, the *Quarterly*, the *London Magazine* and others less famous. The history of these periodicals and the importance they had is a study in itself. Sufficient to say here that they could make or break a literary reputation, that their criteria were often strongly political and that they held a powerful position as arbiters of taste and morality.

Shelley's own place in this commercial world of letters is best assessed by looking at the contacts he made within it and his reaction to some of the writers he knew.

His introduction to London life, the necessary ambience for a young writer, came in 1812 when he encountered the Godwin ménage at the bookshop in Skinner Street. There he met his idol, the philosopher himself, and through him met some of the intellectual radical fringe, including J.F. Newton, author of *Return to Nature*, a work which converted Shelley to the vegetarianism so devoutly recommended in the notes to *Queen Mab*. An enthusiast for off-beat theories, Shelley naturally gravitated to the bohemian circles of the Newtons, a pleasant and cultivated family who seem very much part of our own contemporary scene: as committed health fanatics, given to nudism and a whole-food regimen of nuts, fruit and vegetables they must have represented for him a new and interesting way of life, far removed from the conventionality of Field Place. They introduced him to Mrs Boinville and her *salon* of crotcheteers at Bracknell in Berkshire, satirized for posterity by Peacock; and although Shelley found them mildly stimulating (and was stimulated even more by the charms of her daughter, Cornelia) they were merely a lunatic fringe concerned with politics and philosophy rather than with literature.

His first real contact with a famous writer had been his meeting with Southey in Keswick a year earlier. As a schoolboy he had devoured *The Curse of Kehama* and *Thalaba* and was anxious, when he and Harriet were staying in the Lake District, 'to pay homage to a *really* great man' although he knew that by this time Southey's political opinions were far from being radical. Southey obviously enjoyed his company and recognized in the young man the enthusiast for liberal causes that he himself had embraced in his early years; and Shelley, for his part, was obviously flattered to be able to talk to a famous writer of the senior and much-admired generation of Romantic poets. But within less than a month his attitude had changed:

> Southey the Poet, whose principles were pure & elevated once, is now the servile champion of every abuse and absurdity. I have had much conversation with him. He says 'You will think as I do when you are as old'. I do not feel the least disposition to be Mr S's proselyte.
>
> (Letter to Godwin, 16 January 1812)

In other words Southey, at the ripe old age of thirty-seven was politically unacceptable to him, having turned to the Tories and become a man of the Establishment. The incident is indicative of the gulf between the two generations of Romantic poets: the older poets who had hailed the blissful dawn of freedom had by now joined the ranks of anti-Jacobin opinion, a *volte-face* for which Shelley could not forgive them. His remark about Southey may be dismissed as youthful intolerance, but as late as 1818 he could write to Peacock about Wordsworth, a poet he deeply admired: 'What a beastly and pitiful wretch that Wordsworth! That such a man should be such a poet!' merely because Wordsworth had written an Address to the Freeholders of Westmoreland advising against the election of Brougham. Peacock had agreed, writing 'Now there is a pretty rascal for you', dismissing him with Southey 'and the whole gang' as specimens of 'the degree of moral degradation to which self-sellers can fall'. Harsh words, but no harsher than Hazlitt's, comparing the present day with the early days of the Revolution (Southey had become Poet Laureate in 1813):

> Mr Southey had not surmounted his cap of Liberty with the laurel wreath; nor Mr Wordsworth proclaimed Carnage as 'God's Daughter'; nor Mr Coleridge, to patch up a rotten cause, written the FRIEND. Everything had not then been done...to stop the progress of truth, to stifle the voice of humanity, to break in pieces

and defeat opinion by sophistry, calumny, intimidation, by tampering with the interests of the proud and selfish, the prejudices of the ignorant, the fears of the timid, the scruples of the good, and by resorting to every subterfuge which art could devise to perpetuate the abuses of power.

And harshest of all, because so brilliantly and unsparingly satirical, was Byron's *Vision of Judgment* which despatched Southey once and for all to the mediocrity from which he has never quite recovered.

Shelley met neither Wordsworth nor Coleridge, and his later relationship with Southey was not a happy one as he became involved in a bitter quarrel following an adverse review of *The Revolt of Islam* which he suspected Southey of writing (in fact it was written by John Taylor Coleridge). However, his political animus against these poets did not destroy his appreciation of their true worth, and all left their marks on his own work. Many critics have noted that the paradisal pleasure-domes and gardens and rivers of 'Kubla Khan' are recognizable in Shelley's dream-landscapes: for example in Canto XII of *The Revolt of Islam* the Temple of the Spirit is approached along a stream of 'long and labyrinthine maze' through 'a chasm of cedarn mountains riven', and before the voyage the travellers see

> many a lawny mountain
> With incense-bearing forests.

Wordsworth's influence, too, can be seen in many ways. The 'simple' poet of 'The Idiot Boy' and 'Lucy Gray' had little to say to Shelley, but no poet of his generation could fail to be affected by Wordsworth's fresh and original perception of Nature as a moral force. And Wordsworth, like Shelley, had paid homage to Godwin and Rousseau and had hailed the dawn of freedom if only for a short period. In 1816 the sonnet 'To Wordsworth' expresses Shelley's sorrow at the poet's betrayal of his early ideals, but three years later his feelings took a more satirical turn in *Peter Bell the Third* which celebrates the descent of Wordsworth into dullness. The poem shows a new aspect of Shelley: written in the vein of *Don Juan*, with deliberately contrived and comic rhymes (London, undone, fun done) and dashed off with Byronic carelessness, it attacks Wordsworth on two fronts, political and literary, parodying the original *Peter Bell* with devastating accuracy. It reveals the light-hearted and irreverent side of Shelley which delighted in absurdity, described in Hogg's *Life* and known so well by Mary. There was, she said, 'so much of himself in it'.

His great admiration for the early work of Wordsworth is expressed unstintingly:

> But Peter's verse was clear, and came
>   Announcing from the frozen hearth
> Of a cold age, that none might tame
> The soul of that diviner flame
>   It augured to the Earth . . .

He recognizes the true originality of the poetry:

> Yet his was individual mind,
>   And new created all he saw
> In a new manner,

although for some reason he denies him the gift of imagination, at least no more than 'a pint-pot'. By this he may have meant the kind of invention that could create the fantastic settings and action of *The Revolt of Islam* or of Byron's romantic tales, rather than the true imaginative faculty of which Coleridge wrote and for which Wordsworth has always been justly praised. Shelley certainly venerated, as did Keats, the great imaginative flood of Platonic ideas of his 'Ode on Intimations of Immortality' whose echoes can be heard in *The Triumph of Life* in Rousseau's vision of the dawn of poetic experience. Also it must be remembered that Shelley knew nothing of *The Prelude* since it was not published until after Wordsworth's death.

Nevertheless *Peter Bell the Third* is a damning attack on Wordsworth's literary reputation which had risen, according to Shelley, as his genius declined into gentility and the ultimate awful dullness depicted in Part the Seventh, the brilliantly comic culmination of the poem with its ironic references to some of the better-known ballads. The Poet of Nature has become the Wordsworth of *The Excursion* whose verses were

>   dark and queer:
> They were the ghosts of what they were.

The gap between Shelley and the earlier Romantics was thus more than just a difference in years. He lived in a new political climate of the post-war years and his free-thinking attitude to religious matters was in total opposition to the staid Christianity of the Lake Poets. The authors of *Lyrical Ballads* were by now reviewed more respectfully in the literary journals (although Jeffrey in 1814 could still write of the *Excursion* 'This will never do') except in those of the Left which could not forgive political treachery. Shelley on the other hand, received in his early years little attention and most of that unenthusiastic. His only real champion was the *Examiner*, the literary weekly edited by John and Leigh Hunt; its objective 'to assist in producing Reform in Parliament' and its liberal views on politics and literature were very much after his own heart. The

Hunts were accustomed to being on the wrong side of the law; in 1811, on their acquittal from prosecution by the Government for libel, Shelley wrote to Leigh from Oxford, as a stranger but 'as a common friend of *Liberty*'. The brothers later spent two years in prison for libelling the Prince Regent, Shelley reacting with violent indignation 'at the horrible injustice & tyranny of the sentence'.

With such impeccable credentials, their journal was obviously the one likely to be sympathetic to his writing, and in October 1816 he sent in his 'Hymn to Intellectual Beauty' under the pseudonym 'Elfin Knight' (a Spenserian reference). By the time it was printed in January 1817, he had become friendly with Hunt, who included him, in company with Keats and J.H. Reynolds, in his article on 'Young Poets' of note, singling him out as 'a very striking and original thinker'. During this winter he and Mary became intimate with Hunt and his wife Marianne in their little cottage in the Vale of Health. There they met many of the contributors to the *Examiner*, like Lamb and Hazlitt, and others who enjoyed the hospitality, music and good conversation to be found at the home of the sociable Hunts. Although this was a happy time for Shelley in that he valued Hunt's friendship, he did not always fit in easily with this society; Keats, a frequent visitor there, was somewhat standoffish with him (Hunt thought that he may have had some feeling of social inferiority), Lamb took against him for some mysterious reason, and Hazlitt, a radical after his own persuasion, nevertheless mistrusted him because of 'a fire in his eye, a fever in his blood, a maggot in his brain, a hectic flutter in his speech' which suggested the fanatic rather than the dedicated political thinker.

His closest ties were with Hunt, an amiable man but a third-rate poet, who was indebted to him throughout his life for sums of money which Shelley could ill afford and for the help given to bring him and the entire Hunt family to Italy to launch his new review, the *Liberal*. For this project Shelley enlisted Byron's assistance, but Byron was never an admirer: 'a good man, and a good father – ... and a great coxcomb and a very vulgar person in every thing about him' he wrote to Tom Moore. Similar sentiments were expressed by *Blackwood's* in the famous articles in 1818 'On the Cockney School of Poetry' mocking Hunt as 'the most vulgar of Cockney poetasters' whose influence on Keats was disastrous. The next year (January 1819) the attack turned to Shelley as one of the same Cockney School 'so far as his opinions are concerned' because of his association with Hunt. However, in this review of *The Revolt of Islam*, a poem reviled by the critic for its revolutionary nonsense, Shelley's poetic genius is recognized and he is described as 'a scholar, a gentleman and a poet' in no way resembling his low friends on the *Examiner*. It is a commonplace to deplore Hunt's influence on Keats; on Shelley he appeared to have had very little, and certainly far less than

Peacock whose encouragement in classical studies was of far-reaching importance in his poetic progress.

Hunt remained his friend for life, and included in his *Recollections of Lord Byron and some of his Contemporaries* (1828) is a memoir of Shelley and a long critical review of his work, setting a pattern for the legend of the delicate and angelic poet which was to remain for many years.

Later, from Italy, Shelley looked back with a certain nostalgia to his London literary life. His witty and delightful 'Letter to Maria Gisborne' included sketches of some of his friends in the world of letters there: Godwin, Hunt, Hogg and Peacock are all introduced and so is one whom he had never met but with whom he had so much in common – the great poet Coleridge, 'a hooded eagle among blinking owls', lost in the wilderness of his powerful intellect.

Shelley and Byron

By far the most interesting of all Shelley's friendships was that with Byron, the most celebrated poet of the day. As we have seen, their relationship was one of equals, of aristocrats in exile with much in common although their modes of life were very different. As a critic of his fellow-writers Byron was strongly opinionated and not always reliable. *English Bards and Scotch Reviewers* indicates his early tastes: Augustan satire and a dislike of cant. The Dedication to *Don Juan* is flippant about the Lake Poets, 'shabby fellows' who fail to impress him:

> Scott, Rogers, Campbell, Moore, and Crabbe, will try
> 'Gainst you the question with posterity.

and in similar vein his Journal of 1813 records his opinion of contemporary poetry. At the head of the list is Scott. 'He is undoubtedly the Monarch of Parnassus and the most *English* of bards. I should place Rogers next in the living list (I value him more as the last of the *best* school) – Moore and Campbell both third – Southey and Wordsworth and Coleridge – the rest is πολλοι [the mob].' Hardly an estimate which stands the test of time. For Shelley, however, he had a special admiration springing from their association in Italy, particularly during the last months in Pisa. He told Medwin, 'he is one of the most moral as well as amiable men. I know, I have been intimate with him for two years, and every year has added to my regard for him.'

But what he thought about Shelley's poetry is not easy to say. From his letters we learn that he thought *The Cenci* 'a work of power, and poetry', but there are very few direct critical opinions of Shelley to be found in his Journals. He certainly respected his dedication to the poetic art, and Medwin quotes him as saying: 'There's Shelley

Byron in Albanian Dress *by Thomas Philips (1814)*

has more poetry in him than any man living; and if he were not so mystical, and would not write Utopias and set himself up as a Reformer, his right to rank as a poet, and very highly too, could not fail of being acknowledged.' Reading between the lines one suspects that Byron neither understood nor properly appreciated the true nature of Shelley's genius however much he liked him as a man. For Byron he was obviously not in the class of Scott or Moore, but a phenomenon impossible to place.

Shelley, on the other hand, was liberal in his praise of Byron's poetry, particularly of *Don Juan* which he found not only sublime in its description but in its profound feeling for human emotions. ('Where did you learn all these secrets? I should like to go to school there.') He felt unable to compete with a writer of such formidable reputation, and he was a little envious too: 'I despair of rivalling Lord Byron and there is no other with whom it is worth contending.' A month before he died he wrote to John Gisborne a poignant and self-revealing letter in which he speaks of his unsettled state of mind: his relationship with Mary was not happy and he was obviously suffering some darkness of spirit because on the same day he wrote to Trelawny asking him to buy some prussic acid ('I have no intention of suicide at present, – but I confess it would be a comfort to me to hold in my possession that golden key to the chamber of perpetual rest.') There was some coolness with Byron because of his capriciousness and the kind of society with which he associated; and yet Shelley was able to write about him in words which have become famous, sadly contrasting Byron's achievement with his own lack of a sympathetic audience.

> Lord Byron is in this respect fortunate. He touched a chord to which a million hearts responded, and the coarse music which he produced to please them disciplined him to the perfection to which he now approaches. I do not go on with 'Charles the First'. I feel too little certainty of the future, and too little satisfaction with regard to the past, to undertake any subject seriously and deeply. I stand, as it were, upon a precipice, which I have ascended with great, and cannot descend without *greater*, peril, and I am content if the heaven above me is calm for the passing moment.

In spite of their differences, the time they spent with each other was mutually valuable. They talked endlessly about literature; Shelley urged Byron 'to undertake a great poem' and taught him to appreciate Wordsworth's poetry, and Byron's worldly common-sense must have diverted him from too much cloudy speculation and too much sadness. *Julian and Maddalo* leaves a comfortable image of their talk together:

I might sit
In Maddalo's great palace, and his wit
And subtle talk would cheer the winter night
And make me know myself, and the firelight
Would flash upon our faces, till the day
Might dawn and make me wonder at my stay: . . .

Shelley and Nature

The contemplation of the laws of the universe is connected with an immediate tranquil exaltation of mind, and pure mental enjoyment. The perception of truth is almost as simple a feeling as the perception of beauty.

(Humphrey Davy: the *Director*, No. 19, 1807)

He gives us, for representations of things, rhapsodies of words. He does not lend the colours of imagination and the ornaments of style to the objects of nature, but paints gaudy, flimsy, allegorical pictures on gauze, on the cobwebs of his own brain.

(Hazlitt: on Shelley in *On People of Sense*)

When Shelley in *A Defence of Poetry* wrote that poetry 'strips the veil of familiarity from the world and lays bare the naked and sleeping beauty, which is the spirit of its forms', and that it 'purges from our inward sight the film of familiarity which obscures from us the wonder of our being', he was perhaps consciously quoting Coleridge's famous passage in the *Biographia Literaria*, published some four years earlier. Coleridge says that the aim of Wordsworth in *Lyrical Ballads* was to direct the mind's attention to 'the loveliness and wonders of the world before us; an inexhaustible treasure but for which, in consequence of the film of familiarity and selfish solicitude, we have eyes yet see not, ears that hear not, and hearts that neither feel nor understand'. If Shelley did indeed have this in mind, he must have known that his own poetic objective was far removed from Wordsworth's desire to change conventional poetic responses to Nature by using 'the language really used by men' and by observing the reactions of individuals 'in a state of vivid sensation' in close contact with the natural world. Wordsworth stresses the social benefits of Nature and his attempts to strip away the film of familiarity were addressed to those whose primitive instincts were being dulled by the gross stimulations of city life – a Rousseauistic endeavour with which Shelley would have agreed. But Plato, not Rousseau, lies behind that phrase 'the naked and sleeping beauty, which is the spirit of its forms'. In other words, the beauty of the world is merely phenomenal, the spirit of forms which exist in eternity. Like the garden of the sensitive plant, it is 'a shadow of the dream', and Shelley's aim is to convey the idea of a permanent beauty and truth in contrast to the mutability of human life.

How effectively, then, did he reconcile this Platonic idealism with the appreciation of Nature deeply rooted in Romantic poetry? The view is sometimes put forward that, since his mind was concentrated on the eternal, he had no real feeling for Nature, no feeling proved on the pulses such as Keats had, and that the visible world was of interest to him only in a special symbolic sense. W.H. Auden complained that he could not read Shelley with pleasure: 'Reading him, I feel that he never looked at or listened to anything, except ideas' and he dismissed most of his work as empty and unsympathetic 'because of his inability to record experience'. Dr Leavis, too, in his hostile essay on Shelley in *Revaluation*, attacks him for his 'weak grasp upon the actual' which cannot be excused by 'idealism, Platonism and so on'. The purpose of this section is to show that, on the contrary, his perception of Nature was by no means vague and imprecise, and that his landscapes, however symbolic, were created from careful observation and knowledge.

It is true that for Shelley, as for Socrates, the contemplation of beauty, from which poetic inspiration springs, is a means to the contemplation of the ideal. But 'Poetry...makes immortal all that is best and most beautiful in the world; it arrests the vanishing apparitions which haunt the interlunations of life'. The poet's task, therefore, is to catch the vanishing apparitions in flight, and Shelley is a faithful and sensitive recorder of the sights and sounds and colours of Nature, for a purpose more serious than that of mere sensuous pleasure.

Beauty for Socrates lay in ideas and learning, not in Nature. In the *Phaedrus* he confesses that he never leaves Athens, since trees and fields can teach him nothing (although on this occasion he takes evident delight in a charming country scene) whereas men in cities can. Such a view was hardly possible for poets of Shelley's time. As Wordsworth illustrates in 'Michael', men in cities could teach nothing but lessons of misery and corruption; for Shelley 'Hell is a city much like London', and even Don Juan, that connoisseur of town pleasures, is first introduced to

> That mighty mass of brick and smoke, and shipping,
> Dirty and dusky

through a criminal attack by footpads. The proper study for Romantic poets was not so much man as the effect on man of Nature in all its manifestations: Nature the teacher, guide and inspiration working through the sublime as well as through more domesticated landscapes like those of *Lyrical Ballads*.

Inevitably Shelley was affected by the spirit of the age, and early on inherited the taste for the sublime and picturesque from the Gothic novels he read as a boy; Mrs Radcliffe, for one, had devoted many descriptive pages to the grandiose scenery of France and Italy, the mountains, lakes and rocky pinnacles haunted by brigands. His reading of the Lake Poets and of Rousseau, and his own travels abroad had intensified his feeling for the wilder scenes of Nature; the letters written to Peacock in 1816 from Switzerland, when for the first time he saw the magnificence of the Alps, show his powerful reaction: 'I never knew I never imagined what mountains were before. The immensity of these aerial summits excited, when they suddenly burst upon the sight, a sentiment of extatic wonder, not unallied to madness.' But his emotional turmoil did not prevent his precise and careful observation of the scene; as an amateur scientist he was fascinated by the advance of the glaciers and by the geology of the region; he noted that the 'conical and pyramidal' crystals of the glacier de Boisson were some fifty feet in height, and considered the theory in Buffon's *Natural History* that the earth will one day become a mass of frost; he bought some quartz crystals as a souvenir of his visit. He was, in fact, a man for whom the visible world *did* exist and a man who knew a great deal about its processes.

When he later came to describe the rocks of the icy Caucasus where Prometheus was chained, and the awesome mountains near the cave of Demogorgon, he drew on these memories. The landscape is used now for a special purpose; a philosophical drama is played out in what seem to be dream-settings, inhabited by spirits, furies and fauns, and the characters move across mountains and seas in magic chariots. It is now a symbolic landscape which changes as the drama unfolds, and frozen winter turns to spring as the power of Love is at work; but the details are as exact as in the letters, and the 'crawling glaciers', the 'moon-freezing crystals', the storms howling in the deep abysses of the rocks split by 'Earthquake-fiends' ('the old Earthquake-daemon' of 'Mont Blanc', which had caused the splitting and upheaval of the Alps) and the stalactites, 'the mountain's frozen tears' which hang like 'snow, or silver, or long diamond spires' all lend firm reality to the mythical story of Prometheus.

Shelley's interest in geology, the formation of rocks and crystals and the changing nature of the earth, makes him unique among Romantic poets, and in his aesthetic appreciation of science closer to someone like Ruskin whose enquiring mind explored even more thoroughly the 'inexhaustible treasure' of the natural world. Unlike Keats, who in *Lamia* complained that a scientific understanding of the miracle of the rainbow reduced its mystery and put it 'in the dull catalogue of common things', Shelley felt that knowledge enhanced rather than detracted from the beauty of things, and in this intellectual approach he is truly Platonic.

The *locus classicus* for the argument that Shelley took little heed of the world around him is the song of the Fourth Spirit in Act I of *Prometheus Unbound*, 'On a poet's lips I slept'. The poet is unconcerned with 'mortal blisses'; the life of the mind is what matters:

> He will watch from dawn to gloom
> The lake-reflected sun illume
> The yellow bees in the ivy-bloom,
> Nor heed nor see, what things they be;
> But from these create he can
> Forms more real than living man,
> Nurslings of immortality!

The work of the poet is indeed to 'make immortal all that is best and most beautiful'; yet, whether what he sees is important or not, he has captured in three lines an image of Nature perfect in its detail. And how many poets have even noticed that ivy *has* a bloom? It is necessary to remember that Shelley was born a countryman and according to Mary 'knew every plant by its name and was familiar with the history and habits of every production of the earth'. Those who think of him as a mere intellectual with his head in the Platonic clouds should read some of his letters on this subject; for example, to Hogg he wrote from Italy about the plants in the Pisan countryside, thanking him for sending a milkwort which now 'reposes between the leaves of a folio Plato' and sending in return a mountain flower. 'I shall herborize myself, & will send you as I find them whatever plants are rarest or peculiar to this country. I saw a great number of the Cryptogamia genus the other day which I had never remarked in England'; and when in Switzerland he had bought a collection of seeds of rare Alpine plants with the intention of sowing them in his garden in England. Even the 'visionary flowers' of 'The Question', the 'green cowbind and the moonlight-coloured may' and the other flowers of the English countryside nostalgically remembered from Italy, have the freshness and brightness that comes from loving observation, as do the plants in the garden of 'The Sensitive Plant'.

Knowledgeable as he was about such country matters, he was in one sense an unusual representative of the squirearchy in that he detested blood-sports and felt that botany was a much 'more profitable & innocent an occupation...than that absurd & un-philosophical diversion of killing birds – besides the ill taste of giving pain to sensitive & beautiful animals'.

Shelley's travels and life abroad opened his eyes to new aspects of Nature. In England he had admired in somewhat conventional fashion the grand scenery of Wales and the Lakes; in Switzerland he saw the true sublime, but in Italy the profusion of flowers and trees and above all the beauty of the seascapes added a fresh dimension to his writing. His Preface to *Prometheus Unbound* tells how the rich countryside helped to produce the intoxicating poetry of that particular work; and the Mediterranean was constantly in his mind, whether in the terror of tempest as in 'A Vision of the Sea', or in the summer calm of the 'Ode to the West Wind'. The descriptions in the Ode of the azure moss, the sea-blooms and the 'sapless foliage of the ocean' recall his letter to Peacock (17 December 1818) written after a voyage in the Bay of Naples to see Pompeii and Paestum; the sea was 'so translucent that you could see the hollow caverns clothed with glaucous sea-moss, & the leaves & branches of those delicate weeds that pave the unequal bottom of the water'.

Indeed, very many descriptive passages in his poetry can be shown to be drawn from life. The letters, mostly those to Peacock whose tastes were obviously close to his own, contain a wealth of natural description, not only of landscapes but of weather and cloudscapes. Writing from Bagni di Lucca (25 July 1818) he gives a minute account of the clouds and weather particular to that region, adding 'I take great delight in watching the changes of atmosphere', a remark borne out by many of his poems, notably in the 'Ode to the West Wind' where his picture of the storm in Stanza ii is exact and vivid.

Strangely enough, Dr Leavis cites as an example of Shelley's 'weak grasp upon the actual' this stanza which, on the contrary, demonstrates a perfect observation of a tempestuous sky in the Mediterranean. After the first stanza, whose imagery is of the earth – the dead leaves and winged seeds which will lie in the ground until spring – the focus shifts to the horizon, the meeting-place of Heaven and Ocean where the 'loose clouds', the small dark scud of broken cumulus below the cumulonimbus which will bring the rain, fly like the ghostly dead leaves before the wind; and high above, on the blue sky, are spread the 'locks of the approaching storm' a painstakingly exact description of the thin, mare's-tail cirrus clouds which stream out like the hair of a fierce Maenad. Cirrus, after all, means 'a fringe or filament', fine and thread-like, and the image is brilliantly appropriate visually, as well as suggesting the speed and demented frenzy of the tempest which is to come with 'that magnificent thunder and lightning peculiar to the Cisalpine region', as his note says: again he has noticed the characteristic weather and atmospheric effects of a particular district in Italy. The Ode is an outstanding illustration of Shelley's ability to observe, to understand what he is seeing and to transform it, in this case into a symbolic expression of his divine and prophetic function as a poet.

'The Cloud', too, for all its airy gaiety is a meteorological *tour-de-force*, a series of rapidly changing cloudscapes and impressions of day and night skies noted with remarkable accuracy. In its progress the cloud changes through sun and storm in bright images of light and movement, and Shelley, ever a sky-watcher, observes the clouds which always seem to rest on mountain-tops (lines 13-16), the sky on a calm moonlit night with the stars shining through the 'fleece-like

Study of Cirrus clouds by John Constable

floor' of altocumulus, the rainbows round the sun and moon made by drifting cirrostratus, and the serene evening sky when the wind has dropped and the clouds lie 'still as a brooding dove'. Also he knew that the cumulus clouds manufacture hail (lines 9-13) and that hail generates an electric charge to produce thunder and lightning – a memory no doubt of the lectures of Adam Walker at Syon House and Eton on the principles of electricity.

In Shelley's lifetime weather-watching had become a science, and his interest in clouds and skyscapes may have been stimulated by the work of Luke Howard, a scientist whose 'Essay on Clouds', the first chapter of *The Climate of London* (1818–20), described and classified clouds, giving them names by which we still call them. Goethe certainly knew this book and wrote a number of poems with such titles as 'Nimbus' and 'Cumulus'; it also influenced painters of the period, in particular Turner and Constable, whose many cloud-studies were part of the close analysis of light and colour they made in order to give full visual expression to the variety and fluidity of Nature. Like Constable, whose studies are always meteorologically correct and minutely observed (opposite), Shelley knew that scientific knowledge and an understanding of natural phenomena was an aid, not a hindrance to imaginative perception. 'Poetry', he writes in his *Defence of Poetry*, 'is that which comprehends all science, and that to which all science must be referred.'

Both these poems, the 'Ode to the West Wind' and 'The Cloud', show a characteristically Romantic use of natural phenomena to convey states of mind or philosophical speculation; the same tendency is evident in Keats's Odes and, more relevant to Shelley's Ode, in Coleridge's 'Dejection', in which the ominous night-sky is a sign of the coming storm and the hoped-for return of inspiration to the poet. In this sense Shelley was a thorough Romantic and through his images of the natural world he is making in these poems a philosophical statement heard frequently throughout his work: a denial of death and a proclamation of the power of beauty to survive, although change is inevitable. The Cloud's message is that, after all its transformations, 'I change, but I cannot die'; it is 'a nursling of the sky', one of the nurslings of Immortality from the Fourth Spirit's song in *Prometheus Unbound*. The West Wind is both destroyer and preserver, and its strength is symbolic of the power that the poet must possess to carry out his gift of prophecy. Mutability is inevitable: the seasons must change but apparent death is only the prelude to 'a new birth'. Just as the clarion of spring awakens the earth, so the poet's dead thoughts may be revived by the wind of inspiration.

This theme of mutability ('The flower that smiles today, Tomorrow dies') echoes his Platonic belief that all earthly things are in a state of flux and are shadows of the unchanging eternal reality: 'The One remains, the many change and pass.' He found a similar belief

119

in the works of Spenser, one of his favourite poets. The letters and Journals are full of references to *The Faerie Queene*, and the Mutabilitie Cantos in Book VII were a rich source for his imagination to work on. The Titanesse Mutabilitie, in her attempt to conquer Heaven, surely inspired the aerial flights among the moon and stars of the Witch of Atlas; and the final Canto VIII, following on Spenser's great pageant of Nature – the seasons, months, hours, Life and Death, all subject to change and decay – was much in his mind. Spenser's Platonism is combined with the conception of a Christian Heaven, but the two poets express the same powerful sense of the beauty of the world whose fleeting quality can only be endured if there is something permanent beyond life. Shelley dwells more on the *lacrimae rerum*, but Spenser has a more comfortable hope of Heaven:

> Then gin I thinke on that which Nature sayd,
>   Of that same time when no more Change shall be,
>   But stedfast rest of all things firmely stayd
>   Upon the pillours of Eternity,
>   That is contrayr to Mutabilitie:
>   For, all that moveth, doth in Change delight:
>   But thence-forth all shall rest eternally
>   With Him that is the God of Sabbaoth hight ...

Erasmus Darwin and the Wonders of Science

A poet nearer to his own time saw mutability in more scientific terms:

> While Nature sinks in Time's destructive storms,
> The wrecks of Death are but a change of forms;
> Emerging matter from the grave returns,
> Feels new desires, with new sensation burns.

Erasmus Darwin's *The Temple of Nature* (posthumously published in 1803), from which these lines are taken, was one of the many didactic poems of the eighteenth century intended to entertain and instruct. Darwin (1730–1802), a doctor and grandfather of the famous Charles, had much in common with Shelley, who was reading his poetry as early as 1809: a disciple of the empirical thought of Locke and Hume, he supported the French and American Revolutions and was a keen student of scientific matters. *The Temple of Nature* is an attempt to give a scientific interpretation of the universe, and its wonders are explicated by Urania, the Priestess of Nature, an omniscient guide much like Shelley's Queen Mab. Its subject matter is 'The Origin of Society' and 'The Production of Life', no less. Even more ambitious was *The Botanic Garden*, an

The Sensitive Plant (Mimosa Pudica)

earlier work, written in two sections. The first was the charming *Loves of the Plants*, a presentation of the system of Linnaeus in descriptive and ornate couplets which inform the general public about the sexual classification and properties of plants, among them the Sensitive Plant, 'the chaste MIMOSA' who

> Shuts her sweet eye-lids to approaching night,
> And hails with freshen'd charms the rising light...

a sister to Shelley's plant which 'opened its fan-like leaves to the light, And closed them beneath the kisses of night'.

The second section of *The Botanic Garden* is 'The Economy of Nature', another extraordinary account of the creation of the world, including electrical phenomena and geology among its miscellaneous topics and offering explanations of many oddities of Nature like electric eels and shooting stars. Shelley would have been particularly pleased with the notion of flying-chariots, borne 'through the fields of air' by the power of 'UNCONQUER'D STEAM!'.

Such rare critics as have the necessary knowledge, notably Carl Grabo in *A Newton among Poets*, have shown how well-read Shelley was in the scientific studies of the period and how much of this interest is evident in his poetry. Professor Grabo argues that Erasmus Darwin was an important source for his attempts to synthesize science and metaphysics and that a number of passages, particularly in *Prometheus Unbound*, seem to be suggested by his reading of Darwin. Certainly Darwin's poems, and the copious notes added to them, are a mine of obscure and fascinating information and Shelley, like Coleridge (who incidentally detested Darwin's poetry), had an insatiable curiosity about strange natural phenomena like glow-worms, phosphorescence and the deadly upas tree. His scientific interests extended into the realms of astronomy, electricity and chemistry, subjects which he had explored from his school-days, when he heard Adam Walker lecture. Nor was he content simply to read about these things. One of his prized possessions was a solar microscope, unfortunately sold for £5 in 1814 at a time of financial difficulty; and there are many accounts of his early chemical and electrical experiments, usually spectacular and not well-received by landlords and nervous visitors.

He wrote to Godwin in 1812 about his young days when 'ancient books of Chemistry and Magic were perused with an enthusiasm of wonder almost amounting to belief', and it seems that chemistry, magic and Gothic romance were all one to him then; Godwin's own *St Leon* turned on alchemy and the search for the philosopher's stone. Shelley would have thoroughly agreed with Sir David Brewster, writing in 1832 in his *Letters on Natural Magic*, that 'The science of chemistry has from its infancy been pre-eminently the science of wonders. In her laboratory the alchemist and magician have revelled uncontrolled', and in some ways he never lost that romantic sense of the magical powers of science. In the 'Letter to Maria Gisborne' he paints a comic picture of himself in his room in Leghorn, sitting like 'some weird Archimago' (the magician of *The Faerie Queene*) among scientific bric-à-brac, 'mathematical Instruments, for plans nautical and statical' and books of tables of 'conic sections, spherics, logarithms' with some 'odd volumes of old chemistry'. Also, a reminder of his own chemistry experiments, there is a wooden bowl full of mercury on which he characteristically floats a paper boat: the quicksilver has magic undertones as 'that dew which the gnomes drink When at their subterranean toil they swink', but one hopes that he did not follow their example or even handle it too much since mercury is the element that made hatters mad and a dangerous toy.

It is reasonable to suppose that when Mary Shelley wrote *Frankenstein* she had some help from Shelley in the details of the scientist's education and the long discussions on the wonders of science which led up to his determination to create a living creature. When Frankenstein arrives at the University of Ingolstadt he confesses to having studied, like the young Shelley, many books of alchemy. But at a lecture he hears his chemistry professor utter 'the words of fate, enounced to destroy me', as he expatiates on the miracles performed by the modern scientists, and from that moment he immerses himself in the study of 'natural philosophy and particularly chemistry', anatomy and physiology much as Shelley had done at Oxford when, according to Hogg, his rooms were littered with phials, crucibles and glass jars among other equipment, and the carpets stained with marks of chemical experiments. And it was through galvanism, another of Shelley's interests, that the monster was animated.

So far, then, we can see that Shelley, for all his Platonic idealism, was a man who had eyes for the world around him. His particular interest in electricity, metereology and optics may well account for what seems on the surface to be an abstract approach to Nature. Whereas Keats glories in the colours and rich textures of flowers and fruit, Shelley turns more often to look at the subtle aspects of light and shadow, skies and weather. Typically the 'Hymn to Intellectual Beauty' conceives the spirit of beauty in terms of summer winds, moonbeams, rainbows, mountain mists, clouds and the 'hues and harmony of evening'; he would have perfectly understood what Turner, his great contemporary, was trying to do when he painted atmospheric conditions and nuances of light and water. Not that Shelley lacked a feeling for more earthy things: *Epipsychidion* shows a thoroughly Keatsian abandonment to the senses in his evocation of the island where the air is so 'heavy with the scent of lemon-flowers' and of violets and jonquils, that 'you might faint with that delicious pain'.

Nevertheless it is quite apparent that Shelley's poetry is also full of dream-landscapes with symbolic features frequently related to Platonic thought. For him, as for many Romantic poets, the natural world is alive with some animating principle or spirit; his descriptions of Nature are rarely simply descriptions, but are invested with meaning. The poet and the landscape are often fused, as in 'Ode to the West Wind' in which he seeks to become one with the tempest . In *Alastor* the isolation of the wandering poet is reflected in the loneliness of the countryside, and he becomes identified with it as 'the Spirit of the wind'. In his last hours

> the Poet's blood
> That ever beat in mystic sympathy
> With nature's ebb and flow grew feebler still

and as the moon sinks behind the hills and heaven becomes 'utterly black', he dies, presumably, like Adonais, to survive as a portion of the loveliness which once he graced.

Alastor is particularly interesting in that, although an early poem, it features many of the symbols and images which recur throughout his work. There is certainly plenty of straightforward observation of Nature: here for the first time appear the dead leaves, 'Red, yellow, or ethereally pale', the 'children of the autumnal whirlwind' which are scattered in many later poems (notably in *The Revolt of Islam*, 'Ode to the West Wind', 'The Sensitive Plant', and *The Triumph of Life*). But these and the trees, flowers and rocks of the ever-changing countryside merely add substance to the hallucinatory quality of the Poet's travels through swamps and forests to the ocean shore where Shelley's most personal symbol, 'a little shallop', waits to carry him across a wild sea and then through rocky caverns which lead, by some geographical impossibility, to the edge of a precipice. These features – the boat, the caverns, the river, the sea – are repeated over and over again in his poetry, perhaps most memorably in *Prometheus Unbound* and *The Revolt of Islam*; so is the vision of past ruined civilizations, 'the awful ruins of the days of old' earlier seen in *Queen Mab*. Lifted from Volney's *Ruins* they become one of his favourite symbols of mutability and the ironical fate of what, as in 'Ozymandias', seemed permanent and powerful. Again, in Act IV of *Prometheus Unbound* the crystal sphere of the Spirit of Earth illuminates all the emblems of old glory, the wrecks of 'many a city vast' as well as the skeletons of prehistoric creatures which had made an appearance in Keats's *Endymion*, written a year earlier in 1818.

Neville Rogers in *Shelley at Work* persuasively argues that some of these symbols – the cave, the river, the boat – have strong Platonic or neo-Platonic connotations. *Alastor*, of course, was written before

Shelley had studied Plato in depth, although he had read the dialogues at Oxford. There are certainly suggestions of Platonism in the veiled maiden, the Poet's epipsyche, but it seems more of a personal fantasy with reminiscences of 'Kubla Khan', Southey and imaginative recreation of his own travels. In *The Revolt of Islam* the fantasy becomes more dynamic, invigorated by radical and feminist ideas, and the symbols are more ornately decorated. The little shallop becomes a 'curved shell of hollow pearl' sailing on a gold and purple sea to the paradise island of the Temple of the Spirit, a foretaste of the 'far Eden of the purple East' in *Epipsychidion*. In these two early poems the landscape and the voyages are symbolic of the life of the imagination, seen as a quest, a journey of discovery to find the purpose of existence. As his thought matured the symbols acquired more weight and in *Prometheus Unbound* achieve their full Platonic significance; the scene in the cave of Demogorgon is the prelude to the revelation of the 'real' world of Love, and Asia's lyric 'My soul is an enchanted boat' is mystical expression of the voyage of the soul to a 'diviner day'.

W.B. Yeats in his essay on *The Philosophy of Shelley's Poetry* (1900) interprets Shelley's attitude to Nature as a profoundly mystical one, part of what Yeats calls 'the great Memory that renews the world and men's thoughts age after age'. He sees the recurring images of the rivers and caves as ancient symbols 'from beyond his own mind' and the symbol which he finds the most important is that of the Morning and Evening Star, 'to Shelley's mind the central power of the world', representing the poet's longing for ideal perfection, 'the desire of the moth for the star'.

One outstanding characteristic of a Shelleyan landscape is its fluidity and movement. The Spirit of Nature, or the animating principle which moves and changes all things is for him a turbulent one: not only is everything in a state of flux – the seasons change, the flower dies, the cloud dissolves and is re-created – but the features of the landscape are often in turmoil. Compared with the majestic stillness typical of Wordsworth's natural scenery, Shelley's world is in ceaseless motion:

> Worlds on worlds are rolling ever
> > From creation to decay,
> Like the bubbles on a river
> > Sparkling, bursting, borne away.

His inspiration comes not from the frozen moments of Wordsworth's 'spots of time' but more often from storm and wind. The boat in *Alastor* is swept by a whirlwind through 'a chafèd sea', the waters rush 'in dark tumult thundering', the river twists and winds and eddies with confusing purpose; and the scenery of *The Revolt of Islam* changes with the speed of a nightmare, from the first canto's 'irresistible storm' of darkness and boiling seas to the last journey in Canto XII along the mighty stream with its 'long and labyrinthine maze' through forests and ravines. Shelley's boats and chariots sail and fly through his magic worlds as if to emphasize the restlessness of his spirit or the restlessness of Nature. Even at the end of *Adonais* when calm and peace should prevail, he calls up the image of a tempest-tossed ship, driven out to sea; it may be a remembered echo of Webster's Vittoria Corombona, the White Devil, who cries:

> My soul, like to a ship in a black storm,
> Is driven, I know not whither...

but it betrays an essential Shelleyan lack of repose.

The lyrics of his last years have an evening serenity of their own, but although the rare Spirit of Delight comes in 'tranquil solitude', with the silent forms of snow and 'radiant frost', he still loves 'waves and winds and storms' and can still write to Jane in 'A Recollection';

> Less oft is peace in Shelley's mind
> Than calm in waters, seen.

Peace comes only in dreams of an ideal existence such as that on the Paradisal island of *Epipsychidion*. When in *Prometheus Unbound* the fall of Jupiter heralds the return of the Golden Age the sound is heard of the 'unpastured sea hungering for calm'. Shelley's own hunger for calm and his world-weariness show an unmistakeable death-wish, symbolically figured in the ships, rivers and seas of his poetry, and in the voyages leading to the spiritual calm of another world. He certainly had many times of black despair, but his death-wish is not one that looks forward to total annihilation but to the 'diviner day' of Platonic belief. Like Wordsworth in the 'Ode on Intimations of Immortality' he knew that

> Our Souls have sight of that immortal sea
> Which brought us hither.

Shelley the dramatist : The Cenci

Two aspects of Shelley have not yet been touched on – his work as a dramatist and his translations.

As a dramatist his output was limited to *The Cenci*, the unfinished *Charles the First* and some charming fragments of another uncompleted play about an enchantress and a pirate, set in an Indian isle. There is also a mention in a letter written when he was eighteen, of a tragedy which he proposed to offer to the managements of the Lyceum and Covent Garden, but no more is known of this. The lyric dramas *Prometheus Unbound* and *Hellas* are to be played only in the theatre of the imagination: their unreal settings and companies of

126

flying spirits and furies were hardly suited to the theatre of his time.

The Cenci was another matter; it was intended for a real theatre, Covent Garden (the offer was refused), the heroine was to be played by Eliza O'Neill, a tragic actress greatly admired by him, and he hoped that Edmund Kean would play the wicked Count Cenci. Although not particularly fond of the theatre he shared the ambition of most of the Romantic poets to write a great play. They had all tried, and with little success. Wordsworth's *The Borderers*, Coleridge's *Remorse* (rated high by Shelley) and Keats's *Otho the Great* all reveal a lack of talent in that direction and were not likely to grip any audience; and Byron's dramatic works, including *The Two Foscari, Marino Faliero* and *Sardanapalus*, are now mostly forgotten, although he had a more serious and practical interest in the theatre. The period saw a revival of taste for the Elizabethan and Jacobean writers and dramatists, as the critical essays of Coleridge, Lamb and Hazlitt bear out, but attempts to follow such models inevitably led to pastiche and strained rhetoric. *The Cenci*, although not devoid of these faults, is by far the best of them all, and reveals a new aspect of Shelley as a man interested in the development of character and flesh-and-blood human beings rather than mythological figures or projections of his own personality.

It was the story of the Cenci family that had originally inspired him to write the play. In April 1819 he and Mary had visited the Cenci Palace and the Colonna Palace in Rome and had seen the portrait of Beatrice, 'the most beautiful creature that you can conceive': her story of suffering rape by her father, the plot to kill him and her subsequent trial and execution suggested thrilling possibilities. The struggle of a passionate individual against persecution and the questions raised about the nature of justice were subjects close to his heart. He pinned his hopes on the plot and indeed it was a very good one, full of violent action and turbulent emotions. The Cenci Palace with its dark subterranean chambers and gloomy atmosphere, and the classic Gothic background of a remote castle in the Apennines, recalling the terrors of Mrs Radcliffe's novels, were settings ideally suited to deeds of incest, rape and murder. Altogether it had all the ingredients of a good Jacobean tragedy, including a heroine of truly tragic stature: Beatrice Cenci, like Webster's Vittoria Corombona in *The White Devil*, and her namesake Beatrice in Middleton's *The Changeling*, is a strong and vital character, not afraid to counter evil with evil and meeting death with fortitude 'though wrapped in a strange cloud of crime and shame'. She is a remarkable heroine for Shelley to present, since her progress is a movement from virtue to vice, from the sad and vulnerable girl of Act I to the tragic victim about to meet execution after contriving the murder of her own father. She is not a noble and revolutionary New Woman like Cythna, nor does she meet oppres-

Portrait of Beatrice Cenci, possibly by Guido Reni, in the Palazzo Corsini, Rome

sion by conquering it with pity and love as Prometheus finally does. She has to live in a real world, corrupt and decadent, and is forced to deal with real evil in a practical fashion. Her character compels by its very complexity; on her first appearance Orsino draws attention to

> Her subtle mind, her awe-inspiring gaze
> Whose beams anatomize me nerve by nerve

and her nature has unexpected depths. The change in her personality is carefully drawn as, driven to near-madness by the Count's violation of her and lost in the dark night of the soul, she contemplates suicide but rejects it as forbidden by God. Her thoughts lead to the idea of murder:

> What is this undistinguishable mist
> Of thoughts, which rise, like shadow after shadow
> Darkening each other?

and at once she becomes single-minded and bold in her scheme for justice to be carried out on 'a spirit of deep hell' in human form. To the assassins she says that 'it is a high and holy deed' that they must do, and to her the murder is just in the eyes of the God 'who knew my wrong and made Our speedy act the angel of His wrath'. So convinced is she of the rightness of her action that she behaves as if she and the family are all innocent, protected by Heaven and above earthly law. But earthly law condemns her to trial with her mother and Marzio, the hired killer, and her lies do not save them. At the end she loses faith in all justice:

>   Oh, plead
> With famine, or wind-walking Pestilence,
> Blind lightning, or the deaf sea, not with man!
> Cruel, cold, formal man; righteous in words,
> In deeds a Cain. No, Mother, we must die:
> Since such is the reward of innocent lives;
> Such the alleviation of worst wrongs.
> And whilst our murderers live, and hard, cold men,
> Smiling and slow, walk through a world of tears
> To death as to life's sleep; 'twere just the grave
> Were some strange joy for us.

Her last moments show her resigned to death, 'fear and pain Being subdued' and the gentle ending, as she asks Lucretia to bind up her hair for execution, leaves the audience with the feeling of calm after storm necessary to the end of a tragedy.

It is a full-scale star part and on the rare occasions of the production of *The Cenci* it has been played by such stars as Sybil Thorndike and Barbara Jefford who saw the potential in a character so complex. The plight of Beatrice is not one confined to sixteenth-century Italy. The question she poses is an everlasting one: should the individual take the law into his or her hands when subjected to extreme provocation? It obviously has political connotations, as for example in the case of Charlotte Corday who murdered Marat, a monster less appalling than Count Cenci but responsible in her eyes for the progress of the Terror in France. The theme is a variant also of Shelley's favourite one of 'the One warring with the Evil Principle' and Beatrice stands out from all his poetry as the only truly credible protagonist in the cause.

Difficult as it may be to agree absolutely with Dr Leavis that *The Cenci* 'is very bad indeed', one cannot fail to see that it has many faults. Although the creation of Beatrice is an admirable one and the action of the play well-managed, the spell is constantly broken by intrusive echoes of Shakespeare and Webster. In Act IV, when the murder of the Count is about to take place, one begins to wonder whether the castle is in Italy or in Scotland, and whether the Count's second name is Duncan; one of the hired assassins pleads that he cannot 'kill an old and sleeping man' because of his gray hair and 'reverend brow'. 'Indeed, indeed, I cannot do it.' Lady Macbeth had said much the same:

> Had he not resembled
> My father as he slept, I had done't . . .

and at this point the stychomuthia exactly copies the rapid exchange of Macbeth and his lady:

Olimpio: Did you not call?
Beatrice: When?
Olimpio: Now.

Lady Macbeth: Did you not speak?
Macbeth: When?
Lady Macbeth: Now.

There are many other parallels, not only from *Macbeth* – the dark Cenci Palace and the dreadful happenings there had obviously called up the strongest memories of this play – but from other tragedies of Shakespeare; and the trial of Beatrice has its distinguished predecessor in the trial of Vittoria in *The White Devil*. Few of the other characters come to life; the Count is a pathological monster and the weak and frightened members of the Cenci family have little individuality. The power of the play and the reason that it survives as the best poetic drama of the period lies in Beatrice and Shelley's fascination with her story, which called in question all his pacific views on morality:

...the fit return to make to the most enormous injuries is kindness and forbearance, and a resolution to convert the injurer from his dark passions by peace and love. Revenge, retaliation, atonement, are pernicious mistakes. If Beatrice had thought in this manner she would have been wiser and better; but she would never have been a tragic character.

Charles the First

I mean to write a play, in the spirit of human nature, without prejudice or passion, entitled 'Charles the First'.
(Shelley: Letter to Thomas Medwin, 20 July 1820)

In *The Cenci* Shelley was uncharacteristically subduing his natural instincts to the demands of the theatre. 'I have avoided with great care in writing this play the introduction of what is commonly called mere poetry', he wrote, and it was for this reason that, on receiving a copy, Keats had urged him to 'load every rift with ore'. For once, excited by the Cenci legend, he had concentrated on action and psychological exploration, but what few scenes there are of *Charles the First* suggest a slightly different approach. He began it in 1818 and had books and papers sent to him from England so that he could research the subject. Somehow he was unable to make any progress, set it aside and in 1822 tried again. In that year he wrote to Leigh Hunt that, if completed, it would 'hold a higher rank than the Cenci as a work of art', but completed it was not to be. In fact, the very next day he complained to John Gisborne that 'although the poetry succeeds very well I cannot seize the conception of the subject as a whole yet, & seldom now touch the *canvas*'.

The subject, presumably the downfall of the King and the emergence of Cromwell, must have caught his imagination, as the first scene indicates. The opening Masque of the Inns of Court has immediate dramatic impact and sets the theme of civil conflict as the crowd of citizens watch the extravagant spectacle and exchange their views. Each speaker has a clear identity: the Second Citizen, an old man, foretells the revolution when the land 'will be refreshed with civil blood', and as if to make his point a man enters, branded on the face after punishment at the hands of Archbishop Laud's men. A young man sees only the beauty of the masque

> like the bright procession
> Of skiey visions in a solemn dream

and is rebuked by the citizen who warns him that he must not leave

the broad and plain and beaten road
Although no flowers smile on the trodden dust,
For the violet paths of pleasure.

This image recurs in *The Triumph of Life* (although here the violet paths are thought to be more desirable than the dusty road along which the crowds hurry) and in that poem the chariot has become a sinister version of the chariots of the masque which so enchant the young man and which are decribed by him in terms more suitable to *Prometheus Unbound* than to a London street-scene:

How glorious! See those thronging chariots
Rolling, like painted clouds before the wind,
Behind their solemn steeds: how some are shaped
Like curved sea-shells dyed by the azure depths
Of Indian seas; some like the new-born moon;
And some like cars in which the Romans climbed...

In this scene Shelley achieves a surprising blend of 'mere poetry' with action and political comment; and in it two clearly defined aspects of his personality are dramatically presented – the poetic youth who loves beauty and wants men to 'kill these bitter thoughts' of revenge and bloodshed, and the Puritan radical who rebels against the rottenness of a system which oppresses the poor. From the tensions arising from these incompatible positions a play of some real interest could have resulted; in the conflict between the aesthetic and the political, between Cavalier and Roundhead, he had again, as in *The Cenci*, found a strong plot to work on. It seems, though, that he found the demands of historical drama too difficult. The canvas, as he calls it, was too wide and in need of a number of well-drawn figures, a task beyond his ability.

The following scenes introduce the pro-Catholic Court party, playing politics with the concept of the divine right of kings, and the Puritans whose spokesman is Hampden, about to emigrate to the New World where there will be freedom from the rule of kings and the 'impious rites' of an intolerant Church. In the middle of this sea of political argument are the King and Queen; and although we are not meant, in Tom Paine's words, to pity the plumage and forget the dying bird, these two have a tragic grace, taking refuge from 'the terrors of the time' in the consolation of music and the pictures in the royal gallery. They leave the scene to 'decide where that Correggio shall hang', perhaps a touch significant of Shelley's compassion for their approaching doom, since Correggio was one of his own favourite painters. The danger in which they stand is underlined by Archy, a sad Shakespearean court fool, given to dark prophecies and freakish wit not unlike Shelley's own. He has dramatic possibilities, unfortunately never to

and Machiavelli; or Goethe, Schiller, Wieland, etc. The French language you, like every other respectable woman, already know'.

As an adviser he was well qualified. His own wide reading had, as we have seen, led him into studies of many kinds – political, scientific and philosophical – as well as the mass of English literature which he had absorbed from his earliest years, and the Classical works of Greece and Rome. He read French fluently enough to read the writings of the *philosophes*, of Voltaire, Rousseau, Fénelon, Le Sage and many others, including historians of the French Revolution. By 1814 he was reading Italian and became thoroughly familiar with the literature of the country in which he lived for five years. In German he seemed less at ease, and preferred to read French translations of Kant and Winckelmann (the scholar who in the early eighteenth century had celebrated the aesthetic ideals of Classical antiquity). Unlike Coleridge he did not plunge into the depths of German metaphysics, nor was he significantly affected, as the early Romantics were, by German folk-poetry and ballads, like the collections of Volkslieder by Herder in the late 1770s. But he was a passionate admirer of Goethe, the great poet of Weimar and his own contemporary: *The Sorrows of Young Werther*, the product of Goethe's early Sturm und Drang period, was a novel as influential on the young Shelley as it was on Frankenstein's Monster to whom it was 'a never-ending source of speculation and astonishment'. Above all, *Faust* was a revelation to him: 'I have been reading over & over again *Faust*, & always with sensations which no other composition excites', he wrote to John Gisborne in 1822, adding that he had translated scenes from it, to be published in the *Liberal*, the journal about to be brought out by Leigh Hunt. (In fact, only one scene appeared in the first number.) The *Faust* he read was, of course, Part One of that vast work, which had appeared in 1808; the second part was not completed until 1832, just before Goethe's death. Part One contains the familiar story of Faust, weary of the cloistered life of the scholar and longing for experience and the fierce sensations of real living which will bring him closer to mankind; for this he sells his soul to Mephistopheles, falls in love with Margarete, seduces her and loses her when she becomes mad after she bears his child and kills it, ending her life in a prison cell. Shelley's excitement over *Faust* was increased by what he called 'those astonishing etchings' of Friedrich Retzsch in the English edition of 1820. 'I am never satiated with looking at them', he wrote to Gisborne. 'Margaret in the summer house with Faust! The artist makes one envy his happiness that he can sketch such things with calmness, which I dared only to look upon once, & which made my brain swim round.' Today it is hard to see why he was so enthusiastic: our illustration will seem remarkably crude and ill-drawn, leading one to suspect that Shelley was no great connoisseur of the visual arts (opposite).

The Witches' Revel *or* Walpurgisnacht *by Friedrich Retzsch (1820)*

Shelley chose to translate the Prologue in Heaven and the phantasmagoric night scene on the Hartz Mountains, with choruses of witches and visions of the damned. Of the chorus of archangels in the first scene he wrote that it was impossible to do justice to 'the melody of the versification' of such an astonishing piece, but his lyrics magnificently convey the sense of the spinning Earth and planets in constant motion, and the Ocean and storms of thunder and lightning which sweep around a world 'bright as at Creation's day'. The speed and lightness of his lines are reminiscent of the great choruses in *Hellas* of cosmic harmony and splendour. In contrast come the joky disrespectful speeches of Mephistopheles to the Lord, as they discuss the temptation of Faust:

> I am not in much doubt about my bet,
> And if I lose, then 'tis Your turn to crow; ...

He keeps close to Goethe's changes of tone from sublime poetry to the vulgar speech of everyday, but he sometimes found parts of *Faust* too strong for his fastidious taste and in the next scene omitted two stanzas as being too sexually explicit. His translation of the Walpurgisnacht is brilliantly alive, particularly in the sinister lyrics of the journey of Faust, Mephistopheles and Ignis-Fatuus, the Will o' the Wisp, across the mountains to the Witches' Sabbath:

> The limits of the sphere of dream,
>   The bounds of true and false, are past.
> Lead us on, thou wandering Gleam,
>   Lead us onward, far and fast,
>   To the wide, the desert waste.

Shelley's imagination, always quick to respond to the grotesque and the horrific, as we can see in 'A Vision of the Sea' and 'On the Medusa of Leonardo da Vinci', catches the spirit of the magic May night scene, weird as a painting by Hieronymus Bosch:

> Through the dazzling gloom
> The many-coloured mice, that thread
> The dewy turf beneath our tread,
> In troops each other's motions cross,
> Through the heath and through the moss;
> And, in legions intertangled,
>   The fire-flies flit, and swarm, and throng,
> Till all the mountain depths are spangled.

The incantatory rhythms make evil music for the dialogue of Faust and Mephistopheles, whose black humour mocks 'a world drained to the dregs' and nearing its end. Shelley found in its pessimism a reflection of his own feelings, made more evident in *The Triumph of Life*: 'It deepens the gloom', he wrote, 'And yet the pleasure of sympathizing with emotions known only to few, although they derive their sole charm from despair & a scorn of the narrow good we can attain in our present state, seems more to cure the pain which belongs to them.'

Goethe's *Faust* was one of the great achievements of the Romantic era. Its philosophical implications, the theme of forbidden knowledge, the passion for life and experience and the struggle between the good and evil sides of mankind excited Shelley's imagination and he was overcome by its poetic brilliance and variety. The two passages fully demonstrate Shelley's versatility and his ability to interpret, not merely to translate, his material; Hazlitt, reviewing his posthumous poems in the *Edinburgh Review* of 1824 said that if the volume contained nothing but these scenes from *Faust* 'the intellectual world would receive it with an *All Hail!*'.

He was struck by the similarity between *Faust* and another play, *El Mágico Prodigioso* by Calderón, which he had read when studying Spanish with Maria Gisborne. In 1819 in Leghorn she had taught him the language and he had learned enough to be able to read some plays by Calderón, the seventeenth-century playwright whom he compared to Shakespeare in his fecundity and dramatic power. So quick a pupil was he that in two or three months he could read Spanish with ease and had finished twelve of Calderón's plays, some of which he thought worthy 'to be ranked among the grandest & most perfect productions of the human mind'. By 1820 he could write to Peacock in terms of the highest praise, that 'Plato and Calderón have been my gods', and in the last year of his life he translated three scenes from *El Mágico Prodigioso*. It is the tale of Cyprian, a nobleman of third-century Antioch, who sells his soul to the Devil in exchange for powers to obtain Justina, a virtuous Christian girl unmoved by his declarations of love. He becomes a student of necromancy, spending a year in a dark cave with his master, but when he attempts to claim her by magic means her virtue is too strong and God triumphs over the Devil. Cyprian becomes a convert to the Church, is condemned with Justina to be executed during a purge of Christians in the city, and they are joined in death, having outwitted the forces of darkness.

The scenes chosen are all of temptation by the Devil; first he appears in Court dress, 'a foreign gentleman', to engage in philosophical argument with Cyprian who, in a scholar's dress, seems a typically Shelleyan figure in a setting which we have seen before:

In the sweet solitude of this calm place,
This intricate wild wilderness of trees
And flowers and undergrowth of odorous plants,
Leave me; the books you brought out of the house
To me are ever best society.

Cyprian is puzzled by an idea he has found in Pliny of a God who is 'one supreme goodness, one pure essence', but the Daemon dismisses this as 'a sort of popular philosophy' in a manner reminiscent of the airy agnosticism of *Queen Mab*. This is a scene of gentlemanly conversation but the next appearance of the tempter is more dramatic, on a desolate sea-shore. In a traditional burst of thunder and lightning he enters, as a sailor escaped from the ship-wreck which Cyprian has just witnessed. He reveals himself as a master of the black arts and offers to share the knowledge with Cyprian so that

> Thy wildest dream presented to thy thought
> As object of desire, that shall be thine.

(And again Shelley omits lines which he found too indelicate.) Contrasting with the masculine blank verse of argument in the first scene, the Daemon's speech here is a superb set-piece of Romantic rhetoric, one of Shelley's most splendid achievements in its majestic diction which evokes the violent and unknown powers of Nature. The third extract changes tone yet again, as the Daemon tempts Justina with spirit voices proclaiming the delights of love in seductive songs, translated by Shelley with the lyric grace which seemed to come so easily to him. Although the virtuous Justina instinctively rejects the soft persuasion, its message was the constant theme of Shelley's poetry:

> There is no form in which the fire
>   Of love its traces has impressed not.
> Man lives far more in love's desire
>   Than by life's breath, soon possessed not.
> If all that lives must love or die,
> All shapes on earth, or sea, or sky
> With one consent to Heaven cry
> That the glory far above
> All else in life is —
> Love! oh, Love!

6 A critical examination of some poetry

Shelley is one of the best *artists* of us all: I mean in workmanship of style.

(Wordsworth)

The passages in this section are chosen to illustrate the wide range of Shelley's poetic achievement and his progress from the early romanticism of *Alastor* to the dramatic power of *The Triumph of Life*. It is a pity that long poems can only be represented by short extracts, but he was a poet who found it difficult to compress his ideas except in the lyrics; and these at least are given in their entirety. The extracts illustrate the variety of 'workmanship' in Shelley's use of blank verse, the couplet and the *terza rima*, as well as the various lyric forms; and they are selected, also, to show different aspects of the character and thought of this 'cameleon poet'.

Alastor: or The Spirit of Solitude (*lines 140-191*)

The Poet wandering on, through Arabie   140
And Persia, and the wild Carmanian waste,
And o'er the aërial mountains which pour down
Indus and Oxus from their icy caves,
In joy and exultation held his way;
Till in the vale of Cashmire, far within   145
Its loneliest dell, where odorous plants entwine
Beneath the hollow rocks a natural bower,
Beside a sparkling rivulet he stretched
His languid limbs. A vision on his sleep
There came, a dream of hopes that never yet   150
Had flushed his cheek. He dreamed a veilèd maid
Sate near him, talking in low solemn tones.
Her voice was like the voice of his own soul
Heard in the calm of thought; its music long,
Like woven sounds of streams and breezes, held   155
His inmost sense suspended in its web
Of many-coloured woof and shifting hues.
Knowledge and truth and virtue were her theme,
And lofty hopes of divine liberty,
Thoughts the most dear to him, and poesy,   160
Herself a poet. Soon the solemn mood
Of her pure mind kindled through all her frame
A permeating fire: wild numbers then

Oct 25

O wild West Wind thou breath of Autumn's being
Thou, from whose unseen presence the leaves dead
Are driven, like ghosts from an enchanter fleeing
Yellow & black & pale & hectic red,
Pestilence-stricken multitudes — o Thou
Who chariotest to their dark wintry bed
The winged seeds, where they lie cold & low
Each like a corpse within its grave, until
Thine azure sister of the Spring shall blow
Her clarion o'er the dreaming earth, & fill
[crossed out lines]
With living hues & odours plain & hill
Wild Spirit which art moving everywhere
Destroyer & preserver, hear a hear

Page from the manuscript of 'Ode to the West Wind' in the Bodleian

She raised, with voice stifled in tremulous sobs
Subdued by its own pathos: her fair hands   165
Were bare alone, sweeping from some strange harp
Strange symphony, and in their branching veins
The eloquent blood told an ineffable tale.
The beating of her heart was heard to fill
The pauses of her music, and her breath   170
Tumultuously accorded with those fits
Of intermitted song. Sudden she rose,
As if her heart impatiently endured
Its bursting burthen: at the sound he turned,
And saw by the warm light of their own life   175
Her glowing limbs beneath the sinuous veil
Of woven wind, her outspread arms now bare,
Her dark locks floating in the breath of night,
Her beamy bending eyes, her parted lips
Outstretched, and pale, and quivering eagerly.   180
His strong heart sunk and sickened with excess
Of love. He reared his shuddering limbs and quelled
His gasping breath, and spread his arms to meet
Her panting bosom: . . . she drew back a while,
Then, yielding to the irresistible joy,   185
With frantic gesture and short breathless cry
Folded his frame in her dissolving arms.
Now blackness veiled his dizzy eyes, and night
Involved and swallowed up the vision; sleep,
Like a dark flood suspended in its course,   190
Rolled back its impulse on his vacant brain.

Written in 1815 when he and Mary were living at Bishopsgate, near
Windsor Park. At this time they were neighbours of Peacock who
suggested the title, a Greek work meaning 'evil genius', as applied to
the Spirit of Solitude which destroys the young Poet.

This was his first long and important poem after *Queen Mab*, and
was printed in March 1816 in an edition with a few other poems of
his; it was his first appearance in print to the general public. Much
of the scenery comes from memories of his travels in Switzerland, a
river journey down the Rhine and a more sedate voyage with Mary
and Peacock on the Thames from Windsor to Cricklade. These are
transformed into the dream-like landscape of rivers, mountains and
forests, all elements recognizable in his later poetry, as are the
themes of the solitary Poet, the quest for the ideal and the Romantic
identification of the Poet with Nature.

The Poet, the first of Shelley's solitary heroes, has left his home 'to
seek strange truths in undiscovered lands', and his wanderings take
him through the ruins of ancient cities (one of Shelley's favourite

themes, derived in part from his reading of Volney's *Ruins*) to the Vale of Cashmire. He had always been attracted to India, again a result of his extensive reading; Southey's *Curse of Kehama*, a romance set in that country, had been an early favourite of his, and by 1812 he had read a number of books on India including *The Missionary* by one Miss Owenson, which had greatly pleased him. 'It is really a divine thing' he wrote to Hogg, and the heroine of it, Luxima, a Hindu priestess, probably suggested the veiled maid of *Alastor*, who in her turn may be recognized in the Indian maid of Keats's *Endymion*.

In this passage a number of Shelleyan traits are evident. First we notice his love of exotic and romantic names: Arabie, 'the wild Carmanian waste', Indus and Oxus (and later in the poem, the desolate-sounding 'lone Chorasmian shore'). Then appear the typical 'aerial mountains', 'icy caves' and the lonely dell – features of landscapes to become familiar to readers of his later poetry. In fact, the first eight lines sketch the main landscapes of *Prometheus Unbound*, beginning with Prometheus's ravine of icy rocks and leading to the cave in Act III, sc. 3: 'all overgrown with trailing odorous plants' beside a fountain, a more elaborate dwelling than the Poet's 'loneliest dell, where odorous plants entwine' beside a sparkling rivulet. More elaborate still is the house in *Epipsychidion* also twined with 'the ivy and the wild vine interknit', but all represent his ideal earthly paradise.

Here, too, for the first time appears the ideal woman, the Eve for his Eden. The veiled maid, 'herself a poet', is at the same time his Muse and a figment of an erotic dream, with panting bosom and quivering parted lips. This combination of the divine and erotic is seen at its height in Emilia Viviani, the 'Veiled Glory of this lampless Universe'. In *Alastor* the veiled maid is not so clearly representative of Platonic Beauty as are Emilia and Asia, although he does say that she is like 'the voice of his own soul', the epipsyche that Emilia promised to be but was not. As his Muse she is veiled, like Keats's Moneta; and she sings to him

> sweeping from some strange harp
> Strange symphony

in lines surely inspired by Coleridge's Abyssinian maid in 'Kubla Khan', whose 'symphony and song' also came in a vision. Just as Coleridge was unable to revive within himself her music, so the Poet pursues his ideal inspiration in vain. The vision vanishes, and he wakes with 'vacant brain' to be tormented for the rest of his life by the thought of 'that beautiful shape', lost for ever. This search for the ideal beauty, the romantic quest for the unattainable, is the prototype for much of his poetry and, of course, a basic theme of Romantic literature.

The blank verse has a Miltonic ring (the Milton of *Paradise Lost* Book IV), not only in the use of sonorous place-names but in the generally elevated diction of, for example, lines 158–60. The effect is weakened by an over-indulgent use of cliché: 'sickened with excess of love', 'tremulous sobs' and the banal details of the maid's dark locks, 'beamy eyes', parted lips and so on. She is a figure straight out of a Gothic novel, as sexually inviting as the seductive Matilda in his *Zastrozzi*, who excites her lover to 'an ecstasy of delirious passion' so that 'the fire of voluptuous, of maddening love scorched his veins'. The explicit sexuality of her 'frantic gesture and short breathless cry' is followed by Shelley's equivalent of a discreet row of dots as 'blackness veiled his dizzy eyes'. He has yet to learn to move away from second-rate literary convention, and his vocabulary is limited and repetitive: references to languid limbs, glowing limbs and shuddering limbs within the space of forty lines is hardly forgiveable. Also one notices an excess of adjectives, often well-worn and not particularly well chosen. More interesting is the original and characteristically Shelleyan idea of music 'Like woven sounds of streams and breezes' and the subsequent two lines which attempt to describe the invisible in striking natural terms. The image of the poet's mind, held in a web of changing colours, is something new, a tentative step towards conveying the process of poetic creation which he tries to define again in 'Mont Blanc' and *A Defence of Poetry*.

For all its faults *Alastor* has a true sense of the marvellous and the fairy-tale. Like *Endymion* it is a first serious and ambitious attempt at romantic narrative; insofar as they fail, it is because both poets, young and undisciplined, overload the action with 'poetic' ornamentation and self-indulgent repetition. But in both, the enthusiasm and genuine passion for poetry is unmistakeable.

'Mont Blanc'

I

The everlasting universe of things
Flows through the mind, and rolls its rapid waves,
Now dark—now glittering—now reflecting gloom—
Now lending splendour, where from secret springs
The source of human thought its tribute brings   5
Of waters,—with a sound but half its own,
Such as a feeble brook will oft assume
In the wild woods, among the mountains lone,
Where waterfalls around it leap for ever,
Where woods and winds contend, and a vast river   10
Over its rocks ceaselessly bursts and raves.

II

Thus thou, Ravine of Arve—dark, deep Ravine—

Thou many-coloured, many-voicèd vale,
Over whose pines, and crags, and caverns sail
Fast cloud-shadows and sunbeams: awful scene,   15
Where Power in likeness of the Arve comes down
From the ice-gulfs that gird his secret throne,
Bursting through these dark mountains like the flame
Of lightning through the tempest;—thou dost lie,
Thy giant brood of pines around thee clinging,   20
Children of elder time, in whose devotion
The chainless winds still come and ever came
To drink their odours, and their mighty swinging
To hear—an old and solemn harmony;
Thine earthly rainbows stretched across the sweep   25
Of the aethereal waterfall, whose veil
Robes some unsculptured image; the strange sleep
Which when the voices of the desert fail
Wraps all in its own deep eternity;—
Thy caverns echoing to the Arve's commotion,   30
A loud, lone sound no other sound can tame;
Thou art pervaded with that ceaseless motion,
Thou art the path of that unresting sound—
Dizzy Ravine! and when I gaze on thee
I seem as in a trance sublime and strange   35
To muse on my own separate fantasy,
My own, my human mind, which passively
Now renders and receives fast influencings,
Holding an unremitting interchange
With the clear universe of things around;   40
One legion of wild thoughts, whose wandering wings
Now float above thy darkness and now rest
Where that or thou art no unbidden guest,
In the still cave of the witch Poesy,
Seeking among the shadows that pass by   45
Ghosts of all things that are, some shade of thee,
Some phantom, some faint image; till the breast
From which they fled recalls them, thou art there!

The poem was written after his visit to Chamouni in July 1816,
vividly described in a letter to Peacock, also in Mary's Journal. The
first sight of the great mountains, the vale of the Arve and the glacier
of Boisson made a tremendous impression on him, filling him with 'a
sentiment of extatic wonder, not unallied to madness'. This letter
should be read together with the poem as it shows how Shelley
turned the material of Nature to philosophical use: a metaphysical
poem, it at no time loses the sense of the real world. It should also be
read with 'Hymn to Intellectual Beauty', written at the same period

and concerned with the 'awful power' of the Spirit of Beauty.

Very few Romantic poems can equal 'Mont Blanc' in its evocation of the sublime. Beside it, Byron's attempts in *Childe Harold* seem mere rhetoric. Wordsworth's description of Snowdon in Book XIV of *The Prelude*, and of the Simplon Pass in Book VI, are comparable in grandeur, although the account of the first sight of Mont Blanc itself in Book VI (lines 524–40) is strangely muted. He seems dismayed by the 'soulless image' of the mountain, and turns with an obvious sense of relief to the Vale of Chamouni 'which reconciled us to realities' with its pleasant rural scene of reapers binding the sheaves and girls spreading the hay. Dr Leavis, however, in making a comparison with Wordsworth, sees 'Mont Blanc' as an example of Shelley's 'ecstatic dissipation', confused and unsure in its grasp of 'the world of common perception', a view which I do not share.

From the beginning Shelley establishes the two-fold vision of this difficult and subtle poem. The first lines denote that the subject is to be one of the central Romantic topics, that of the relationship of 'The everlasting universe of things' with the poet's mind, and therefore the nature of poetic creation. This is made more clear at the end of stanza II. The 'everlasting universe' is also linked with the Power of line 16, 'in likeness of the Arve', although by the end of the poem Mont Blanc itself comes to symbolize the Power, 'the secret strength of things'. What Shelley means by the 'Power' is debatable: it may be the world-spirit which rules the universe, and by analogy, the spirit of poetry; or it may be the power of the Sublime, just as the 'Hymn to Intellectual Beauty' celebrates the 'awful power' of Beauty.

It could be argued at length (although space forbids it here) that these two poems are essays on the two great aesthetic distinctions of the eighteenth century. Shelley must surely have read Burke's *A Philosophical Inquiry into the Origin of our Ideas of the Sublime and the Beautiful*, so popular that it went into many editions from 1756 onwards, and had a strong effect on current aesthetic theory. The Beautiful, celebrated by Shelley in the 'Hymn' in delicate and graceful imagery, according to Burke 'excites in the soul that feeling, which is called love' (as the last line of the poem indicates) and is associated with soft colours and music just as is Shelley's 'Spirit fair'. But the Sublime 'excites ideas of pain and danger' and is concerned with vastness, silence, darkness, magnificence and solitude. Burke's opening lines on the subject are very relevant to 'Mont Blanc': The passion caused by the great and sublime in nature... is Astonishment; and astonishment is that state of the soul in which all motions are suspended, with some degree of horror.' Astonishment and horror are indeed the keynotes of the poem.

Stanza I makes a general statement: like a great river, the universe in all its aspects affects the mind of man. The mind itself has a secret source of inspiration, 'the secret springs' which well up from some mysterious power, but beside the immense force of Nature it is merely a 'feeble brook'. Stanza II extends and illustrates this theme. Shelley gives a brilliant impression of the ravine of the Arve, with its crags and waterfalls, the rainbows in the veils of spray (see the 'Hymn', line 19) and the sound of the 'chainless winds'. The ravine represents 'the everlasting universe of things' in its varied aspects: it is many-coloured, many-voiced, and the vast river of Stanza I is the Arve, a 'Power' which from its secret throne shapes the scene, forcing its path through the rocks and roaring through the caverns in ceaseless motion. Shelley relates what he sees to his own poetic imagination (lines 35–48). Like Coleridge in 'Dejection' or 'Kubla Khan', he has found in Nature an image for the creative activity of the poet. Coleridge in 'Dejection' believes that 'We receive but what we give'; for Shelley the mind

> passively
> Now renders and receives fast influencings

(not the most felicitous line of the poem) and is involved in 'an unremitting interchange' with Nature, as the first stanza had indicated.

His image of the mind also suggests the Platonic nature of the poem; the imagination is sometimes a 'legion of wild thoughts', perhaps like the 'Fast cloud-shadows and sunbeams' (line 15) which float above the darkness of the ravine, and sometimes it is at rest 'In the still cave of the witch Poesy', seeing, like the prisoners in Plato's cave, the phantoms of reality pass by. The theme of illusion and reality is carried on in the next stanza with the suggestion that in sleep we may dream of 'a remoter world' (but more 'real') and like Keats he wonders 'Do I wake or sleep?'. These first two stanzas suggest aspects of poetic creativity: the frenzy of 'wild thoughts' and the contemplative thought in the 'still cave'. In 'Kubla Khan' Coleridge had stressed the Dionysiac nature of the poet, and the river in that poem can be compared to Shelley's 'vast river' symbolizing the uncontrollable force of the imagination. Shelley's 'Power', like the Arve, comes from a 'secret throne' as

> the flame
> Of lightning through the tempest;

and his mind, like the ravine, is pervaded 'with that ceaseless motion'. The voice of poetry is 'A loud, lone sound no other sound can tame'.

The mood of 'Mont Blanc' is of ecstasy 'not unallied to madness' and the language reflects both the wildness (note the verbs: *springs*, *leap*, *bursts*, *raves*) and the awesome splendour of the scene. Neither the word nor the concept of Beauty is mentioned. The ravine is dark, and the sound of the wind in the pines is 'an old and solemn harmony'; the Power is violent, like lightning in a storm, and the waterfalls veil some mysterious 'unsculptured image'. Just as Milton in 'Il Penseroso' calls up gloomy and majestic sights and sounds, so Shelley appropriately sees the Sublime in pictures of ever-increasing harshness, death and ruin which become more horrific in Stanzas III and IV. The landscape has a sinister life of its own: the Arve is a monarch in a secret kingdom, the pines cling to the rocks like a giant brood of 'Children of elder time' and later in Stanza IV the glaciers 'creep like snakes that watch their prey'. In every way the poem is in accordance with Burke's conception of the Sublime: it evokes terror, a sense of awful solitude and danger. At one point Burke quotes *Paradise Lost* (Book II, lines 618 ff), a description of 'many a frozen, many a fiery Alp', a scene of desolation which may have come to Shelley's mind: certainly much of the diction in the poem is Miltonic, especially in Stanza IV.

Prometheus Unbound (*Act I, lines 380-409*)

Prometheus.   Evil minds   380
Change good to their own nature. I gave all
He has; and in return he chains me here
Years, ages, night and day: whether the Sun
Split my parched skin, or in the moony night
The crystal-wingèd snow cling round my hair: 385
Whilst my belovèd race is trampled down
By his thought-executing ministers.
Such is the tyrant's recompense: 'tis just:
He who is evil can receive no good;
And for a world bestowed, or a friend lost,   390
He can feel hate, fear, shame; not gratitude:
He but requites me for his own misdeed.
Kindness to such is keen reproach, which breaks
With bitter stings the light sleep of Revenge.
Submission, thou dost know I cannot try: 395
For what submission but that fatal word,
The death-seal of mankind's captivity,
Like the Sicilian's hair-suspended sword,
Which trembles o'er his crown, would he accept,
Or could I yield? Which yet I will not yield.   400
Let others flatter Crime, where it sits throned
In brief Omnipotence: secure are they:
For Justice, when triumphant, will weep down
Pity, not punishment, on her own wrongs,
Too much avenged by those who err. I wait,   405
Enduring thus, the retributive hour

> Which since we spake is even nearer now.
> But hark, the hell-hounds clamour: fear delay:
> Behold! Heaven lowers under thy Father's frown.

Act I of *Prometheus Unbound* was composed in 1818 at Este, soon after the Shelleys had come to Italy. It was published in 1820 in London by C. and J. Ollier.

This passage of blank verse should be compared with the extract from *Alastor* as an indication of how Shelley, within the space of three years, has tightened and disciplined his earlier 'poetic' diction. These lines have a true sense of the dramatic: words are used not in a self-indulgent way but to convey the character of the speaker as clearly as the ideas that Shelley is expounding.

As we have seen, this first Act is devoted to Prometheus and his sufferings, and the verse is much firmer, more masculine than in Act II in which Asia is the central figure. Mercury, Jupiter's messenger, has reluctantly brought the Furies to torture him, 'a doom of new revenge', and Prometheus answers him. He reiterates his refusal to bow to the tyrant, voicing his expectation that right must triumph in the end and that 'the retributive hour' is at hand. Shelley's ideas on the nature of despotism and his optimistic belief in change are strongly expressed: Godwinian justice will prevail, and the tyrant will receive 'pity, not punishment', sorrow more than anger in the true Godwinian spirit of reason. He is thinking of the excesses of the French Revolution and repeating what he had said in the Preface to *The Revolt of Islam* about 'the atrocities of the demagogues', the Terror which had so shocked the civilized world.

These lines show perfect control of the blank verse. It never becomes over-rhetorical, as Shelley often does at moments of emotion, but maintains a tone of quiet bitterness and stoicism, in keeping with the character of Prometheus. The lines are broken to reflect thought and feeling, as in the staccato 'I gave all He has', followed by the long dragging syllables of 'Years, ages, night and day', the seemingly endless period of his suffering. Similarly the chopped rhythm of 'He can feel hate, fear, shame; not gratitude' or 'Or could I yield? Which yet I will not yield' catch the defiant mood. There is nothing here of the luxuriant or delicate imagery usually associated with Shelley; only in the fifth and sixth lines does he call up the cold images of 'crystal-wingèd snow' and 'moony night' as a reminder of the agony of Prometheus among the 'crawling glaciers' and 'moon-freezing crystals' in the first moments of the drama. This is not self-indulgence in 'poetic' language but essential to the situation, as is the simile of the sword of Damocles (line 399). Otherwise the diction is spare and direct, conveying bitterness and defiance in the hard, cutting sounds of 'Split my parched skin', 'Kindness to such is keen reproach', 'bitter stings', 'the hell-hounds clamour'. The rhetoric is controlled, since it is the language of sober argument, sharpened by the single dramatic question and at the end by the phrases 'But hark' and 'Behold!' to draw attention to the appearance of the Furies.

Prometheus Unbound represents Shelley's blank verse at his finest, and in it he creates remarkable dramatic and lyrical effects. To appreciate his versatility compare this extract with, for example, the dialogue of the Fauns (Act II, sc. 2, lines 64–97) or Panthea's speech (Act II, sc. 5, lines 16-36) in which the verse is flowing and strongly musical.

Julian and Maddalo (*lines 1-35*)

```
I rode one evening with Count Maddalo
Upon the bank of land which breaks the flow
Of Adria towards Venice: a bare strand
Of hillocks, heaped from ever-shifting sand,
Matted with thistles and amphibious weeds,              5
Such as from earth's embrace the salt ooze breeds,
Is this; an uninhabited sea-side,
Which the lone fisher, when his nets are dried,
Abandons; and no other object breaks
The waste, but one dwarf tree and some few stakes       10
Broken and unrepaired, and the tide makes
A narrow space of level sand thereon,
Where 'twas our wont to ride while day went down.
This ride was my delight. I love all waste
And solitary places; where we taste                     15
The pleasure of believing what we see
Is boundless, as we wish our souls to be:
And such was this wide ocean, and this shore
More barren than its billows; and yet more
Than all, with a remembered friend I love              20
To ride as then I rode;—for the winds drove
The living spray along the sunny air
Into our faces; the blue heavens were bare,
Stripped to their depths by the awakening north;
And, from the waves, sound like delight broke forth    25
Harmonising with solitude, and sent
Into our hearts aëreal merriment.
So, as we rode, we talked; and the swift thought,
Winging itself with laughter, lingered not,
But flew from brain to brain,—such glee was ours,      30
Charged with light memories of remembered hours,
None slow enough for sadness: till we came
Homeward, which always makes the spirit tame.
```

150

This day had been cheerful but cold, and now
The sun was sinking, and the wind also.   35

Written in 1818, after Shelley had been to Venice for the first time to
discuss with Byron the future of Claire's child, Allegra, who was
staying there with a Mr and Mrs Hoppner. She is the 'serious,
subtle, wild yet gentle being' referred to later in the poem, a child for
whom he had a special affection and over whose welfare he took
immense trouble. He wrote to Mary describing the encounter with
Byron; they went in his gondola 'across the laguna to a long sandy
island' where they mounted the horses waiting for them and rode
along the sands, talking. This occasion provides the opening part of
Julian and Maddalo.

The extract is chosen to illustrate Shelley's powers as a realistic
descriptive writer, a quality in his poetry sometimes forgotten. His
fondness for dream-landscapes did not prevent him from observing
Nature with a clear and thoughtful eye, as the section on 'Shelley
and Nature' has tried to show. The setting of lagoon and sandbank
is as detailed and strongly drawn as Crabbe's picture of the seashore
in 'Peter Grimes', and like Crabbe he paints it in uncompromisingly
bleak images. The thistles, amphibious weeds, the one dwarf tree
and the broken stakes are the sharp vertical strokes in a landscape as
flat and empty as that of 'Ozymandias'. Each detail is carefully
selected and arranged as a painter might do, to convey the atmosphere he needs. The thistles are matted, a word which suggests the
thickly clumped plants, also a sense of the unkempt and wild, as in
matted hair; the idea of an uncared-for stretch of land continues in
the single tree, dwarfed as if unable to grow in such unhospitable
surroundings, and the broken and unrepaired stakes. It is a place
abandoned even by the fisherman (he is 'lone' to emphasize the
desolation); the key-words are '*bare*', '*waste*', '*barren*', '*uninhabited*'.
And yet the stark beginning with its romantic statement, typical of
Shelley, that 'I love all waste And solitary places', leads on to an
unexpectedly cheerful and bracing description of the ride along the
shore. 'Bracing' is the exact adjective: in the colourless scene the sky
has the clear, cold blue that comes when it is swept by the north
wind, which whips up the 'living spray' in the faces of the two riders.
It becomes exhilarating, the sound of the sea delights them and they
take pleasure in each other's conversation until, as evening draws
on, their laughter turns to more serious talk.

It is very strong and clear-cut writing with none of the feminine
softness usually associated with Shelley's natural description. After
the sharp visual impact of the first dozen lines one is given a physical
sense of the wind which 'drove' the spray and of the energetic action
of riding communicated in the sounds of *swift, flew, winging, lingered,
light*. The passage has the effect of speech, in keeping with the

narrative 'I', and the couplets have a free, almost conversational rhythm with great variety of phrase lengths and changes of speed. There are many run-on lines, some broken to stress a point as in line 7 with the emphatic 'Is this;' or line 9, 'Abandons;' and others, as in lines 14–17, because Shelley is here becoming more personal and confidential. As they ride the impetus of the lines increases: in lines 21–23 the drive of the metre, with the two final strong beats on line 21, mimics the force of the wind, and the long lifting and rippling rhythms of lines 25–26 follow the sound of the waves and their 'aëreal merriment'. The speed of their progress along the shore is halted by the heavy syllables of 'Homeward' and the slowing down of the regular line 'The sun was sinking, and the wind also'.

The whole poem is remarkable for its shifts of tone and its descriptive virtuosity, of which this passage demonstrates only a little. The colourless landscape and the easy camaraderie of the riders is soon followed by one of Shelley's most highly-coloured and Turneresque sunsets and a deeper change of mood to an ominous sense of death ('if you can't swim Beware of Providence') and silence, as the night falls.

'Letter to Maria Gisborne'

                    I recall
My thoughts, and bid you look upon the night.
As water does a sponge, so the moonlight   255
Fills the void, hollow, universal air—
What see you?—unpavilioned Heaven is fair,
Whether the moon, into her chamber gone,
Leaves midnight to the golden stars, or wan
Climbs with diminished beams the azure steep;   260
Or whether clouds sail o'er the inverse deep,
Piloted by the many-wandering blast,
And the rare stars rush through them dim and fast:—
All this is beautiful in every land.—
But what see you beside?—a shabby stand   265
Of Hackney coaches—a brick house or wall
Fencing some lonely court, white with the scrawl
Of our unhappy politics;—or worse—
A wretched woman reeling by, whose curse
Mixed with the watchman's, partner of her trade,   270
You must accept in place of serenade—
Or yellow-haired Pollonia murmuring
To Henry, some unutterable thing.
I see a chaos of green leaves and fruit
Built round dark caverns, even to the root   275
Of the living stems that feed them—in whose bowers

There sleep in their dark dew the folded flowers;
Beyond, the surface of the unsickled corn
Trembles not in the slumbering air, and borne
In circles quaint, and ever-changing dance,   280
Like wingèd stars the fire-flies flash and glance,
Pale in the open moonshine, but each one
Under the dark trees seems a little sun,
A meteor tamed; a fixed star gone astray
From the silver regions of the milky way;—   285
Afar the Contadino's song is heard,
Rude, but made sweet by distance—and a bird
Which cannot be the Nightingale, and yet
I know none else that sings so sweet as it
At this late hour;—and then all is still—   290
Now—Italy or London, which you will!

Written in July 1820, when Shelley was living in the Gisbornes'
house at Leghorn.

This is chosen as an example of Shelley's mature style, using the
couplet in free and easy epistolary manner, in a more familiar vein
than the couplets of *Julian and Maddalo*. It also illustrates the side of
Shelley known to his friends: a sympathetic correspondent (he puts
himself in Mrs Gisborne's place, imagining what she sees around
her) and one with the ability to make magic out of the ordinary.

The earlier part of the poem lists the pleasures of the London
literary scene. Now he tells her to look at the night sky which they
are both seeing ('All this is beautiful in every land'), and he
imagines the sordid reality of London that she has around her –
hackney cabs, prostitutes and a sight only too familiar to city-
dwellers, then as now, the political graffiti scrawled on a slum wall.
He, on the other hand, is part of the lovely Italian night, with its
flowers and fire-flies and the song of birds and Italian voices.

The whole passage communicates by its liveliness, even restlessness. Everything in it seems alive: the moon climbs the sky, the
clouds sail, the stars rush through them, the Italian night is a 'chaos'
of vegetation, the fire-flies 'flash and glance' like 'wingèd stars'. His
world is one of living Nature: the 'living stems', the flowers sleeping
in 'dark dew', the air 'slumbering' over the cornfields, and the dark
trees, all suggest a world of harmony and richness, a night-scene
created by Shelley as sensitively as that of Coleridge's 'Frost at
Midnight'. The harmony is intensified by the use of many liquid
sounds (*trembles, slumbering, silver, milky, still* and so on) and sibilants
which catch the flickering quality of the fire-flies. In contrast, the
sketches of London are static and harsh: the hard consonants
(*Hackney, brick, scrawled*) reflect the ugliness of the slum scene with its
lonely court and 'shabby stand' of cabs; nothing seems alive but the

drunken prostitute and the watchman, whose cursing voices are the equivalent of the Italian birdsong and serenade. It is an unhappy scene with a background of 'unhappy politics'. The passage proves again that he could write with a sure sense of reality, evoking a city-scene as clearly as the view from his own window in Leghorn.

The opening lines are especially characteristic of Shelley, in his love of night skies, introduced by that arresting quasi-scientific image of the moonlight saturating the empty air 'as water does a sponge'. The moon is personified as a woman 'into her chamber gone', like the 'dying lady' in 'The Waning Moon' who 'totters forth, wrapped in a gauzy veil'; and again as climbing the sky, wan and diminished like the moon in 'Art thou pale for weariness'. Lines 261–3 recall 'The Cloud', where the stars on a windy night

> whirl and flee
> Like a swarm of golden bees

as the clouds are blown by 'the many-wandering blast'.

The rapid movement of his ideas and images is perfectly matched in his remarkably flexible and free use of the couplet. The first dozen lines tend to be end-stopped although the internal rhythm is broken in various ways, to catch the rhythm of the spoken word. For example, in line 256 the breaks come with the commas after 'void' and 'hollow' and in the next line the question creates a natural pause. The inversion at the beginning of line 263 hurries along the rhythm, just as the stars rush through the clouds. The six lines of the London scene are run-on to give a broken effect, almost prosaic (suitably, as the scene is the antithesis of poetic), culminating in the ironic and regularly accented 'You must accept in place of serenade'. Throughout the poem, in its shifts from wit to imaginative description, he maintains this tone of inspired and delightful conversation; and a closer study of the metrics will reveal what Wordsworth meant when he so highly praised Shelley for his 'workmanship of style'.

The next three extracts represent another aspect of Shelley, that of his skill as a writer of lyrics, for which he has always had a very high reputation. His extraordinary technical ability must have come in part from his intimate knowledge of Classical poetry, but he also had an intuitive response to the movement and music of words. He can catch, for example, the flight of the skylark:

> Higher still and higher
>   From the earth thou springest
> Like a cloud of fire;
>   The blue deep thou wingest,
> And singing still dost soar, and soaring ever singest.

154

This is a stanza in which the modulated trochaic metre of the four short lines lifts and takes wing with the thin light syllables to the certain flight of the long iambic line. The subject may be ethereal, a blithe spirit, but the verbs are strong and physically carry the verse up and up to the skylark's height. As well as the majestic choruses he can write lyrics swift and impetuous as 'The Cloud' or 'Arethusa', or delicate as the dialogue of 'The Two Spirits'. For him the writing of songs and lyrics seemed as natural and easy as breathing. John Stuart Mill, in his essay 'Two Kinds of Poetry', defines lyric poetry as that 'most natural to a really poetic temperament, and least capable of being successfully imitated by one not so endowed by nature', adding that, because of his sensibility and the vividness of his emotions, Shelley was at his greatest in short poems and lyrics in which 'the overruling influence of some one state of feeling' was the unifying power.

Hellas: *the last Chorus (lines 1060 to the end)*

Chorus.

The world's great age begins anew,   1060
   The golden years return,
The earth doth like a snake renew
   Her winter weeds outworn:
Heaven smiles, and faiths and empires gleam,
Like wrecks of a dissolving dream.   1065

A brighter Hellas rears its mountains
   From waves serener far;
A new Peneus rolls his fountains
   Against the morning star.
Where fairer Tempes bloom, there sleep   1070
Young Cyclads on a sunnier deep.

A loftier Argo cleaves the main,
   Fraught with a later prize;
Another Orpheus sings again,
   And loves, and weeps and dies.   1075
A new Ulysses leaves once more
Calypso for his native shore.

Oh, write no more the tale of Troy,
   If earth Death's scroll must be!
Nor mix with Laian rage the joy   1080
   Which dawns upon the free:
Although a subtler Sphinx renew
Riddles of death Thebes never knew.

Another Athens shall arise,
    And to remoter time   1085
Bequeath, like sunset to the skies,
    The splendour of its prime;
And leave, if nought so bright may live,
All earth can take or Heaven can give.

Saturn and Love their long repose   1090
    Shall burst, more bright and good
Than all who fell, than One who rose,
    Than many unsubdued:
Not gold, not blood, their altar dowers,
But votive tears and symbol flowers.   1095

Oh, cease! must hate and death return?
    Cease! must men kill and die?
Cease! drain not to its dregs the urn
    Of bitter prophecy.
The world is weary of the past,   1100
Oh, might it die or rest at last!

Hellas was written in 1821 at Pisa and published by C. and J. Ollier in the spring of 1822. It was composed at a time when, as Mary's note says, 'the South of Europe was in a state of great political excitement', and the success of movements for national liberation in Spain and Italy had inspired Shelley to look forward to Greek independence from the Turks. *Hellas* was the result of this political enthusiasm as well as the expression of his passion for Greece and all it stood for. The modern Greek in his eyes was the descendant of 'those glorious beings' of Classical days and therefore capable of bringing about the regeneration of their country. He added his own notes to *Hellas* including two on this extract, of which the first refers to the prophetic nature of the Chorus; it is, he says, for this reason 'indistinct and obscure' as if he were looking through a glass darkly.

If indeed it is obscure, much of it can be clarified when we recognize that the Chorus is directly inspired by Virgil's Fourth Eclogue, the Pollio, although the last stanza is pure Shelley in its despair at the unreason of mankind. The Pollio, so called because it was written in the consulship of C. Asinius Pollio, (40 BC) and possibly in honour of the expected birth of his child, is a famous vision of a new Golden Age. The child, Virgil sings, will have the gift of divine life and will see the Iron Age pass away, as prophesied by the Cumaean Sibyl, and Saturn's reign return; *iam regnat Apollo* – now Apollo is King and art and poetry will flourish. Virgil speaks of the great new era of fertility, peace and plenty, although some traces of old sin remain to tempt men once again to put to sea like the

Argonauts in search of the Golden Fleece, and to fight another war with Troy; but in time all will be settled and return to the primal natural scene.

This eclogue was from early days thought to be a link with Christianity in that it foretells the coming of a Messiah, the divine child, in accordance with Isaiah's prophecy. Shelley in his first note quotes from both Virgil and Isaiah, and throughout the Chorus there are close and clear references to the Pollio.

The Chorus is perhaps his finest and most lyrical statement of a theme always in his mind; every one of the major poems looks forward to a new Eden, and even in the early *Queen Mab* are images taken directly from Virgil's Eclogue, of a golden age when poison-plants are no more and the herds no longer fear the lion (*Queen Mab*, Stanza VIII). But in *Hellas* for the first time, the promise seemed about to be fulfilled: the preceding Semichorus exults that Greece 'which was dead, is arisen!' and at last the shadows, seen in Platonic terms from 'the walls of our prison', vanish in the brilliant light of reality. These shadows are the old ideologies and empires which dissolve like dreams in the brightness of morning.

The first stanza of the Chorus makes the triumphant statement of the return of the Golden Age with the arresting image of the snake. In the Pollio Virgil says that the serpent shall perish (*occidet et serpens*) but Shelley instead sees it as the symbol of eternity, constantly renewed, casting off its winter skin in springtime to emerge fresh and new. The 'winter weeds' suggest both mourning to be discarded (like a widow's weeds) and the weeds of the field which will give way to fertile crops. Greece, like the snake, rises in renewed beauty and the second stanza celebrates this in images of light and peace, evoking the scenery of the Classical world – the blossoming vale of Tempe, the River Peneus and the Cycladean Islands asleep on a calm sea, a typically Shelleyan landscape. After this the Chorus closely follows Virgil in its references to the Argonauts and the Trojan War: but Shelley sees these episodes as part of the inevitable cycle of history in which man seeks adventure, love and power. There will always be those who voyage out in search of gold, the tragic Orpheus figure of the poet and lover will be there in every age as will the wanderer Ulysses leaving the Isle of Calypso for his home. Shelley, unlike Virgil, rejects the idea of new wars – 'Oh, write no more the tale of Troy' – and prays that freedom will come to Greece unmixed with rage and further oppression; at the back of his mind was the thought of the French Revolution. The golden years of Saturn will be celebrated not with gold and blood (images often associated in his poetry with the career of Napoleon, as in 'Lines' written on hearing of his death: 'Napoleon's fierce spirit rolled In terror and blood and gold') but with regret for the past and peaceful offerings of flowers. The gods who, in the earlier Chorus 'Worlds on worlds are rolling ever' had fled 'from the folding-star of Bethlehem' and the oppression of Christianity, will return. Apollo, Pan and Love are to be preferred to 'One who rose', Jesus, because as Shelley's note indicates, Christianity brought with it 'every aggravation of atrocity and variety of torture', although Christ himself had 'a sublime human character'.

The last stanza, however, seems characteristically to deny all that has gone before. He has implied the inevitable cycle of history but now longs for it to stand still; worlds are rolling ever, but there must be a break in the pattern so that hate and death need not return. The triumphant paean 'The world's great age begins anew' ends in the dying fall of 'Oh, might it die or rest at last!' as if his prophetic vision had run out and he has become a mere mortal faced with the world as it is rather than what it might be. There is a certain ambiguity in 'it' in the last line. Is it the past which should die, or is it the world itself? Either way, the last two lines have a sad and wistful cadence.

The Chorus is in effect an answer to the earlier Chorus: 'Worlds on worlds are rolling ever' which concludes with Earth and the pagan gods wailing for 'the golden years' which have vanished because

> killing Truth had glared on them;
> Our hills and seas and streams,
> Dispeopled of their dreams,
> Their waters turned to blood, their dew to tears...

Shelley's nostalgic longing for the Arcadian past is in the true Romantic tradition, echoing Coleridge's lines in *The Piccolomini* (Act II, sc.4) translated from Schiller:

> The intelligible forms of ancient poets,
> The fair humanities of old religion,
> The Power, the Beauty, and the Majesty,
> That had their haunts in dale, or piny mountain,
> Or forest by slow stream, or pebbly spring,
> Or chasms and wat'ry depths; all these have vanished.
> They live no longer in the faith of reason!

With lyric simplicity this last Chorus from *Hellas* thus brings together ideas and feelings central to Romantic poetry. In the spirit of the age the poet fills the rôles of prophet and enthusiast for political freedom; at the same time he expresses the sense of a magical pantheistic past and departed glory, and the despair of one who realizes that his vision is hardly likely to come true.

158

'Song'

I

Rarely, rarely, comest thou,
　Spirit of Delight!
Wherefore hast thou left me now
　Many a day and night?
Many a weary night and day　　　　　5
'Tis since thou art fled away.

II

How shall ever one like me
　Win thee back again?
With the joyous and the free
　Thou wilt scoff at pain.　　　　　10
Spirit false! thou hast forgot
　All but those who need thee not.

III

As a lizard with the shade
　Of a trembling leaf,
Thou with sorrow art dismayed;　　　　15
　Even the sighs of grief
Reproach thee, that thou art not near,
And reproach thou wilt not hear.

IV

Let me set my mournful ditty
　To a merry measure;　　　　　20
Thou wilt never come for pity,
　Thou wilt come for pleasure;
Pity then will cut away
Those cruel wings, and thou wilt stay.

V

I love all that thou lovest,　　　　　25
　Spirit of Delight!
The fresh Earth in new leaves dressed,
　And the starry night;
Autumn evening, and the morn
When the golden mists are born.　　　　30

VI

I love snow, and all the forms
　Of the radiant frost;
I love waves, and winds, and storms,
　Everything almost
Which is Nature's, and may be　　　　35
Untainted by man's misery.

I love tranquil solitude,
    And such society
As is quiet, wise, and good;
    Between thee and me   40
What difference? but thou dost possess
The things I seek, not love them less.

I love Love—though he has wings,
    And like light can flee,
But above all other things,   45
    Spirit, I love thee—
Thou art love and life! Oh, come,
Make once more my heart thy home.

One of Shelley's late lyrics, characteristic in its lightness and grace
and in its tone of underlying melancholy – underlying because the
metre is 'a merry measure', intended to court the capricious Spirit of
Delight and win its favours. The Spirit is one of Shelley's lesser
spirits, not of the importance of the Spirits of Nature, of Beauty or of
Earth which appear in his other works. It is interesting that Burke,
in his distinction between the Sublime and the Beautiful, categorizes
'delight' as 'the sensation which accompanies the removal of pain'
and is to be thus distinguished from simple 'pleasure'. This is
certainly true of the mood of this lyric, suggesting as it does the
desire for an end to sadness. But at no point is one conscious of the
excess of self-pity which mars, for example 'Stanzas written in
Dejection, near Naples'. Sadness is suggested in 'many a weary
night and day' and in references to pain and grief, but the half-
teasing address to the Spirit has an urbanity implying that any self-
indulgence would be unmannerly. The tone is perfectly sustained:

    Between thee and me
    What difference?

is that of whimsical reproof in a conversation between equals, as is

    Spirit false! thou hast forgot
    All but those who need thee not.

The trochaic metre has a few variants and irregularities (lines 17,
24, 34, 41) emphasizing the conversational style, and the words used
are mostly light, short and airy, appropriate to the Spirit they are
invoking. Occasionally they carry weight, as in the opening stress on
'Rarely, rarely' or 'Reproach thee', but on the whole Shelley uses
many thin vowel sounds (*spirit, pity, lizard, mists, winds*) and sibilants
(Stanzas 5 and 6). The word 'delight' itself suggests lightness and
liberation. The last stanza, the most deeply felt and one of longing, is

free in its use of labial sounds, and here the emphasis falls, after earlier tentative gestures, on the positive 'Oh, come', just as 'Rarely, rarely' stresses the pleading tone which opens the poem.

Characteristic also of Shelley are the swift sketches of the seasons, and his choice of solitude or a small company of sympathetic friends. The poem, technically a triumph of tone and delicacy, shows the gently humorous side of him, so often praised by his friends.

'To Jane: The Recollection'

I

Now the last day of many days,
    All beautiful and bright as thou,
        The loveliest and the last, is dead,
Rise, Memory, and write its praise!
    Up,—to thy wonted work! come, trace   5
        The epitaph of glory fled,—
For now the Earth has changed its face,
    A frown is on the Heaven's brow.

II

We wandered to the Pine Forest
    That skirts the Ocean's foam,   10
The lightest wind was in its nest,
    The tempest in its home.
The whispering waves were half asleep,
    The clouds were gone to play.
And on the bosom of the deep   15
    The smile of Heaven lay;
It seemed as if the hour were one
    Sent from beyond the skies,
Which scattered from above the sun
    A light of Paradise.   20

III

We paused amid the pines that stood
    The giants of the waste,
Tortured by storms to shapes as rude
    As serpents interlaced,
And soothed by every azure breath,   25
    That under Heaven is blown,
To harmonies and hues beneath,
    As tender as its own;
Now all the tree-tops lay asleep,
    Like green waves on the sea,   30
As still as in the silent deep
    The ocean woods may be.

How calm it was!—the silence there
   By such a chain was bound
That even the busy woodpecker   35
   Made stiller by her sound
The inviolable quietness;
   The breath of peace we drew
With its soft motion made not less
   The calm that round us grew.   40
There seemed from the remotest seat
   Of the white mountain waste,
To the soft flower beneath our feet,
   A magic circle traced,—
A spirit interfused around,   45
   A thrilling, silent life,—
To momentary peace it bound
   Our mortal nature's strife;
And still I felt the centre of
   The magic circle there   50
Was one fair form that filled with love
   The lifeless atmosphere.

V

We paused beside the pools that lie
   Under the forest bough,—
Each seemed as 'twere a little sky   55
   Gulfed in a world below;
A firmament of purple light
   Which in the dark earth lay,
More boundless than the depth of night,
   And purer than the day—   60
In which the lovely forests grew,
   As in the upper air,
More perfect both in shape and hue
   Than any spreading there.
There lay the glade and neighbouring lawn,   65
   And through the dark green wood
The white sun twinkling like the dawn
   Out of a speckled cloud.
Sweet views which in our world above
   Can never well be seen,   70
Were imaged by the water's love
   Of that fair forest green.
And all was interfused beneath
   With an Elysian glow,
An atmosphere without a breath,   75

A softer day below.
Like one beloved the scene had lent
    To the dark water's breast,
Its every leaf and lineament
    With more than truth expressed;   80
Until an envious wind crept by,
    Like an unwelcome thought,
Which from the mind's too faithful eye
    Blots one dear image out.
Though thou art ever fair and kind,   85
    The forests ever green,
Less oft is peace in Shelley's mind,
    Than calm in waters, seen.

This is one of the group of poems of 1822 written to Jane Williams, the common-law wife of Edward Williams who died with Shelley on the *Don Juan*. Jane was beautiful and serene, 'a sort of spirit of embodied peace in our circle of tempests', not an intellectual like Mary but musical and a sympathetic listener. From admiration Shelley's feelings changed to love, but, since she was devoted to her husband it was a love which could not be fulfilled. At this time Mary was pregnant and unhappy, and he felt that their marriage was strained; in his longing for affection and understanding he turned to Jane and to her were written 'The Guitar' ('Ariel to Miranda'), 'The Invitation' and 'The Magnetic Lady to her Patient'. She was 'best and brightest', 'Radiant Sister of the Day', the source of both comfort and sadness and she, too, felt the strong attraction expressed in these poems.

'The Recollection' is a delicate and subtle statement of their relationship, the memory of a perfect day spent together, an 'epitaph of glory fled'. In the very first lines Shelley touches on the fleeting quality of experience: the day is dead and will not come again. Their walk in the pine forest of the Cascine at the edge of the sea is like a walk in Paradise under a smiling sky; the tortured shapes of the pines are 'as serpents interlaced', a hint that Paradise cannot last, but calm and harmony prevail to create a mystical stillness as if a magic circle is drawn round them. She is at the centre of it all, the 'one fair form that filled with love The lifeless atmosphere'. They move on to look into the pools under the trees, and see the reflections of a world transfigured 'with an Elysian glow', a world more perfect than the one they know. It is as if Shelley is contemplating the ultimate Platonic reality of beauty and love:

Sweet views which in our world above
    Can never well be seen

but the wind stirs the water and the vision disappears as the perfect day is to disappear.

> The Earth has changed its face,
> A frown is on the Heaven's brow.

and the broken surface of the pool becomes a symbol of Shelley's broken peace of mind and the impermanence of their relationship.

The lyrics to Jane must be read as a group. This one is obviously linked to 'The Guitar' in its reference to *The Tempest* and the magic circle drawn by Prospero which binds them in a spell. Trelawny tells us that it was Shelley's favourite play and these poems are pervaded with a sense of the sea and the music of that enchanted island. Perhaps when he spoke of Jane as the spirit of peace 'in our circle of tempests' this was in his mind and gave rise to the poem. Certainly no other of his lyrics conveys a moment of mystical union as eloquently as this one does. The short lines and light movement of the verses accentuate the fragility of the passing moments; the language has a simplicity which eschews elaborate imagery and overheated adjectives. The effect is tender and infinitely sad, yet there is no over-indulgence in melancholy. The mood of the golden day is expressed in soft tranquil sounds – *lightest, smile, whispering, silent, Paradise* – and gentle images: the clouds 'were gone to play', the wind 'was in its nest'. Even the twisted pines are 'soothed by every azure breath' and lie asleep like the ocean woods under the sea (a memory of the 'Ode to the West Wind'). The sounds die down to the absolute calm of the silent moment:

> A spirit interfused around,
>   A thrilling, silent life

and the following image of the reflections in the pools sustains the sense of wonder in the 'purple light' in the dark water, and the lightly fanciful notion of

> the water's love
> Of that fair forest green.

It has all the qualities of a Romantic poem – the concentration on personal emotion, the identification of feeling with landscape, and the sense of a spirit in Nature; but the sensibility which shapes it is unmistakably that of Shelley in the delicacy with which the scene is evoked. The few descriptive touches of the sea, the pines and the flowers at their feet are all closely linked to the changing mood of the two lovers, and in five stanzas a miniature human drama is played out, coming full circle from the opening note of regret to the muted ending. If one had to choose a poem to illustrate Shelley's supreme mastery of the lyric art – leaving aside the great choruses and songs of *Prometheus Unbound* and *Hellas* – it might well be 'The Recollection'.

164

The Triumph of Life (*lines 41-111*)

As in that trance of wondrous thought I lay,
This was the tenour of my waking dream:—
Methought I sate beside a public way

Thick strewn with summer dust, and a great stream
Of people there was hurrying to and fro,   45
Numerous as gnats upon the evening gleam,

All hastening onward, yet none seemed to know
Whither he went, or whence he came, or why
He made one of the multitude, and so

Was borne amid the crowd, as through the sky   50
One of the million leaves of summer's bier;
Old age and youth, manhood and infancy,

Mixed in one mighty torrent did appear,
Some flying from the thing they feared, and some
Seeking the object of another's fear;   55

And others, as with steps towards the tomb,
Pored on the trodden worms that crawled beneath,
And others mournfully within the gloom

Of their own shadow walked, and called it death;
And some fled from it as it were a ghost,   60
Half fainting in the affliction of vain breath:

But more, with motions which each other crossed,
Pursued or shunned the shadows the clouds threw,
Or birds within the noonday aether lost,

Upon that path where flowers never grew,—   65
And, weary with vain toil and faint for thirst,
Heard not the fountains, whose melodious dew

Out of their mossy cells forever burst;
Nor felt the breeze which from the forest told
Of grassy paths and wood-lawns interspersed   70

With overarching elms and caverns cold,
And violet banks where sweet dreams brood, but they
Pursued their serious folly as of old.

And as I gazed, methought that in the way
The throng grew wilder, as the woods of June   75
When the south wind shakes the extinguished day,

And a cold glare, intenser than the noon,
But icy cold, obscured with blinding light
The sun, as he the stars. Like the young moon—

When on the sunlit limits of the night   80
Her white shell trembles amid crimson air,
And whilst the sleeping tempest gathers might—

Doth, as the herald of its coming, bear
The ghost of its dead mother, whose dim form
Bends in dark aether from her infant's chair,—   85

So came a chariot on the silent storm
Of its own rushing splendour, and a Shape
So sate within, as one whom years deform,

Beneath a dusky hood and double cape,
Crouching within the shadow of a tomb;   90
And o'er what seemed the head a cloud-like crape

Was bent, a dun and faint aethereal gloom
Tempering the light. Upon the chariot-beam
A Janus-visaged Shadow did assume

The guidance of that wonder-wingèd team;   95
The shapes which drew it in thick lightenings
Were lost:—I heard alone on the air's soft stream

The music of their ever-moving wings.
All the four faces of that Charioteer
Had their eyes banded; little profit brings   100

Speed in the van and blindness in the rear,
Nor then avail the beams that quench the sun,—
Or that with banded eyes could pierce the sphere

Of all that is, has been or will be done;
So ill was the car guided — but it passed   105
With solemn speed majestically on.

The crowd gave way, and I arose aghast,
Or seemed to rise, so mighty was the trance,
And saw, like clouds upon the thunder-blast,

The million with fierce song and maniac dance   110
Raging around——

This was Shelley's last poem, uncompleted at his death. Begun in
1822 when the Shelleys were living in Casa Magni at Terenzo, it was
left, as Mary wrote, 'in so unfinished a state that I arranged it in its
present form with great difficulty'. The text therefore offers many

The Triumph of Chastity *by Luca Signorelli, showing in the background chariots and figures as in* The Triumph of Life

problems, as well as lacunae, and there are many variants and emendations made by critics and editors (such as William Rossetti who altered words and sense quite freely). For our purpose, the text used here is from the standard Oxford edition of Thomas Hutchinson, as being the most easily available and one of the more acceptable versions. He does, however, omit the ending of the manuscript, subsequently edited to read

> 'Then what is Life?, I said ... the cripple cast
> His eye upon the car which now had rolled
> Onward, as if that look must be the last,
> And answered ... 'Happy those for whom the fold
> Of

And the rest is unfortunately silence. This version does make it plain that the final question is that of the poet, not that of Rousseau as the Oxford edition implies. Any consideration of the poem is therefore beset with problems of interpretation, but without becoming too involved in such arguments one can at least consider the form and sources of the poem and point to some fundamental ideas and images. While looking at the extract it is particularly important to keep in mind the rest of the poem, since the poet's waking dream and Rousseau's (lines 308 ff) have many parallels.

At dawn the poet is lying under a chestnut tree on the Apennine Hills, the ocean below him. The birds and flowers awaken with the sunrise, but the poet, after a wakeful night, falls into a trance 'which was not slumber' but a 'waking dream'. He sees a road in summertime, dusty and thronged with people, much as Langland in *Piers Plowman* looks on 'a fair field full of folk' in his May morning dream. They seem to have no purpose as they drift along, ignoring the beauty of the woods and flowers by the roadside. Suddenly a rushing chariot appears, a shape huddled within it, and driven by a charioteer who has four faces, looking in all directions but blindfolded. The crowds are swept along by it; all kinds of people are there and in front of the chariot are some who dance a wild bacchanal.

The spring morning setting, repeated in Rousseau's dream ('In the April prime') is the May morning *reverdi* (re-greening) theme common in medieval literature, and is the framework for Petrarch's *Triumph of Love*, the main source for Shelley's poem. The title comes from it, as does the style. Petrarch's *Trionfi*, which had a powerful influence on medieval art and literature, are written in *terza rima* and celebrate such subjects as the Triumph of Chastity (p. 167), of Time, of Death and of Love, and form in their entirety a kind of spiritual autobiography of the poet, culminating in the *Triumph of Eternity*, a vision of a new world of God's salvation, much as Dante's *Divine Comedy* ends in the vision of paradise. One might hazard a guess that

Shelley intended to end his Triumph with a similar 'transformation scene'.

The word 'Triumph' denotes the Roman triumphal procession, with captives led beside the victorious chariot and spoils of war; in Shelley's poem a triumphal arch is mentioned (line 439), 'a moving arch of victory' in the form of a rainbow. Petrarch, using the same concept, opens his poem with a spring morning dream in which he sees a chariot surrounded by throngs of lovers; at one point a shade suddenly appears beside him and is questioned by him, in the same way that Rousseau appears. Many other parallels between the two poems have been noted.

Also, Shelley's reading of Dante has a strong influence on *The Triumph of Life*, not only in his use of the *terza rima*. The first part of *The Divine Comedy*, the *Inferno*, begins with Dante emerging from a dark wood to morning brightness after a wakeful night (as in the opening of *The Triumph of Life*). Guided by Virgil through the circles of Hell he sees the ugly figures of the damned, punished for their earthly vices and crimes; and Shelley's presentation of the victims of the procession of Life is very close in tone to Dante, a combination of horror and contemplative gravity although lacking in Dante's supreme power of unexpectedly vivid detail.

The third significant source is Virgil's *Aeneid*, particularly Book VI, the descent to the Underworld. He is remembering this when he describes 'the great stream of people' flying like 'the million leaves of summer's bier', an image repeated in lines 75 and 76 and again at the end of the poem (lines 528 ff). It is a famous and often-repeated simile (and often repeated by Shelley himself), originally found in Homer, appearing in the *Inferno* and later in *Paradise Lost*. But it is seen at its most poignant in the *Aeneid*, which is what Shelley must have had in mind. Here the shades in the Underworld rush to the banks of Acheron stretching their arms in longing to the further shore. They come 'thick as the leaves of the forest that at autumn's first frost dropping fall' (*quam multa in silvis autumni frigore primo Lapsa cadunt folia*). Virgil likens them also to flocks of migrating birds and Shelley follows this in 'birds within the noonday aether lost'.

The poem thus has a traditional framework and structure of classical inspiration, and like *Adonais* has a complex texture rich in associations. Shelley has taken over themes and images from other poets but *The Triumph of Life* is throughout marked with his own unmistakable stamp.

Shelley uses the difficult *terza rima* form, which he had earlier attempted in *Prince Athanase* and had completely mastered in the 'Ode to the West Wind'. In this passage he handles it to brilliant effect; it is eminently suitable to his purpose, as the interlocking patterns of the rhyme-scheme create a sense of speed and urgency, and maintain the feeling of the hurrying crowds and flying chariot.

The lines run on so skilfully that it is hard to find a pause at the end of a triad. To intensify the restless surging movement of the narrative he used images of gnats, falling leaves, birds and clouds, and later in the section following this extract, those of moths and whirlwinds. And since the poem is about death, and the Underworld of Virgil and Dante is in his mind, these images have a ghostly and sinister quality. The dropping leaves are 'of summer's bier', the clouds throw shadows, the birds are lost. The first few triads pile on words to increase this sense of the misery of lost souls: *dust, gloom, death, shadows, ghost, fear, fainting, fled, mournfully* – all thrown into relief by the subsequent cool beauty of the woodland, the 'over-arching elms' and banks of violets.

As the crowds suddenly become wilder a cold nightmarish glare lights up the scene, and the chariot comes, likened to the new moon seen in a crimson sunset and foretelling tempest, bearing the 'ghost of its dead mother'; this recalls Coleridge's 'Dejection' Ode and its ominous prophecy of the coming storm ('I see the old moon in her lap, foretelling The coming on of rain and squally blast'). The chariot itself is thus associated with doom and despair; it is not like the beautiful magic chariots of *Prometheus Unbound* and *Queen Mab*, but is closer in spirit to the Juggernaut in Southey's *Curse of Kehama*, a dreadful machine which 'rolls on and crushes all', followed by a wild rout of fanatics. It is splendid, the chariot of a Roman triumph, but its occupants and the charioteer are figures of horror, only hinted at. Instead of describing the Shape, Shelley suggests something evil and frightening: it is deformed, and wears a dusky hood, like a creature 'crouching within the shadow of a tomb'. In a marvellously sinister stroke he speaks of the cloudy fabric 'o'er what seemed the head', and uses the heavy adjective 'dun' to describe the gloom. It is the Chariot of Life bearing Death within it, and driven by a blind force. Shelley points out the uselessness of 'Speed in the van and blindness in the rear' (a bitter paraphrase of Gray's 'Youth on the prow, and Pleasure at the helm'?), but its progress is inevitable, since it represents Destiny. We remember the lines in *Hellas* when

> The world's eyeless charioteer,
>   Destiny, is hurrying by.

The arrival of the chariot is the culmination of a passage in which the speed of the action has remorselessly increased as the dream takes possession of the poet: the crowds are first of all hurrying, hastening, then flying and then as the chariot comes in 'rushing splendour' they are whipped up to a frenzy and end 'raging around', greeting it as a conqueror. There is too the movement from darkness to light: the doomed victims are seen in shadows like gnats 'upon the evening gleam' until the blinding light of the chariot floods the scene, to represent, as some critics suggest, the cold light of reason or materialism.

The extract is remarkable for its narrative drive, its visual sharpness and its tone of growing horror, rising to 'and I arose aghast' as the crowds turn from aimlessness to a bacchanal, the 'maniac dance' of death. The discipline of the *terza rima* form curbs Shelley's tendency to rhetoric and rhapsody: the result is a poem of unusual strength achieving descriptive and emotional effects which point to a new development of his poetic power.

Some critical judgements of Shelley

During his lifetime Shelley's poetry was not widely known. Harsh words were said by critics on his atheism, the immorality of his private life and his subversive political views. On this last score, as we have seen, his association with the Hunts laid him open to attacks from the Tory reviewers; Lockhart in *Blackwood's* wrote a rousting review of *The Revolt of Islam*, describing it as a contemptible product of the Cockney school, dangerous and perverted in its ideology. On moral grounds *The Cenci* drew even stronger complaints from the critic of the *Literary Gazette*: 'Of all the abominations which intellectual perversion, and poetical atheism, have produced in our times, this tragedy appears to us to be the most abominable'. He met with prejudice on all sides, and of all kinds; only the more liberal periodicals like the *Examiner* and the short-lived *Liberal* consistently praised his work, although the imaginative scope and the beauty of language of *Prometheus Unbound* could not fail to win the admiration of other discerning critics.

One growing audience for his poetry was the working-class readership, particularly that of the radical Left. Robert Owen, the philanthropical mill-owner of the New Lanark experiment, followed his Godwinian principles and popularized them during the 1830s and 40s in his own magazines and periodicals for working-men; and when in 1836 the Chartist Movement was begun by the London Working Men's Association, *Queen Mab* (in the pirated edition of 1821, the occasion of a *cause célèbre* in which the bookseller William Clarke was imprisoned) and 'The Mask of Anarchy' were part of its inspirational literature. Shelley himself would have disapproved of the influence which *Queen Mab* came to exert; on hearing of this 1821 edition he wrote to Leigh Hunt that the poem was crude and immature, 'better fitted to injure than to serve the cause of freedom'. Charles Kingsley's novel *Alton Locke*, written in 1850 but concerned with the period between 1838 and 1842, the growing years of Chartism, is interesting in that it points to two attitudes to Shelley current in those years. One is of the hero who, in a lecture to a working-men's club, applauds 'the true nobleness of a man, whom neither birth nor education could blind to the evils of society; who, for the sake of the suffering many, could trample under foot his hereditary pride, and become an outcast for the People's Cause' (a somewhat exaggerated claim); the other is of the educated middle-class, in the person of a dean who deplores the influence of the poet on the young Alton Locke: 'He is a guide as irregular in taste, as unorthodox in doctrine; though there are some pretty things in him now and then.'

Although the passing of the Reform Bill in 1832 gradually brought about a more just society, Shelley's optimistic vision of 'man Equal, unclassed, tribeless, and nationless' had by no means materialized (and in its fullest sense probably never will). However, the ideal was central to the socialist tradition, and no less an authority than Karl Marx considered him to be a precursor of the socialist millennium. His popularity among the politically committed survived the century; the last literary radical of any consequence to emphasize this aspect of Shelley was George Bernard Shaw, who absorbed his ideas on both philosophical anarchism and vegetarianism, recognizing, him as a poet of ideas and not merely the simple singing bird of the anthologies.

Mary's publication of *Posthumous Poems* in 1824, and later of the six volumes of his works (1839–40) established him as a poet of note to a wider reading public. Even so, critical views were divided. Browning's early poem *Pauline* (1833) apostrophizes him as 'Sun-treader – life and light be thine for ever', a rare spirit and singer of 'sweet imaginings'. Both Meredith and Swinburne, who in particular had an ear tuned to the Classical measures of lyric verse, acclaimed his poetic worth. Some lesser writers turned Shelley into a cult-figure: James Thomson (1834–1882) was such an admirer that he wrote under the name of Bysshe Vanolis (the last an anagram of the German poet Novalis), and Francis Thompson's *Shelley* (1909) presents him as a divine child, an estimate very hard to swallow. But there were dissident voices: Tennyson and William Morris were not enthusiastic, Arnold's opinion of the 'beautiful *but ineffectual* angel' was less than laudatory, and the image of the 'one frail Form, A phantom among men' did not go down well, even allowing for the radical views, with the muscular Christianity of Kingsley who said that reading Shelley was like sipping Eau-de-Cologne in secret. Gerard Manley Hopkins, in a letter to Patmore, made the more usual complaint about 'the specious Liberal stuff that crazed Shelley'.

Lady Shelley's dedication to the Shelley cult led her to make the formidable collection of letters, papers and manuscripts which provided more material for the biographers. With the foundation of the Shelley Society in 1886 he had become an established poet, although most of his reputation still rested on the much-anthologized lyrics rather than on the philosophical breadth of his major poetry. Even so, final respectability was not his until 1954, when the Keats-Shelley Memorial Association erected in Poets' Corner in Westminster Abbey two small oval tablets by Frank Dobson, incised with the names Keats and Shelley, placed just above the memorial to Shakespeare.

The twentieth-century criticism of Shelley is no less of a battleground. After the First World War the climate of literary opinion was not receptive to his philosophical ideas, nor to what C.S. Lewis called the 'enchantment' of his poetry, too other-worldly at a time when it was more natural to be disillusioned and down-to-earth. By the 1930s the Georgian poets, cultivating their gardens in the Home Counties, were out of favour; wit and intelligence were more to contemporary taste and the Romantic poet most in tune with the age was Byron in his satirical vein, taken by Auden as his model for the verse *Letter to Lord Byron* of 1937. A few years before, in 1933, T.S. Eliot's damning and influential essay on 'Shelley and Keats' had reversed all notions of the angelic and divine poet; he was dismissed as 'humourless, pedantic, self-centred, and sometimes almost a blackguard', his letters 'insufferably dull', his mind 'a very confused one' and his poetry 'an affair of adolescence' not for the mature reader. Shelley, he says, had 'to a high degree the unusual faculty of passionate apprehension of abstract ideas' but – and an unsurmountable but – he finds the ideas repellent or merely silly, and implies that the poetry suffers thereby. A more detailed attack from a critic of distinction comes in F.R. Leavis's essay in *Revaluation* (1936) which incidentally takes Mr Eliot to task for neglecting to make a proper enquiry into the poetry. For Dr Leavis feeling has nothing to do with thinking in Shelley's work, and the dissociated sensibility (of which Mr Eliot had written in another context) operates in the void, surrendering 'to a kind of hypnotic rote of favourite images, associations and words', to produce often bad and imprecise poetry. His aim is to prove that Shelley, having no grasp 'of the world of common perception' and lacking emotional discipline, is not a great poet nor even a very good one. His case is weakened by the analyses of 'Ode to the West Wind' and 'When the lamp is shattered', since in both these poems his reading seems to be inaccurate and mistaken.

A more profitable and less destructive enquiry originated in W.B. Yeats's essay on 'The Philosophy of Shelley's Poetry' (1900) which opened up the paths of Platonism and the study of Shelley's symbolism as representing memories of ancient myths. These lines of investigation led to a particularly rewarding field, although not until the 1940s, when substantial work done by J.A. Notopolous on *The Platonism of Shelley*, followed by Neville Rogers's *Shelley at Work* and his annotated edition of the poems (so far only two volumes), all laying strong emphasis on Shelley's Platonic thought. The only danger with such intense concentration on this theme is that in the end one can hardly see the wood for the Platonic trees, important as the emphasis certainly is. From this groundwork have come valuable studies of Shelley's imagery and symbolism, such as Peter Butter's *Shelley's Idols of the Cave* (1954) and Harold Bloom's *Shelley's Myth-making* (1959).

Shelley seems once more in favour, and perhaps less difficult to appreciate now that so much intelligent criticism has been directed to the thought behind his poetry; even so, he is not an easy poet unless one accepts him merely as a maker of music, of sound without sense, as Mr Eliot will have it. But his preoccupations are those which many contemporary readers can share: among them the devotion to freedom, the consciousness that hate is self-destructive and the sense of science as a liberating force. Equally he would have found much to enjoy in our age, not least the voyages into space, prefigured in *Queen Mab*, and the miracles of physics and modern technology, dreamed of in *Prometheus Unbound* as features of the millennium.

Part Three
Reference Section

The Shelley circle: family and friends

MRS BOINVILLE, 17?–1847, née Harriet Collins, and sister of J.F. Newton's wife. She married a distinguished Frenchman, Jean-Baptiste Chastel de Boinville, who died in 1813 in the retreat from Moscow. In that same year Shelley met her in London and was impressed by her sympathetic character, her intelligence and the fact that grief had turned her hair white; he called her Maimuna, a character in Southey's *Thalaba* who also had a youthful face 'And yet her hair was grey'. She later moved to Bracknell and when the young Shelleys also moved there to High Elms House they frequented her salon. As his marriage to Harriet became more difficult he moved into her household, 'the delightful tranquillity of this happy home', and became rather too fond of her daughter Cornelia Turner. Mrs Boinville was kind to him, nursing him on an occasion when, in the frenzy of his divided feelings for Mary and Harriet, he took an overdose of laudanum. However, she disapproved of his relationship with Mary and after they eloped did not meet him again.

BYRON, GEORGE GORDON, sixth lord, 1788–1824. Educated at Harrow and Trinity College, Cambridge. By the time he met Shelley in June 1816 when they were staying on Lake Geneva, he was already an established and famous poet; among other productions, *Childe Harold*, 'The Corsair', 'The Bride of Abydos' and similar romantic tales, had assured his literary reputation although his moral reputation was in ruins among respectable society after the scandal of his relationship with his half-sister Augusta and the breakdown of his marriage which caused him to leave England. Before he left, Claire Clairmont had become one of his many conquests (although it seems that she had virtually forced herself on him) and in 1817 bore his child Allegra who died of typhus in 1822. During the years in Italy he wrote *Don Juan*, his greatest achievement. There also he was involved in the revolutionary politics of the Carbonari, and later with the cause of freedom in Greece in its conflict with the Turks. In 1823 he went to Cephalonia and then to Missolonghi, where he died of fever on 19 April 1824.

CLAIRMONT, CLARA MARY JANE, 1798–1879, later known as Claire; daughter of Godwin's second wife. After Shelley's elopement with Mary she became a permanent attachment to their household. An enigmatic character, moody, wayward and from all accounts much more attractive than the rather heavy portrait by Amelia Curran (p. 178) would suggest. Her relationship with Shelley is one of the

unresolved mysteries for his biographers. That he loved her is certain: in 1821 he wrote to her when she was away in Florence: 'Do not think that my affection & anxiety for you ever cease, or that I ever love you less although that love has been & still must be a source of disquietude to me –.' Also certain is that Mary found her constant presence irritating and was jealous of her closeness to her husband. The birth of Allegra (thought by some to be Shelley's child) led to endless arguments with Byron about the child's upbringing, Shelley tirelessly acting as mediator between them. After Shelley's death she lived the rest of her long life in various cities of Europe, with one spell in London; at one time she worked as a governess in Moscow, described in fascinating detail in her Journals and letters to Mary. She became a Catholic and never married, although Trelawny was obviously very attracted to her. Her death at the age of eighty-one in Florence and her romantic life-story with its undisclosed secrets was the basis for the short novel by Henry James, *The Aspern Papers*.

GISBORNE, MARIA, 1770–1836, daughter of a rich merchant. She made an early marriage to an architect, William Reveley, and was attached to the liberal and radical circles around Godwin. On the death of Mary Wollstonecraft Godwin she looked after Mary and Fanny for a while, and when her husband died in 1799 Godwin at once proposed to her. She refused him, married John Gisborne, a businessman, and went with him to Rome in 1801. They settled at Leghorn where, in 1818, they met the Shelleys and became close friends, she teaching him Spanish. In 1820, after a trip to London, there was some unexplained break in their intimacy; its cause partly lay in a scheme devised by her son, Henry Reveley, an engineer, to build a steam-boat. Shelley had become interested in it and decided to put money into the project, but when the idea was abandoned, became angry and disappointed.

GODWIN, WILLIAM, 1756–1836, son of a Dissenting minister from Wisbech, Cambridgeshire. In 1797 he married Mary Wollstonecraft who died in giving birth to Mary. In 1801 he married Mrs Clairmont, a widow with two children (Charles and Clara), and by her had a son, William. *Political Justice* (1793) was the work which brought him fame, but his literary output was considerable, including the novels *Caleb Williams* (1794), *St Leon* (1799), *Fleetwood* (1805) and *Mandeville* (1817). When Shelley met him, he and Mrs Godwin were running a bookshop and publishing business in Skinner Street, Holborn. In spite of all the money he extracted from his son-in-law he became bankrupt in 1822, but managed for the rest of his life to

Claire Clairmont

survive by literary work of all kinds (and with financial aid from his friends), including a vast *History of the Commonwealth*.

HITCHENER, ELIZABETH, 1782?–1822, a schoolmistress at Hurst-pierpoint, Sussex, whom Shelley met when staying with his uncle Captain Pilfold in 1811. Her father, once a smuggler, now kept a local public-house. A woman of intellectual and philosophical interests, 'of extraordinary talents', as Shelley described her, she seemd to him a soul-mate who shared his radical ideas. Their long correspondence, carried on over a year or more, is extremely interesting in that it is concerned with many of the topics which absorbed him at this time. He finally persuaded her to give up her teaching position and join him at Lynmouth in July 1812; Harriet, on meeting her, was not so impressed. She wrote to a friend: 'She is very busy writing for the good of mankind. She is very dark in complexion, with a great quantity of long black hair. She talks a great deal. If you like great talkers she will suit you.' Shelley, typically, had expected too much of her: in a few months his 'Sister of my soul' had become the Brown Demon, 'an artful, superficial, ugly, hermaphroditical beast of a woman' and to get rid of her he agreed to pay her £100 a year. She later became a governess on the Continent, married an Austrian officer and when the marriage broke up, returned to England to start a school at Edmonton.

HOGG, THOMAS JEFFERSON, 1792–1862, fellow-undergraduate of Shelley's at University College, Oxford. There they jointly produced a set of burlesque verses attributed to one Margaret Nicholson, a mad washer-woman who had tried to assassinate George III, and then the ill-fated *Necessity of Atheism* for which they were both sent down. He remained a close friend throughout Shelley's lifetime, so closely involved that he not only attempted to seduce Harriet, but briefly shared Mary's favours, this time with Shelley's approval; Shelley wrote to him offering 'your share of our common treasure', a 'participated pleasure', and after his death Hogg, true to form, transferred his affections to Shelley's last love, Jane Williams, who, in 1827 agreed to live with him. He became an unsuccessful barrister and a literary man of sufficient merit to be given material by the Shelley family for a biography which ended after the unfavourable reception of the first two volumes.

HUNT, JAMES HENRY LEIGH, 1784–1859, poet, essayist, critic and founder with his brother John of the *Examiner* (1808), a weekly newspaper of liberal views. They were prosecuted in 1811 for an article on military flogging, but acquitted; on this occasion Shelley wrote from Oxford to congratulate them. In 1812 they were sent to prison for forthright comments on the Prince Regent. Later, in 1816,

Shelley and Mary often visited James Hunt's house in the Vale of Health, Hampstead, where they met other writers. In 1821 Shelley and Byron asked him to join them in the production of a new magazine, the *Liberal*, and it was after meeting the Hunt family at Leghorn that Shelley's boat was wrecked. He and his wife Marianne, who bore him seven children, were close friends of the Shelleys and he was of great assistance to Mary in her work of publishing the poems after Shelley's death. A prolific but not particularly good poet ('The Story of Rimini' is perhaps his best known long poem), he was a kind man with many friends, cheerful and lively; the allegation that he was the model for the flibbertigibbet Mr Skimpole in Dickens's *Bleak House* caused him much pain.

IMLAY, FANNY, 1794–1816, illegitimate daughter of Mary Wollstonecraft and Gilbert Imlay, an American who in 1793 met Mary in France and lived with her there and in London until 1795 when he left her. When Mary married Godwin, Fanny was brought up as his own daughter; she was a rather plain girl, somewhat melancholy in contrast to the sprightly Claire and Mary. Godwin in a letter describes her as 'of a quiet, modest, unshowy disposition'. Her suicide in October 1816, by taking an overdose of laudanum, was a great shock to Shelley. In her suicide note she speaks of herself as 'a being whose birth was unfortunate, and whose life has only been a series of pain to those persons who have hurt their health in endeavouring to promote her welfare'.

LIND, DR JAMES, 1736–1812, physician to the royal household at Windsor at the time when Shelley was at Eton. His learning and kindness were a great help to the schoolboy, and he is thought to be the model for the sage Zonoras in 'Prince Athanase', 'an old, old man, with hair of silver white' who introduced his student to the works of Plato. In his early days as a ship's surgeon he had visited China, and the novelist Fanny Burney speaks of 'his love of Eastern wonders and his taste for tricks, conundrums and queer things' which must have been particularly pleasing to Shelley.

MEDWIN, THOMAS, 1788–1869, Shelley's cousin, at school with him at Syon House. He joined the army, went to India with the Dragoons, where he met Edward Williams, and retired on half-pay shortly before he went to Italy in 1821. There he joined the circle around Shelley, and like Trelawny took note of both Shelley and Byron as subjects of literary interest. After Byron's death he published in 1824 a *Journal of the Conversations of Lord Byron*, long before his biography of Shelley, which did not come out till 1849. He wrote poetry (and had a good appreciation of Shelley's work), a novel and various sketches and essays.

NEWTON, JOHN FRANK, 1767–1837, one of the more interesting characters whom Shelley met at the Godwins' house. He was a strict vegetarian, author of *The Return to Nature, A Defence of the Vegetable Regimen* (1811), a book which had great influence on Shelley as the notes to *Queen Mab* show. He claimed that vegetarianism had cured his chronic asthma and the meals of fruit, grains and vegetables provided by the hospitable Newtons apparently converted Shelley and even Hogg, at least for a time. Cornelia, his wife, was the sister of Mrs Boinville.

PEACOCK, THOMAS LOVE, 1785–1866, poet, novelist, scholar and critic. In 1819 he became an official at the East India House but was able at the same time to keep on his literary career. For an account of his novels see pp. 17–20; a work equally relevant to a study of Shelley is his essay *The Four Ages of Poetry* (1820), a satirical attack on the poets of his time which provoked Shelley to respond with *A Defence of Poetry*. One of his daughters became the wife of George Meredith, but the marriage did not last; its breakdown is related in Meredith's sonnet-sequence *Modern Love*.

SHELLEY, SIR BYSSHE, 1731–1815, Shelley's grandfather. (See pp. 29 ff)

SHELLEY, CHARLES BYSSHE, 1814–1825, Harriet's second child, born after Shelley had left her for Mary. After her suicide he and his sister were in the care of Eliza Westbrook. The Chancery suit initiated by her and her father ensured that Shelley did not have the custody of the children; the Court decided that his immorality and atheism made him an unfit person to bring them up. After Shelley's death, Charles went to live at Field Place with his grandfather, and like his father was sent to Syon House. He died of tuberculosis, and is buried in Warnham Church.

SHELLEY, CLARA EVERINA, 1817–1818, Mary's second child. She died in Venice, as Shelley said 'of a disorder peculiar to the climate'. Everina was the name of Mary Wollstonecraft's sister.

SHELLEY, ELENA ADELAIDE, 1818–1820. The mysterious 'Neapolitan charge', often thought to be the child of Claire and Shelley (or so was the scandal put out by the Shelley nursemaid, Elise). Her birth was registered by him in February 1819, naming himself as father and Mary as mother. On 7 July 1820 he wrote to the Gisbornes: 'My Neapolitan charge is dead. It seems as if the destruction that is consuming me were as an atmosphere which wrapt & infected everything connected with me.'

SHELLEY, IANTHE, 1813–1876, Harriet's first child. (See under Charles Bysshe Shelley.) She was brought up by Eliza Westbrook, and in 1837 married Edward Jeffries Esdaile of Cothelstone House; the volume of early minor poems known as the Esdaile Manuscript was in her possession, and stayed in the family until 1962.

SHELLEY, LADY JANE, 1820–1899, née Gibson. As a young widow, Jane St John met Mary Shelley in 1847 and became her friend, admirer and later the wife of her son Percy Florence. They had no children and she devoted herself to collecting and editing Shelley's papers, letters and manuscripts and preserving mementoes of him. Her influence on his reputation was very great, although in her desire to present an idealized image of the poet she destroyed some letters and omitted sections of others when they were published. She and her husband commissioned Hogg to write the biography which was never finished because they disapproved of it. She also commissioned the statue of the dead poet in University College, Oxford (p. 8).

SHELLEY, MARY WOLLSTONECRAFT, 1797–1851, daughter of Mary Wollstonecraft and Godwin, and Shelley's second wife. Born into a literary family her own career as an author began early with the *History of a Six Weeks' Tour* (1817), an account of the travels after the elopement. This was followed by *Frankenstein* (1818) and other novels written after Shelley's death, including *The Last Man* (1826), *Lodore* (1835), *Falkner* (1837) and many short stories, all written to support herself and her son. As Claire wrote: 'In our family if you cannot write an epic poem or novel that by its originality knocks all other novels on the head, you are a despicable creature, not worth acknowledging.'

SHELLEY, PERCY FLORENCE, 1819–1889, Mary's last child, born in Florence, and the only one of her children to survive infancy. As a widow with very little money she had a struggle to bring him up. As he was now the heir to the estate, she hoped that Sir Timothy would help, but he offered to do so only on the condition that the child was given over to his care. She refused, receiving from him a few small allowances; her literary work helped to provide for them both, and she was able to send him to Harrow and then to Trinity College, Cambridge, where he took his degree in 1841. On the death of Sir Timothy in 1844 he became baronet, coming into his inheritance. In 1848 he married Jane St John, and they moved to live at Boscombe Manor, Bournemouth.

SHELLEY, SIR TIMOTHY, 1753–1844, Shelley's father (see biographical section *passim*). After the death of his son he would allow no biography to be published, and allowed Mary to issue the poems of 1839 and 1840 only on condition that she included no memoir.

SHELLEY, WILLIAM, 1816–1819, first son of Mary and Shelley, born when they were living at Bishopsgate; a much adored child whose pet-name was Willmouse. Shelley wrote of 'his beauty, the silken fineness of his hair, the transparence of his complexion, the animation and deep blue colour of his eyes' and addressed two short poems to him – one written while he was still alive, 'The billows on the beach are leaping around it, The bark is weak and frail' and one after his death. He was buried in the Protestant Cemetery in Rome.

SMITH, HORACE, 1779–1849, a banker, also a poet who was one of the visitors to Hunt's cottage in Hampstead where he met the Shelleys. They became friends and Smith, a generous man, was of great financial help to him, often doing small commissions and sending books when he was abroad. In the course of their correspondence Shelley asked him to advance money to purchase a harp for Jane, but this was apparently too much for Smith and he refused, much to Shelley's annoyance. He is celebrated in the 'Letter to Maria Gisborne' as a worldly and cultivated man, combining 'Wit and sense, Virtue and human knowledge'. With his brother James he is famous for *Rejected Addresses* (1812), a set of verse parodies whose victims included Wordsworth, Coleridge, Southey and Byron.

SOUTHEY, ROBERT, 1774–1843, usually associated with the Lake poets, although his work has little in common with theirs. Educated at Westminster School and Balliol College, Oxford. In 1803 he went to live at Greta Hall, Keswick, where Shelley and Harriet visited him. His early radical views on politics and religion had changed, and in 1813 he became Poet Laureate. He wrote many historical works, including a *Life of Nelson* and a history of the Peninsular War, but the long poems like *Thalaba* (1801), *Madoc* (1805) and *The Curse of Kehama* (1810) first brought him literary fame and had much influence on Shelley as a young man. Southey's opinion of Shelley changed after the desertion and suicide of Harriet; in 1820, when Shelley had written to him, assuming mistakenly that he was the author of an adverse review of *The Revolt of Islam*, there followed an exchange of bitter letters, in the course of which Southey harshly reprimanded him for immorality and general depravity of character.

TRELAWNY, EDWARD JOHN, 1792–1881 (see Chapter 1). After Shelley's death he left with Byron in 1823 for Cephalonia, to assist in the Greek fight for independence, and his recollections of Byron are coupled with those of Shelley in the memoir he wrote. His own life-story is difficult to disentangle from his romantic fabrications, as in the quasi-autobiographical *Adventures of a Younger Son*. Attractive to (and attracted by) women, he made three marriages and had designs on both Mary and Claire. He was the model for the old seaman in the famous painting by Millais, 'The North-West Passage'.

VIVIANI, EMILIA, 1799–1836, daughter of the Governor of Pisa, and a pupil in the convent school of St Anna, where the Shelleys were taken by an Italian friend to meet her. They were charmed by her beauty, and Shelley in particular was affected by her longing for freedom from the convent walls. His obsession with her resulted in *Epipsychidion*, but when he heard that she had decided to marry a suitor of her father's choice, his disillusionment was complete. Her marriage was unhappy, she bore four children who all died, and after a few years she returned to her father's house.

WALKER, ADAM, 1731–1821, popular lecturer and inventor. He had great public success with his lectures on astronomy and natural philosophy, and was engaged to speak at various public schools, including Eton College, where Shelley heard him. He had also lectured and demonstrated experiments at Syon House.

WESTBROOK, ELIZA, 1781–?, Harriet's sister, some fourteen years older. A powerful character, she encouraged the relationship of Shelley and Harriet, and after their marriage moved in to live with them. Although at first he thought her 'a very clever girl tho' rather affected' he became more and more irritated by her managing ways ('Eliza keeps our common stock of money for safety in some hole or corner of her dress – she gives it out as we want it'). It is likely that her continued presence helped to disrupt their marriage as Harriet was of a docile nature and regarded Eliza as 'my more than mother'. After Harriet's suicide Shelley alleged that 'the beastly viper' had virtually murdered her sister. She and Mr Westbrook brought the case against him as unfit to keep the children and she obtained custody of Ianthe. In 1822 she married Robert Beauchamp of Tetton House, Somerset.

WESTBROOK, HARRIET, 1795–1816. After her suicide Godwin (whose doctrines she had blamed for Shelley's treatment of her) put about the story that she had been unfaithful with a Guards Officer, Colonel Maxwell; however, the circumstances leading to her death remain a mystery, and it is still not known where she is buried. Although intelligent and willing to learn, she found it difficult to keep up with Shelley's intellectual pursuits; also at heart she was a conventional girl, carefully brought up (she once hoped to marry a clergyman) and was hardly suited to the high-minded bohemian existence of her married life.

WILLIAMS, EDWARD ELLERKER, 1793–1822, born in India, and after a few years at Eton joined the navy at the age of eleven. He later transferred to the Dragoons of the East India Company and retired as a lieutenant on half-pay in 1816. He came to Europe with Jane, who had left her husband, and in Geneva met Medwin who told them of his admiration for Shelley. They soon became part of the circle of friends at Pisa; Shelley went sailing with Williams, and the next year the couple shared the Casa Magni with them, before the fatal shipwreck.

WILLIAMS, JANE, 179?–1884, common law wife of Edward Williams, and later 'married' to T.J. Hogg. The subject of a group of Shelley's late poems (see pp. 161–4).

WOLLSTONECRAFT, MARY, 1759–1797, mother of Mary Shelley and of Fanny Imlay. A writer with strong feminist and liberal views. In her early life she became, so Godwin wrote in his Life of her, 'a democrat and republican in all their sternness'; she met many of the radical intellectuals of the time, including Holcroft and Tom Paine, also the painter Fuseli, with whom she became infatuated. She lived in France from 1792 to 1795, and there she fell in love with Gilbert Imlay and gave birth to Fanny. He left her, and on returning to London she lived with and subsequently married Godwin, dying very soon after the birth of Mary. She is remembered for *A Vindication of the Rights of Woman* (1792) but she wrote also the semi-autobiographical novels *Mary* (1788) and *The Wrongs of Woman*, unfinished at her death. A strongly-motivated and remarkable character, she was much admired by Shelley for her sensibility and breadth of vision in her writings on the education and liberation of women.

The traveller: a Shelley gazetteer

MR GLOWRY: You will see many fine old ruins, Mr Cypress;
crumbling pillars, and mossy walls – many a one-legged Venus
and headless Minerva – many a Neptune buried in sand – many a
Jupiter turned topsy-turvy – many a perforated Bacchus doing
duty as a waterpipe – many reminiscences of the ancient world,
which I hope was better worth living in than the modern...
MR CYPRESS: It is something to seek, Mr Glowry. The mind is
restless, and must persist in seeking, though to find is to be
disappointed.

Peacock in this passage from *Nightmare Abbey* manages to kill two
birds with one satiric stone: the tourist, in search of the wonders of
the past, and the Romantic poet (Mr Cypress is a persona of Byron,
just about to leave England after the breakdown of his marriage) in
search of himself. The poets of the Romantic period were, with a few
exceptions, insatiable travellers for one or both of these reasons.
Among the less restless souls were Blake and Clare, the one content
to remain for most of his time in London travelling only in his
visionary world, and the other regretfully leaving Helpstone, his
native village, to move four miles away to Northborough before
becoming an inmate of an asylum. Crabbe, as a clergyman, moved
only from one living to another (Rutland, Lincolnshire, Leicestershire,
and Wiltshire), finding human nature more absorbing than foreign
scenery.
Wordsworth in *The Prelude* (Book III) wrote:

> A traveller I am,
> Whose tale is only of himself

and indeed his Continental tours (France, Germany, Belgium, Italy,
Switzerland) are diligently recorded in his poetry, as are his
impressions of Scotland, the Western Isles and the Isle of Man. Like
many other tourists he went to look at Fingal's Cave on Staffa, in
pious memory of Macpherson's *Ossian* and, of course, in Europe
Mont Blanc and the Grande Chartreuse were essential points in the
guide-book. Significantly, one of the central characters in *The
Excursion* is the Wanderer. Coleridge, like Wordsworth, dallied with
the idea of emigrating to found a Pantisocratic community on the
banks of the Susquehanna, but never got there; he did spend nearly
four years in Malta and in Mediterranean regions and toured
Germany with the Wordsworths. Southey went to Spain and
Portugal, and Keats visited Ireland and many English places of

A map to show places associated with Shelley

note, and made the final journey to Rome. Byron was the only one of them affluent enough to embark on the Grand Tour, although Sir Timothy Shelley, who himself had made the trip, offered his son the chance on his expulsion from Oxford, as a cure for his tiresome atheism.

In fact, travel and tourism supplied important raw material for much Romantic poetry. One thinks at once of *The Prelude*, *Childe Harold*, and *Don Juan*, all of which maintain the reader's interest through a long poem by setting the central figure of the poet, or his hero, against an ever-changing backdrop of the sublime (Wordsworth crossing the Alps) or the exotic (Don Juan in Turkey and Russia); the more highly-coloured, as in Byron's Turkish tales or Moore's *Lalla Rookh*, the more the public liked it.

Shelley was the greatest wanderer of them all, as the maps of his travels indicate. The personal complications of his life, the two marriages and his financial difficulties accounted for much of his restless existence. Sometimes also the dictates of health forced him to move; it will be remembered that he left for Italy at the suggestion of his physician. There was also the Romantic search for the ideal ambience; and even when it was discovered, as often seemed the case, he found some reason to leave it, in much the same way as he reacted to many personal relationships, expecting too much and turning away in disillusionment. He was a perfect example of Mr Cypress's declaration that 'the mind is restless, and must persist' in seeking, though to find is to be disappointed'.

WEST SUSSEX Shelley's birthplace and home, Field Place, Warnham, near Horsham, still stands amongst its parkland and gardens. The gardens are occasionally open to the public for charity, but the house is private. In the village of Warnham the Parish Church of St. Margaret has memorials to Timothy Shelley (father of Sir Bysshe) and his American wife, Joanna; also here is the Field Place Chapel which contains tablets to Hellen and Elizabeth (Shelley's sisters) and to his son Charles. The parish register in the church records the baptism of the poet.

In Horsham, St. Mary's Parish Church has a tablet on the west wall commemorating Shelley, and there are memorials to his grandfather, parents and other ancestors. The family vault is also in this church. In Horsham, too, is Sir Bysshe's house, Arun House in Denne Road.

Also in this County, near Arundel, seat of the Duke of Norfolk, is Sir Bysshe's country house, Castle Goring, its Gothic façade just visible from the A27. It is now used as a language school and is gradually being restored from its ruined state. Near Cuckfield lived his uncle, Captain Pilfold, at Nelson Place, and in nearby Hurstpierpoint Miss Hitchener was schoolmistress.

OXFORD   The principal Shelley memorial in England is in University College, where Onslow Ford's dramatic marble monument of the drowned poet is set alone in a panelled room under a dome; this was completed in 1894, commissioned by Lady Shelley (see p. 8). At the Bodleian Library is a large collection of Shelley relics, including most of his note-books and many other manuscripts given by Lady Shelley and Sir John Shelley-Rolls, a descendant of Shelley's younger brother, John. Visitors can see miniatures of the poet and Mary, and some personal mementoes including the guitar given to Jane and his own blue-and-white enamel snuffbox inscribed 'Liberty and Free Election'. The library also has portraits of the Shelley family, but these are not on view.

LONDON   Much of Shelley's life centred on London. His sisters were at Clapham Academy and through them he met Harriet Westbrook. After his expulsion from Oxford in 1811 he lodged with Hogg at 11 Poland Street in Soho, and it was from London that he eloped with Harriet. Their daughter Ianthe was born while they were staying at Cook's Hotel in Albemarle Street. He met the Godwin household in their bookshop in Skinner Street, Holborn, and he and Mary declared their mutual love in St Pancras Churchyard at Mary Wollstonecraft's tomb. On their return from the elopement to France they lived in various London lodgings. London was also the scene of Harriet's suicide by drowning in the Serpentine, and of the marriage to Mary at St Mildred's in Bread Street. They were frequent visitors at Leigh Hunt's cottage in the Vale of Health, Hampstead.

BERKSHIRE   Shelley was at Eton College from 1804 to 1810 and later came back to this County when, after the birth of Ianthe, he and Harriet moved to High Elms, Bracknell, a house belonging to Mrs Boinville who lived nearby. In August 1815 he and Mary took a cottage at Bishopsgate, near Windsor Park, hidden among the woods and near to Virginia Water; here he wrote *Alastor*, and they stayed till the spring of 1816.

BUCKINGHAMSHIRE   In 1817 Shelley and Mary lived in Albion House, Marlow, a pleasant house with Gothic windows, still to be seen although not open to the public. They were happy there with their son William, and Claire with her Allegra. Peacock was a neighbour at 47 West Street. Shelley enjoyed the garden with 'firs and cypresses intermixed with apple trees now in blossom' and they had a boat on the river. Here he read the classics with Peacock, but his health was not good and in February 1818 they left, departing a month later for Italy.

190

The drawing-room of Field Place drawn by Shelley's sister, Elizabeth

CUMBRIA   In the winter of 1811–12 Shelley and Harriet stayed in Keswick in Chestnut Cottage, and while there visited Southey at Greta Hall; they also visited the Duke of Norfolk in his country house, Greystoke. They returned to the Lakes in 1813, hoping but failing to find a suitable house to rent.

DEVON   In the summer of 1812 Shelley and Harriet moved to a cottage in Lynmouth, now called Shelley's Cottage. After the arrest of their Irish servant for distributing the *Declaration of Rights* they left before the arrival of Godwin, who had been asked by them to stay. Godwin wrote to his wife: 'They lived here nine weeks and three days. They went away in a hurry, in debt to her [the landlady] and two more.'

DORSET   Shelley's son, Percy Florence, and his wife lived at Boscombe Manor, near Bournemouth. When Mary died in 1851 he had a vault made in the grounds of St Peter's, a church recently built (consecrated in 1845) in the centre of Bournemouth. Here her body was buried and later the remains of Godwin and Mary Wollstonecraft were brought from St Pancras churchyard in London. He and Lady Jane were also buried in the same family vault, which is alleged to contain Shelley's heart. This had been snatched from his funeral pyre by Trelawny and finally came into the possession of Sir Percy, although there are many versions of the story. It seems a strange resting-place for it, although the churchyard on its wooded slope has a certain romantic charm. In 1854 Sir Percy commissioned a memorial to Shelley intended for the interior of the church. Carved in marble by Henry Weekes, the figure of the drowned poet held by his wife in the style of Michelangelo's Pietà in Rome surmounts a tablet commemorating his death with a verse from *Adonais*. The authorities of St Peter's thought it not suitable for the church, and it was placed in the ancient and beautiful Priory at Christchurch, one of their many fine monuments.

Boscombe Manor is now occupied by the Bournemouth and Poole College of Art. On the ground floor are two rooms which house the Shelley Museum, a fine collection of pictures, photographs and other Shelley memorabilia, together with a reference library. In 1972, on the 150th anniversary of Shelley's death, Miss Margaret Brown, who had gathered together many of these pieces, opened a museum in the Casa Magni itself in Terenzo, but in 1979 the house was sold and the collection was given its new home by the Bournemouth Borough Council. For students of Shelley it is an important and fascinating collection, and Miss Brown, the Hon. Keeper, is enthusiastic and full of helpful information to visitors.

EDINBURGH   In August 1811 Shelley and Harriet eloped to Edinburgh, via York, by mail-coach, and here they were married; Hogg joined them and they remained in Edinburgh, staying at 60 George Street, seeing the sights ('Holyrood, Arthur's Seat & the Castle will of course be objects of my attention').

DUBLIN   Harriet and Shelley arrived here in February 1812, staying in Sackville Street and later at 17 Grafton Street. His pamphlets to the Irish were printed here; he visited Curran who lived on St Stephen's Green and spoke to the Aggregrate of the Catholics of Ireland in the theatre in Fishamble Street.

CWM ELAN   near Rhayader in Radnorshire (Powys) was the home of Shelley's cousin Thomas Grove, whose sister Harriet was Shelley's first love. He first visited Cwm Elan in July 1811 and had his first sight of mountain scenery 'excessively grand'. When he and Harriet left Dublin in 1812 they came to Nantgwillt, a house and farm a mile away from the Grove estate. This was a large property: a house with seven bedrooms and 200 acres of arable land which he hoped to farm. 'We are now embosomed in the solitude of mountains woods & rivers, silent, solitary, and old, far from any town' he wrote to Miss Hitchener and tried to persuade her to join them in his project. Unfortunately he could not raise the necessary £500 to buy the furniture and farm stock and after two months or so they had to leave.

TREMADOC   After they left Lynmouth they travelled to North Wales and came to Tremadoc in Carnarvonshire (Gwynedd), a village being developed by William Alexander Madocks, philanthropist and MP for Boston. It was constructed on land being reclaimed from the sea and Shelley became an enthusiastic supporter of the scheme, lending money for the purpose of extending the embankment there. They lived in a house rented from Madocks, called Tan-yr-allt, 'our beautiful Welsh cottage' set in the wild scenery of Snowdon. It seemed yet another idyllic retreat, but in February 1813 came the mysterious attack by an unknown man who broke into the house at night and according to both the Shelleys, fired at him, knocking him to the ground after a struggle. Shocked by this attempt at 'an atrocious assassination' they hastily departed once again, returning to Dublin.

Shelley's wanderings in Europe were too extensive to be recorded here in detail. The places listed below are those particularly associated with him, or those where he stayed for some length of time. His letters reveal him as an untiring tourist, excited by the beauty of the countryside and the wealth of painting and sculpture

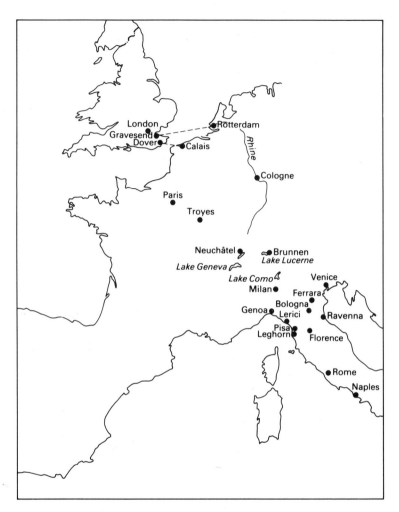

A map to show Shelley's travels in Europe

in the galleries and palaces of Italy. He had a good eye not only for landscape but for noting such scenes as that in Rome, in St Peter's Square, where he saw 300 fettered criminals 'sit in long rows hoeing out the weeds between the pavement stones', their chains clanking discordantly. Inspired as he was by Italy, he saw its limitations, contrasting the nobility of the ancient ruins with the 'filthy modern inhabitants' whose manners and way of life constantly offended him: 'What do you think? young women of rank actually eat – you will never guess what – *garlick*', he complained, and deplored the degeneracy of the country.

FRANCE AND GERMANY His first travel abroad was occasioned by his elopement with Mary. With Claire they went to Paris, then crossed over into Switzerland (Brunnen on Lake Lucerne) but hastily returned to England as they began to run out of money; they journeyed up the Rhine to Cologne, and sailed from Rotterdam in Holland. This is all related in detail in *A History of a Six Weeks' Tour* (1817).

LAKE GENEVA (LAC LÉMAN) In May 1816 with Mary and Claire he crossed the Jura and the Alps to arrive at the Lake. They lived in the Maison Chappuis at Montalègre, Byron staying nearby at the Villa Diodati. With Byron he took a week's journey on the Lake, at one point being almost wrecked in a storm; en route they saw the Castle of Chillon, Clarens (site of *La Nouvelle Héloïse*), Lausanne (Gibbon's house), Vevey and Evian. In July he went to 'the famous Valley of Chamouni' to see Mont Blanc and the source of the Arveiron, Mecca of all tourists in search of the sublime: 'the entire mass of the population subsist on the weakness & credulity of travellers as leeches subsist on the blood of the sick'. His letters to Peacock give a full account of these journeys.

ITALY
MILAN In April 1818 they arrived in Milan and began to look for a house on Lake Como, hoping to take the Villa Pliniana, a half-ruined palace. They did not, but Como gave him his first sight of the rich vegetation of Italy, the olives, orange and lemon trees, vineyards and myrtles.

BAGNI DI LUCCA In June 1818 they took a house here, the Casa Bertini, in the hills near Pisa.

FLORENCE In 1818 he passed through Florence, 'the most beautiful city I ever saw', with Claire en route for Venice, and in September 1819 took an apartment there in the Palazzo Marini in the Via Valfonda, near Santa Maria Novella. His second son, Percy

Florence, was born and baptized here. The winter was cold, but Shelley spent much time in the Uffizi Gallery where he was particularly moved by the sculpture of Niobe and her children, by Scopas, and when he returned to Florence in 1821 in search of a house to rent for the season, he went back to look at it again, contemplating it for hours on end and moved by 'the sublime emotions such spectacles create'.

VENICE He came to Venice for the first time in August 1818 with Claire, crossing the lagoon in a gondola in the middle of a storm. The purpose of the visit was to see Byron about Allegra, and it was the occasion of *Julian and Maddalo*. In September he returned, Mary following with their daughter Clara, who died here of dysentery. A letter to Peacock eloquently describes the city 'wonderfully fine' but degraded by its subjection to the Austrian rule.

ESTE Byron lent them his villa at Este, Il Capuccini, built on the site of a Capuchin convent and looking across the plain of Lombardy to the Apennines. It was a pleasant house, with a pergola of vines and a summer house where Shelley worked. They stayed here from August 1818 to November.

NAPLES Shelley and Mary came here at the end of November 1818, staying at 250 Riviera di Chiaia, near the Royal Gardens. Here they stayed till February 1819 sightseeing and travelling to look at the Bay of Baiae, Lake Avernus, and the Graeco-Roman cities of Pompeii, Paestum and Herculaneum, all described in vivid detail in letters to Peacock. They went to the opera and to the picture gallery, the Studii, where Shelley noted with pleasure paintings by Raphael, Titian and Guido; his taste was for the gentle and sensuous rather than the tormented shapes of Michelangelo's *Last Judgment* which he saw there, the first study for the great fresco in the Sistine Chapel in Rome.

FERRARA The home of the powerful Este family. Shelley came here in November 1818 and his letters show him as the indefatigable tourist. He went to the Cathedral, the fine public library of 160,000 books including manuscripts of Tasso and Ariosto, and to the tomb of Ariosto and the prison where Tasso died.

BOLOGNA Visited after Ferrara en route for Rome. He saw the Cathedral, the Accademia delle Belle Arte and many palaces. His letters descibe in detail some of the paintings, particularly praising Correggio, Raphael and Guido (his taste again for the gentle and spiritual).

RAVENNA In August 1821 he went to see Byron, then staying in a splendid palace there, and visited Allegra in her convent. He and Byron rode in the pine woods every day, and he visited the Church of S. Vitale, famous for its mosaics, and the tomb of Galla Placidia; he also 'worshipped the sacred spot' of Dante's tomb.

ROME In November 1818 Shelley and Mary arrived for a brief visit to 'this capital of the vanished world' which impressed him more deeply than any other city he had seen. He visited the Forum and Colosseum every day, walking among the wild flowers, myrtles and fig-trees and meditating on the past history of Rome. In March 1819 he returned; this time the Baths of Caracalla astonished him by the grandeur of the ruins, its 'vast desolation' softened by flowering trees and shrubs. Like the tourists of today he marvelled at the city of palaces and temples, the triumphal arches, obelisks and fountains, particularly Bernini's fountain in the Piazza Navona and the celebrated Fontana di Trevi. He went to St Peter's, the Vatican Museum, and the Pantheon by moonlight, its dome at that time open to the sky. In the palaces he saw paintings and sculpture, and in the Palazzo Colonna he was especially struck by the picture of Beatrice Cenci. It is now in the Palazzo Corsini (catalogued as possibly by Guido Reni, and possibly of Beatrice), the portrait of a slender brown-eyed girl in a white turban and flowing gown, hardly the suffering martyr described by him in the preface to the play.

In Rome his son William died and was buried in the Protestant Cemetery, within the old walls of the city; his grave-stone does not mark his resting-place, since when the grave was opened so that he could be buried near his father, the body of an adult man was found in it. His stone is in the old part of the Cemetery, not far from the tombs of Keats and Severn, and close to the Pyramid of Cestius. Shelley's own grave, next to that of Trelawny, is in the newer part in a shady corner near the tower.

The Keats-Shelley Museum, at the foot of the Spanish Steps in the house where Keats died, has an important collection of Shelleyana, including letters, books and paintings.

PISA In May 1818 Shelley's first impression of Pisa, where they stayed briefly, was of 'a large disagreeable city almost without inhabitants'. But in January 1820 they returned and remained there for most of the remainder of his life, with visits to Livorno some fourteen miles away and in the summer to the Baths of S. Giuliano, a watering-place near Pisa, where for his health he took the warm baths from the natural springs. Here Medwin joined them. In Pisa, too, Shelley met Emilia Viviani at the Convent of S. Anna and in 1821 the Williamses arrived, followed by Trelawny. In this year Shelley and Mary moved into an apartment in the Tre Palazzi di

The Funeral of Shelley: The Last Rite at Viareggio (1889). *Louis Edward Fournier's romantic version. Trelawny, Leigh Hunt and Byron are the mourners beside the pyre*

Chiesa on the Lung' Arno, the Williamses living on the floor below. Opposite was Byron's Palazzo Lanfranchi where he came with La Guiccioli.

LERICI   On 1 May 1822 they left Pisa for the sea-coast, to move into the Casa Magni at Terenzo, a few miles from Lerici on the Gulf of Spezia. The house, long and low, was shared with Claire and the Williamses and their two children; it was uncomfortable and overcrowded and Mary, who was pregnant (she had a miscarriage while there) hated it and found the local people savage and rough. From here Shelley sailed to Genoa to meet Hunt and on returning was drowned.

Further reading

Editions of Shelley's works

The textual problems of Shelley scholarship are of such complexity that no really authoritative complete edition of his works has yet appeared. His note-books and manuscripts are often extremely difficult to decipher and in the past editors, unable to consult all the material which is now available, relied as much on intuition as on painful scholarship to interpret his intentions. The Julian edition of *The Complete Works* (eds. Ingpen and Peck: Benn 1926–30, and 1965) is the best and most complete; its ten volumes include the poems, prose and letters; but since many readers will not have ready access to this edition I have used in this book the Oxford edition of the poetry, compiled by Thomas Hutchinson in 1904 and subsequently revised by G.M. Matthews in 1970. A two-volume edition prepared by Mr Matthews is to be issued by Longman, and will then be the authoritative text.

A new Oxford edition of the poems is also being prepared by Neville Rogers; so far two volumes have appeared, covering works up to and including 1817 (Oxford, Clarendon Press, 1972 and 1975). He devotes much space to notes and interpretations of individual poems, strongly biassed to a Platonic view of Shelley. He has also edited the Clarendon edition of the *Esdaile Poems* (Oxford, 1966), early poems written before the marriage to Mary; Shelley gave the note-book in which they were transcribed to Harriet, and after her death it was in the possession of their daughter, Ianthe, and her descendants until 1962, when it was purchased by the Carl Pforzheimer Library in the USA. Kenneth Neill Cameron also did an edition of it for the Pforzheimer Foundation published by Knopf in 1964, and this has what he calls 'a minimum clean-up text' with many informative notes and commentary.

The *Letters*, edited by F.L. Jones in two volumes (Oxford, Clarendon Press, 1964), unfortunately now out of print, are of invaluable assistance in an understanding of the poetry and the man. Also edited by Mr Jones are the *Letters* of Mary Shelley and her *Journal* (University of Oklahoma Press, 1944 and 1947). A fuller edition of Mary's letters is being prepared under the editorship of Betty Bennett; Volume I, the first of three, came out in 1980 (Johns Hopkins University Press).

For the prose, including the two early novels, the Julian edition is essential.

Biography

The standard biography is by Newman Ivey White (2 volumes, Knopf, 1940; single volume, 1945), a fine and readable work presenting a full-length picture of Shelley in all his varied aspects. The early accounts, discussed in Chapter 1:

Hogg, T.J., *Life of Percy Bysshe Shelley* (2 volumes, 1858, Oxford University Press, 1906)

Medwin, Thomas, *Life of Percy Bysshe Shelley* (2 volumes, 1848, later edition, Oxford University Press, 1913)

Peacock, T.L., *Memoirs of Shelley* (1858–1860); revised edition by H. Mills (Hart-Davis, 1970)

Trelawny, E.J., *Recollections of the Last Days of Shelley* (1858), revised edition by J.E. Morpurgo (Folio Society, 1952)

Of later biographies Edmund Blunden's *Shelley, A Life Story* (Collins, 1946), an account of one poet by another, is full of sympathetic insight and particularly informative on the years in England and his relationship with the Hunt circle. Roger Ingpen's *Shelley in England* (Kegan Paul, 1917) also fully documents the formative years. Kenneth Neill Cameron has written at length: *The Young Shelley: Genesis of a Radical* (New York, Macmillan, 1950) concentrates on his political writings; and his later *Shelley: The Golden Years* (Harvard University Press, 1974) is a detailed account of the last years in England and his life in Italy, complete with notes and critical assessments of both poetry and prose.

John Buxton's *Byron and Shelley* (Macmillan, 1968) is particularly interesting on the relationship of these two and their mutual influence.

To these could be added two background books: H.N. Brailsford's *Shelley, Godwin and their Circle* (Oxford University Press, 1913) helpful in assessing the part played by Godwin and the early Radicals in Shelley's political education; Leigh Hunt's *Autobiography* (1850) has much first-hand information about Shelley's life and the political climate of the day. For a good pictorial account Claire Tomalin's *Shelley and his World* (Thames & Hudson, 1980) supplies over a hundred illustrations of people and places from contemporary pictures and drawings.

Critical studies

A very short list from the huge mass of critical work on Shelley. The critical reception accorded his work is now studied and anthologized in *Shelley: The Critical Heritage*, edited by J.E. Barcus (Routledge & Kegan Paul, 1975).

Carl Grabo's *A Newton among Poets* (University of North Carolina, 1930) is still the best account of his interest in science and use of it in his poetry, especially in *Prometheus Unbound*. Peter Butter's *Shelley's Idols of the Cave* (Edinburgh University Press, 1954) also has good material on his scientific thought but mainly concentrates on poetic symbolism.

Neville Rogers's *Shelley at Work* (Oxford, Clarendon Press, 1967) studies the symbolism and discusses both the thought and imagery in wholly Platonic terms. A less one-sided view is taken by Carlos Baker in *Shelley's Major Poetry: The Fabric of a Vision* (Princeton University Press, 1948 and 1961) which is straightforward and helpful in identifying sources and ideas of the longer poetry. Influential articles mentioned in the text are those by T.S. Eliot in his essay on Shelley in *The Use of Poetry and the Use of Criticism* (Faber and Faber, 1934) and by F.R. Leavis in *Revaluation: Tradition and Development in English Poetry* (Chatto and Windus, 1936). These are both hostile; at the other extreme is the essay of W.B. Yeats on 'The Philosophy of Shelley's Poetry' reprinted in *Essays and Introductions* (Macmillan, 1961). In defence of Shelley is the essay by C.S. Lewis, 'Shelley, Dryden and Mr Eliot' in *Rehabilitations and other Essays* (Oxford University Press, 1939).

General Index

Shelley's Poetry and Prose